Fodor's

LOS CABOS

W9-AUO-074

WELCOME TO LOS CABOS

With coastline that stretches from the Sea of Cortez to the Pacific Ocean, and 350 sunny days a year, Los Cabos is Mexico's ultimate seaside escape. It's endless summer at the tip of the Baja Peninsula, and surfers, golfers, divers, and hikers come here for year-round water sports and outdoor activities. The sister towns of Cabo San Lucas and San José del Cabo offer distinct experiences that range from all-night bar crawls to Thursday night Art Walks. Between them the Corridor presents all-inclusive resorts with everything for the perfect honeymoon or family vacation.

TOP REASONS TO GO

★ **Beaches:** More than 50 miles of gorgeous strands with towering rock formations.

★ **Golf:** Spectacular views from greens designed by the world's best course architects.

★ **Nightlife:** Cabo's after-dark, into-the-dawn party scene draws a loud, festive crowd.

★ **Sportfishing:** Beginners and pros drop a line in the "Marlin Capital of the World."

★ **Whale Watching:** The gentle giants that migrate here swim right next to the boats.

★ **Spas:** Desert healing treatments in sumptuous resort wellness centers.

917.224
F653Lo
4th ed.
2015

Fodor's LOS CABOS

Publisher: Amanda D'Acierno, *Senior Vice President*

Editorial: Arabella Bowen, *Editor in Chief*; Linda Cabasin, *Editorial Director*

Design: Tina Malaney, *Associate Art Director*; Chie Ushio, *Senior Designer*; Ann McBride, *Production Designer*

Photography: Jennifer Arnow, *Senior Photo Editor*; Jennifer Romains, *Photo Researcher*

Production: Linda Schmidt, *Managing Editor*; Evangelos Vasilakis, *Associate Managing Editor*; Angela L. McLean, *Senior Production Manager*

Maps: Rebecca Baer, *Senior Map Editor*; Mark Stroud (Moon Street Cartography), David Lindroth, Inc., *Cartographers*

Sales: Jacqueline Lebow, *Sales Director*

Marketing & Publicity: Heather Dalton, *Marketing Director*; Katherine Punia, *Publicity Director*

Business & Operations: Susan Livingston, *Vice President, Strategic Business Planning*; Sue Daulton, *Vice President, Operations*

Fodors.com: Megan Bell, *Executive Director, Revenue & Business Development*; Yasmin Marinaro, *Senior Director, Marketing & Partnerships*

Copyright © 2015 by Fodor's Travel, a division of Random House LLC

Writers: Marlise Kast–Myers, Chris Sands

Editor: Eric Wechter

Production Editor: Carolyn Roth

4th Edition

ISBN 978-0-8041-4360-8

ISSN 2326–4152

SPECIAL SALES

This book is available at special discounts for bulk purchases for sales promotions or premiums. For more information, e-mail specialmarkets@penguinrandomhouse.com

PRINTED IN THE UNITED STATES OF AMERICA

10 9 8 7 6 5 4 3 2 1

CONTENTS

Fodor's Features

CONTENTS

ABOUT THIS GUIDE

Fodor's Recommendations

Everything in this guide is worth doing—we don't cover what isn't—but exceptional sights, hotels, and restaurants are recognized with additional accolades. **Fodor's Choice★** indicates our top recommendations; and **Best Bets** call attention to notable hotels and restaurants in various categories. Care to nominate a new place? Visit Fodors.com/contact-us.

Trip Costs

We list prices wherever possible to help you budget well. Hotel and restaurant price categories from **$** to **$$$$** are noted alongside each recommendation. For hotels, we include the lowest cost of a standard double room in high season. For restaurants, we cite the average price of a main course at dinner or, if dinner isn't served, at lunch. For attractions, we always list adult admission fees; discounts are usually available for children, students, and senior citizens.

Hotels

Our local writers vet every hotel to recommend the best overnights in each price category, from budget to expensive. Unless otherwise specified, you can expect private bath, phone, and TV in your room. For expanded hotel reviews, facilities, and deals visit Fodors.com.

Top Picks	Hotels & Restaurants
★ **Fodor's**Choice	🏨 Hotel
Listings	🛏 Number of rooms
⊠ Address	⊠ Branch address
⊠ Branch address	⊠ Meal plans
☎ Telephone	✗ Restaurant
🖷 Fax	⌦ Reservations
⊕ Website	🏛 Dress code
✉ E-mail	▭ No credit cards
🎫 Admission fee	$ Price
⊙ Open/closed times	**Other**
Ⓜ Subway	⇨ See also
✢ Directions or Map coordinates	☞ Take note
	🏌 Golf facilities

Restaurants

Unless we state otherwise, restaurants are open for lunch and dinner daily. We mention dress code only when there's a specific requirement and reservations only when they're essential or not accepted. To make restaurant reservations, visit Fodors.com.

Credit Cards

The hotels and restaurants in this guide typically accept credit cards. If not, we'll say so.

EUGENE FODOR

Hungarian-born Eugene Fodor (1905–91) began his travel career as an interpreter on a French cruise ship. The experience inspired him to write *On the Continent* (1936), the first guidebook to receive annual updates and discuss a country's way of life as well as its sights. Fodor later joined the U.S. Army and worked for the OSS in World War II. After the war, he kept up his intelligence work while expanding his guidebook series. During the Cold War, many guides were written by fellow agents who understood the value of insider information. Today's guides continue Fodor's legacy by providing travelers with timely coverage, insider tips, and cultural context.

EXPERIENCE LOS CABOS

LOS CABOS PLANNER

When to Go

Although Los Cabos hotels are often busiest starting in mid-October for the sportfishing season, the high season doesn't technically begin until mid-December, running through the end of Easter week. It's during this busy period that you'll pay the highest hotel and golf rates. Spring break, which can stagger over several weeks in March and April, is also a particularly crowded and raucous time. Downtown Cabo gets very busy, especially on weekends, throughout the year. Whale-watching season (December–April) coincides with high season, but whale-watchers tend to stay in La Paz, not Los Cabos.

The Pacific hurricane season mirrors that of the Atlantic and Caribbean, so there is always a slight chance of a hurricane from August through late October. Although hurricanes rarely hit Los Cabos head-on, the effects can reverberate when a large hurricane hits Mexico's Pacific coast. Though much less frequent than Atlantic hurricanes, Pacific hurricanes do occur and can cause significant damage. Still, most summer tropical storms pass through quickly, even during the so-called short "rainy" season, from July through October.

Getting Here and Around

Visitors fly nonstop to Los Cabos from all over the United States, and to La Paz from some U.S. cities. Via nonstop service, Los Cabos is about 2 hours from San Diego, 2½ hours from Los Angeles, 2¾ hours from Houston, 2¾ hours from Dallas/Fort Worth, and 2 hours from Phoenix.

Flying time from New York to Mexico City, where you must switch planes to continue to Los Cabos, is 5 hours. Los Cabos is about a 2-hour flight from Mexico City.

CABAJA Rental Cars. Consider renting an auto from CABAJA Rental Cars, in San Diego. It's one of the few American car-rental companies that permits, and encourages, taking cars south of the border. ⊠ *9245 Jamacha Blvd., Spring Valley, CA* ☎ *888/470–7368, 619/470–7368* ⊕ *www.cabaja.com.*

Lewis & Lewis Insurance. For affordable insurance for your own car, that covers you in Mexico, try Lewis & Lewis Insurance. ⊠ *2950 31st. Street, Suite 140, Santa Monica, CA* ☎ *310/399–0800, 800/966–6830* ⊕ *www.mexicanautoinsurance.com.*

Safety

Los Cabos is one of the safest areas in Mexico, but standard precautions always apply: Use your security safe in hotel rooms. Distribute your cash, credit cards, and IDs between a deep front pocket, an inside jacket pocket, and a hidden money pouch. Don't carry excessive amounts of cash. Leave your passport behind, with your other valuables, in your in-room safe—and be sure to make copies of your passport and credit cards and leave an extra copy with someone back home.

WHAT'S NEW IN LOS CABOS

San José del Cabo Grows Up

The same gnawing question has always confronted visitors planning a trip to Los Cabos: Do I stay in San José del Cabo or in Cabo San Lucas? Most visitors have always opted for the flash and glitter of the latter. San José's hoteliers and restaurateurs have stopped trying to compete on San Lucas's terms, opting instead to market their community for what it is.

The city has truly come into its own. San José's *zócalo* (central plaza) has been jazzed up with a lighted fountain and gazebo; old haciendas have been transformed into trendy restaurants and charming inns. And the city's art scene is thriving with a high-season **Thursday Night Art Walk,** where those interested in art can visit participating galleries and enjoy free drinks and live music. Several farms on the outskirts of San José are capitalizing on the organic food movement with their farm-to-table restaurants. By adding cooking schools, markets, and tours, these desert draws are more of an experience than just an ordinary meal.

Greens Galore

Golf is the name of the game in Los Cabos. There are multiple courses tied to names that read like a who's who of golf legends and course designers: Jack Nicklaus, Greg Norman, Davis Love III, Phil Mickelson, Tom Weiskopf, Robert Trent Jones II, Tom Fazio, and most recently Tiger Woods. Baja golf is more than just Los Cabos: courses line the entire peninsula, if not in the same density as at its southern extreme.

The Rise of Todos Santos

Once the province of surfers—the undertow is wicked here, making for some amazing waves, but risky swimming— this town overlooking the western cape about an hour north of Cabo San Lucas is home to a growing artists' community. Just don't call Todos Santos Baja's "hot" new destination, because folks here aren't interested in becoming another Los Cabos, thank you very much. But "genteel" and "refined" and "preserving Mexican culture"? Absolutely, those descriptions apply.

New Terminal at SJD

Aeropuerto Internacional de Los Cabos (SJD) is Mexico's seventh-busiest airport. A new international terminal opened in 2013, which slightly eased congestion for the more than 3 million passengers who pass through annually.

Border Crossing 2014–15

U.S. citizens need to have their paperwork in order to return to the United States from Mexico by land or sea. Those aged 16 years and older need to carry a passport or passport card. Children 15 and under are only required to provide a birth certificate if traveling with their parents or an organized group. When departing, you'll need to present the Tourist Card (FMT card) that was given to you upon entry, otherwise you will be subject to a fine. If you plan on bringing back tequila or wine, U.S. Customs allows American citizens to import 1 liter of alcohol duty free. A 10% tax is applied to anything more than 1 liter.

Note that if you return from a cruise and your itinerary also took you beyond Mexico, a full-fledged passport is necessary for reentry to the United States. All travelers, regardless of age, require a passport when returning by air from Mexico. See the U.S. Department of Homeland Security's website (⊕ *www.dhs.gov*) for more information.

WHAT'S WHERE

1 San José del Cabo. Thirty-two kilometers (20 miles) east of Cabo San Lucas, San José, the elder sister, has remained the smaller, quieter, and more traditional of the two siblings. Its 18th-century colonial architecture, artsy vibe, and quality restaurants are great for those who like to be within driving distance, not right in the middle, of the happening spots.

2 The Corridor. Along this stretch of road, which connects San José to Cabo, exclusive, guard-gated resort complexes have taken over much of the waterfront with their sprawling villas, golf courses, and shopping centers such as Las Tiendas de Palmilla, an upscale, open-to-the-public mall.

3 Cabo San Lucas. Cabo San Lucas is at the very end of the Carretera Transpeninsular (Highway 1). Cabo has always been the more gregarious, outspoken of the sisters. The sportfishing fleet is anchored

here, and cruise ships anchored off the marina tender passengers into town. Trendy restaurants and bars line the streets and massive hotels have risen all along the beachfront. Here, you'll find Bahía Cabo San Lucas (Cabo Bay), the towering Land's End Rocks, and the famed arched landmark, El Arco.

4 Todos Santos. Only an hour north of Cabo San Lucas, Todos Santos lies close enough to be part of the Los Cabos experience—but still be that proverbial world away. This *típico* town on the West Cape is home to a growing expat community, as well as some cozy lodgings and restaurants.

5 La Paz. The capital of southern Baja is a "big little" city, one of the most authentic on the peninsula. La Paz is a laid-back community with excellent scuba diving and sportfishing in the Sea of Cortez. Its lovely oceanfront *malecón* features a number of good restaurants and hotels.

6 Baja California. The beaches and seafood of Rosarito, Ensenada, and Puerto Nuevo draw retirees, RV'ers, and, during spring break, crowds of wild college kids; the Valle de Guadalupe provides respite and fantastic vineyards.

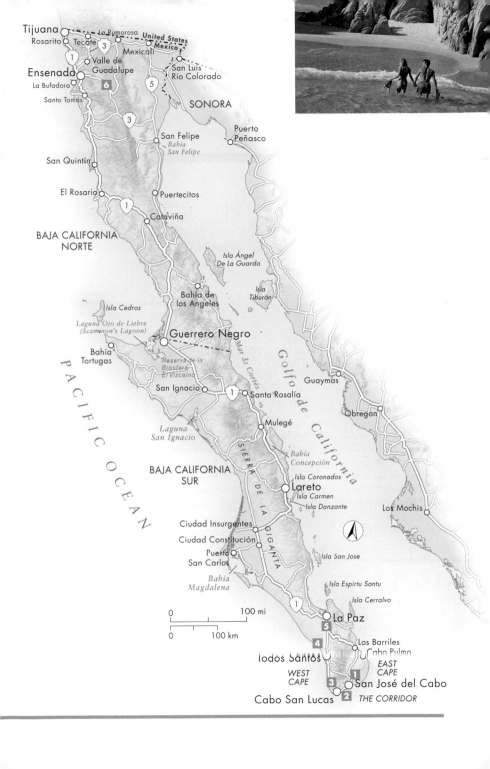

Tijuana
Rosarito
Tecate
La Rumorosa
United States
Mexico
Valle de
Guadalupe
Mexicali
San Luis
Río Colorado

Ensenada
La Bufadora
Santo Tomás

SONORA

San Felipe
*Bahía
San Felipe*

San Quintín

Puerto
Peñasco

El Rosario

Puertecitos

Cataviña

BAJA CALIFORNIA
NORTE

Isla Ángel
De la Guarda

Isla Cedros

Isla
Tiburón

Bahía de
los Angeles

Laguna Ojo de Liebre
(Scammon's Lagoon)

Guerrero Negro

Bahía
Tortugas

*Reserva de la
Biosfera
El Vizcaíno*

San Ignacio

Santa Rosalía

Guaymas

PACIFIC OCEAN

Laguna
San Ignacio

Mulegé

Obregon

Golfo de California

Mar de Cortés

SIERRA   DE   LA   GIGANTA

*Bahía
Concepción*

BAJA CALIFORNIA
SUR

Isla Coronados

Loreto

Isla Carmen

Los Mochis

Isla Danzante

Ciudad Insurgentes

Ciudad Constitución

Puerto
San Carlos

*Bahía
Magdalena*

Isla San Jose

Isla Espíritu Santu

Isla Cerralvo

0   100 mi

0   100 km

La Paz

5

Todos Santos

4

Los Barriles
Cabo Pulmo

WEST
CAPE

EAST
CAPE

1

San José del Cabo

3

2

Cabo San Lucas

THE CORRIDOR

LOS CABOS
TOP ATTRACTIONS

Gray Whales, Cabos San Lucas, San José del Cabo, Todos Santos, La Paz

(A) All the commercialism of this part of Mexico evaporates at the stunning sight of the annual whale migration—seasonally, December through April—down Baja's west coast and up the east. You might have arrived by plane, RV, or cruise ship, but these 45-ton creatures swam all the way from Alaska.

Puerto Nuevo, Baja California

(B) Who crosses international borders for lunch or dinner? People who live in San Diego do. About 48 km (30 miles) south of the U.S. border lies a town they've nicknamed "Newport"—not to be confused with Newport Beach farther north in Orange County. Puerto Nuevo is famous for its lobster, and the season runs October through March. Of course, if you're already in Baja, you can approach the town's dozen–plus lobster restaurants from the south, too.

Land's End, Ĉabo San Lucas, Los Cabos

(C) This is it. It's the end of the line. The sight of the towering granite formations here lets you know that you've arrived at the tip of the Baja Peninsula. El Arco ("the arch") has become Los Cabos' most iconic symbol—an odd choice, perhaps, for something so stark and natural to represent a place so entrenched in commerce. Yet all the sleek hotels and shopping malls nearby can't deflect from the end-of-the-world feel you get when you arrive.

Parque Nacional Marino Cabo Pulmo, Cabo Pulmo, Baja Sur

(D) Labeled "The Aquarium of the World" by Jacques Cousteau, the 25,000-year-old coral reef here is the only living coral reef on North America's west coast. Its eight reef fingers attract more than 2,000 different kinds of marine organisms, including almost 250 species of tropical fish. Toss in the sunken wreck of a tuna boat nearby

and you have one of Baja's top snorkeling and diving destinations.

Valle de Guadalupe, near Ensenada, Baja California

You may know about Corona beer, tequila, and margaritas, but did you know that 90% of Mexico's wine came from Baja California? An anomaly in Baja's desert climate produces the Guadalupe Valley, a cooler, Napa-like pocket that cultivates several varieties of grapes and produces several of the world's best (but not best known) wines. Many of the vineyards are open to tours and samplings, some to meals and overnight stays, and all, of course, to purchases.

Boulevard Mijares San José del Cabo

(E) Shops, trendy restaurants, and a couple boutique hotels line this pleasant street running south from San José's expansive central plaza. Marking this zócalo is the Misión de San José del Cabo Anuiti church, founded by the Jesuit Priest,

Nicolas Tamaral in 1730. As the heat of the day dissipates— usually after evening mass—locals and visitors alike emerge to partake of the boulevard's attractions. Between November and June, this area is bustling with travelers who come for the Art Walk that takes place on Thursday from 5 to 9.

Malecón, La Paz, Baja Sur

(F) What's Baja's best ocean-side walk? The marina boardwalk in Cabo San Lucas gets most votes, but for a far more authentic Mexican experience, head three hours north to the seaside promenade in southern Baja's largest city. This is urban renewal at its best, with attractive landscaping for the entire 5 km (3 miles) of the malecón's length. The walkway comes alive as evening approaches and residents throng the walkway for their evening paseo.

LOS CABOS TOP EXPERIENCES

Wine-tasting in Valle de Guadalupe

In the past decade, Valle de Guadalupe has gone from a handful of vineyards squeezing their grapes, to more than 100 in production, many of which open their cellars. The best way to experience the region is by wine tasting your way through the *Ruta del Vino* (wine route). Even if you aren't a wine connoisseur, this valley just 20 minutes from the coast is worth a visit. Some of the more established wineries double as boutique hotels, meaning you can enjoy a room with a sprawling view (wine tasting and tour included). This wine-and-travel combo lends itself to wine tasting by day and organic cuisine by night. Because the valley is made up of farmland, international chefs are flocking to the area in hopes of creating the next farm-to-table experience. The most exciting time to visit Valle de Guadalupe is in August when wineries celebrate the harvest, but be sure to make reservations at least three months in advance.

Fishing for Marlin

Let's start with the sport that originally put Los Cabos on the map, and keeps it there—fishing! Even for someone who has never been fishing, plying the indigo seas while savoring the stunning scenery from a new perspective makes for an amazing day. Boats from 23 to 110 feet long are available, and you can pay from $250 to $5,000 for the experience. Everyone, even non-anglers, will get excited when the line goes screaming out behind a jumping marlin, as it "greyhounds" off into the ocean. Catch (and, of course, release) all billfish—e.g. marlin and sailfish—but enjoy telling your tale.

"Under the Boardwalk, Down by the Sea"

If you arrive in Cabo San Lucas on a cruise, you'll disembark at its marina boardwalk. Approach from any other direction and you'll still find your way here. Known as the Marina Golden Zone, this stretch is lined with restaurants and bars that are terrific for people-watching, and complete with an air-conditioned shopping mall to pop into when the afternoon heat gets you down. Perhaps no place in Baja pulses to the tourist beat quite the way Cabo's marina does. Yes, it's undeniably touristy, but we look at it this way: can all those visitors possibly be wrong?

Whale-Watching

The giant gray whales are snowbirds, too. Thousands of these mammoth cetaceans make their lengthy migrations between December and April, swimming nearly 10,000 km (6,000 miles) from Alaska and Canada to mate and give birth in Baja's warm(ish), west-coast lagoons; they make the trip without even stopping to eat, they're in such a rush to get to Mexico (we know how they feel).

Once the whales arrive, they cavort, spy-hop (poking their heads straight out of the water), and generally enjoy the seas of Baja, just like their human counterparts. A number of whale-watching tours are available, most of them centered around Scammon's Lagoon, San Ignacio Lagoon, and Magdalena Bay, where tourists go in *pangas* (small boats) out into the lagoons. Oftentimes, the whales and their new babies will approach the boat, rubbing against it, and looking with their sweet brown eyes at the people inside.

Maya Temazcal

Los Cabos has the spas, where giving yourself up to utter pampering and exotic treatments is just another day's vacation, but don't forget about the *temazcal*. This Mayan sweat-lodge experience at the Pueblo Bonito Pacífica Resort, Hacienda Encantada, and Yhi Spa at Me by Meliá is spiritual in nature, working over your psyche as much as your body. Lead by a *temazcalero*, this ritual is a group experience, within a traditional enclosure, and incorporates bathing, steam at high temperatures, and medicinal plants. It requires an almost meditative commitment because extreme emotions often surface in these conditions. Your reward? A feeling of having been completely cleansed and renewed.

Viewing Art in San José del Cabo

Art lovers unite on Thursday evenings in San José del Cabo, where the Art District Association is behind the Thursday Night Art Walk. With at least 15 impressive art galleries to visit in several square blocks, the district is located north and west of the town's centuries-old church. The Art Walk takes place from 5 to 9 pm, November to June. The informal, unguided tour makes for a fun opportunity to drink (free) wine, and be amazed by all forms and variations of art, from amber jewelry and photography to Huichol beadwork and very pricey sculptures from top Mexican artists.

Hitting the Surf

It's during the hot summer months, when tropical storms kick up giant waves, that you'll find the best surfing in these parts. If you are inspired to learn the sport, a number of tour operators offer lessons. By far, though, the easiest way to make this happen is to book a room at the boutique Cabo Surf Hotel, with perhaps the most prime Los Cabos surf location. Right out in front of the hotel are three top breaks, Old Man's, La Roca, and Acapulquito, all gentle, forgiving, feathering waves. The Mike Doyle Surf School has taken up residence in the hotel, and has 100 boards of all sizes, shapes, lengths, and compositions to encourage the beginner as well as outfit more advanced surfers.

Tequila Tasting

What better place to enjoy and learn about tequila than in festive Los Cabos? Tequila tasting options abound: Toss down a couple of 70¢ shots of Cuervo. Order $2.80 shots of Don Julio with your lobster omelet at the open-air Crazy Lobster restaurant. Take a tequila class at Pancho's Restaurant & Tequila Museum from a certified "Tequila Ambassador." Enjoy the world's finest tequilas in the exclusive ambience of Las Ventanas al Paraíso resort. Los Cabos is *the* place to put tequila to the test.

Without a doubt, every bar and restaurant in Los Cabos offers a great selection; there are at least five "local" Cabo tequilas (though they're not grown or bottled in Baja but on Mexico's mainland, and then given company labels). Cabo Wabo makes a famed line of tequilas, and the Cabo Surf Hotel has its own namesake in the tequila world, as has the Hotel California in Todos Santos and Nick-San in Cabo San Lucas and Shoppes at Palmilla. Las Varitas, a popular Cabo dance club located near ME Cabo Hotel by Meliá, also slapped its name on the stuff.

GREAT ITINERARIES

Each of these fills one day. Together they touch on some of Los Cabos' most quintessential experiences from boating to El Arco and visiting the blown-glass factory, to grabbing a beer at a local brewpub and discovering Cabo's Marina Golden Zone.

Learn the Lay of the Land

On Day 1 take it easy, enjoy your hotel, take a swim in the pool, and get to know the beach in your general area. If staying in Cabo, meander around town, mentally noting the many restaurants and shops on the way that you might wish to sample later. Walking the length of the marina boardwalk will introduce you to Cabo's notorious party central: From the boardwalk's western end beginning near the **Marina Fiesta Hotel**, you'll pass through the marina's Golden Zone (along which is the infamous **Nowhere ¿Bar?**). If you make it all the way to the **Wyndham Hotel**, you've essentially completed the marina walk. Note that it's here where you can catch a boat for sunset cruises, whale-watching, and sportfishing.

Traversing the Corridor

To see the Corridor and make it over to San José del Cabo from Cabos San Lucas, it's most convenient and least expensive if you rent a car for a couple of days. (Taxis are frightfully expensive, and buses limit you to their schedule and stops.) Shop around for rentals and you'll be amazed at the range; Alamo and Cactus Car include insurance in their rates. Take your time driving along the Corridor, both to enjoy the sights of the coast, as well as to become accustomed to the unique traits of this quirky highway. On and off ramps are challenging, as you'll see. About mid-Corridor you pass **Playa Santa María** and **Chileno Bay**, fun for stops to sun, swim,

and snorkel. Bring your own equipment and refreshments.

As you near San José del Cabo, you can't miss the **Tiendas de Palmilla** (Palmilla Shopping Center) across from the **One&Only Palmilla Resort**. "Tiendas" comprises upscale shops and some excellent restaurants, including Nick-San. (Walmart, Costco, and Sam's Club have also set up shop along Highway 1 for more basic shopping needs.) Heading farther east, you'll shortly see a turnout and large parking lot—a great panoramic overlook of the Sea of Cortez. It's a lovely spot to watch the surf at the **Old Man's break**, to your right, in front of the **Cabo Surf Hotel**.

Beachy, Happy People

For a small deposit, many hotels provide beach towels, coolers, and umbrellas, or you can rent these from **Trader Dicks**, near the Costa Azul beach. Dicks also fixes good box lunches. The 7 Seas restaurant at Cabo Surf Hotel will deliver cocktails beachside, meaning you don't even have to leave your sunning spot for a margarita. To get to the most pristine beaches along the Sea of Cortez, head east out of San José del Cabo by car. At the corner of Boulevard Mijares and Calle Benito Juárez in San José, turn east at the sign marked "pueblo la playa." The paved street soon becomes a dirt road that leads to the small fishing villages of **La Playa** (The Beach) and **La Playita** (The Little Beach), about 1½ km (½ mile) from San José. As the gateway between San Jose del Cabo and the East Cape coastline, this area known as Puerto Los Cabos is marked by a series of roundabouts that branch to the marina, Cacti Mundo (cactus world gardens), organic farms (Flora Farms and Los Tamarindos), and luxury resorts like Secrets and JW Marriott.

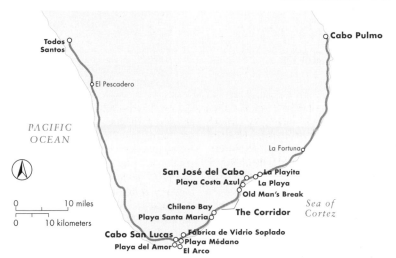

Todos
Santos

Cabo Pulmo

El Pescadero

PACIFIC
OCEAN

La Fortuna

San José del Cabo — La Playita
Playa Costa Azul — La Playa
Old Man's Break

0   10 miles
0   10 kilometers

Chileno Bay
Playa Santa Maria — The Corridor

Sea of
Cortez

Cabo San Lucas — Fábrica de Vidrio Soplado
Playa Médano
Playa del Amor — El Arco

From La Playita, drive 60 km (37 miles) up the coast to the ecological reserve **Cabo Pulmo,** home of Baja Sur's largest coral reef. Water depths range from 15 to 130 feet, and colorful marine animals live among the reef and shipwrecks. When hunger pangs call, stroll up the beach from Cabo Pulmo to **Tito's** for a fish taco and an ice-cold cerveza. Try to get back to La Playa by late afternoon to avoid driving the East Cape's dirt road at night. Stop for some fresh seafood and a frozen margarita at **Buzzard's Bar and Grill** right near the beach just north of La Playa. San José is 10 minutes away.

Artsy Los Cabos

Set out from Cabo San Lucas for the **Fábrica de Vidrio Soplado** (Blown-Glass Factory)—a bit hard to find if you're driving yourself. First head toward San José on Avenida Lázaro Cárdenas, which becomes Highway 1. Turn left at the stoplight and signs for the bypass to Todos Santos; then look for signs to the factory. It's in an industrial area two blocks northwest of Highway 1. At the factory, you can watch the talented artisans use a process little changed since it was first developed some 4,000 years ago.

From the factory, head east for the 20-minute drive to San José del Cabo. Park at the south end of Boulevard Mijares near the Tropicana Inn, since parking is limited from here on in. Grab some lunch at **Baja Brewing Company,** located on Avenida Morelos. The pub has a tasty San José Especial cerveza, and offers international fare to go along with it. Then stroll through the central plaza, or zócalo, directly in front of the **Mision de San José del Cabo Anuiti** (mission church) and take in the several art galleries north and west of the church.

For dinner, try Don Sanchez's in San Jose proper, where Canadian-born chef Tadd Chapman is elevating the presentation of local ingredients and Mexican wines.

Alternatively, from the glass factory, head north on Highway 19 for the one-hour drive to the laid-back town of Todos Santos. Lunch at **El Gusto!** restaurant in the Posada La Poza hotel promises to be one of the most sumptuous you'll get in Baja. (Reservations are a must.) Spend the afternoon visiting in-town galleries near the **Misión de Nuestra Señora de Pilar** (Mission of Our Lady of Pilar) church.

CRUISING TO LOS CABOS

Cruise lines with itineraries to Los Cabos and Baja California include Carnival, Celebrity, Crystal, Cunard, Holland America, Lindblad Expeditions, Norwegian, Oceania, Princess, Regent Seven Seas, Royal Caribbean, Seabourn, and Silversea. Most depart from Los Angeles (Long Beach), San Diego, San Francisco, Seattle, Fort Lauderdale, Miami, New York, San Juan, Vancouver, and even Southampton, England, or Bridgetown, Barbados. Most cruises to Baja dock at Cabo San Lucas, with a few calling at Ensenada, La Paz, and Loreto.

Terrific shopping, dining, beaches, and shore excursions and the unforgettable view of Los Arcos upon approach make Cabo San Lucas a crowd-pleaser among cruise ports. Ships need to drop anchor and tender passengers to the marina, about a 10-minute trip. Ensenada is a favorite stop on shorter Baja cruises. Its modern Cruise Port Village terminal berths two full-size ships at a time. La Paz, on the Sea of Cortez, wins rave reviews as being the most "authentically Mexican" of Baja's cruise destinations. A few large ships dock at its port of Pichilingue, about 16 km (10 miles) north of town. Smaller boats can berth at La Paz itself. It's back to the need for tenders at the port of Loreto, north of Pichilingue.

Carnival. Carnival is known for its large-volume cruises and template approach to its ships, two factors that probably help keep fares accessible. Boats in its Mexican fleet have more than 1,000 staterooms; at the time of this writing the newest ship, *Vista*, is scheduled to be inaugurated in 2016. Seven-night Mexican Riviera trips out of Los Angeles or San Diego hit Cabo San Lucas and, occasionally, La Paz, among other Pacific ports in Mexico.

Carnival wrote the book on Baja-only cruises, with three- or four-day itineraries out of Los Angeles or San Diego to Ensenada. Las Vegas–style shows and passenger participation is the norm. ☎ 888/227–6482 ⊕ *www.carnival.com*.

Celebrity. Spacious accommodations and the guest-lectured Enrichment Series are hallmarks of Celebrity cruises. Its *Millennium, Infinity,* and *Century* ply the Panama Canal east- and westbound on 13- to 17-day itineraries, hitting Cabo San Lucas along the way, with an extensive choice of departure ports (Fort Lauderdale, Los Angeles, Miami, San Diego, San Juan, or Seattle). ☎ 800/647–2251 ⊕ *www.celebritycruises.com*.

Crystal. Crystal is known for combining large ships with grandeur, opulence, and impeccable service. Its *Crystal Symphony* calls at Cabo San Lucas on a variety of itineraries from New York (18 days) and Los Angeles (10 days). ☎ 800/722–0021 ⊕ *www.crystalcruises.com*.

Holland America. The venerable Holland America line leaves from and returns to San Diego or Fort Lauderdale. Panama Canal cruises spanning 14-, 17-, 20-, 28-, and 29-day itineraries on the MS *Statendam* include stops in Cabo San Lucas, while a 21-day Hawaii-Mexico on the *Veendam* calls at Cabo San Lucas and other Mexican ports. ☎ 877/932–4259 ⊕ *www.hollandamerica.com*.

Lindblad Expeditions. Lindblad's smaller *Sea Lion* and *Sea Bird* take you where the other guys can't go, for an active, nature-themed Baja cruise experience. Eight- to 15-day excursions embark in La Paz and nose around the islands of the Sea of Cortez. Its kayaks and Zodiacs launch from the ship to provide you with unparalleled opportunity to watch whales, dolphins,

and seabirds. ☎ *800/EXPEDITION* ⊕ *www.expeditions.com.*

Norwegian Cruise Lines. Its tagline is "whatever floats your boat," and Norwegian *is* known for its relatively freewheeling style and variety of activities and excursions. Seven-day cruises on the *Star* depart from Los Angeles, with full days in Cabo San Lucas, and Panama Canal cruises on the *Jewel, Sun*, and *Pearl* from 14 to 17 days all call on Cabo San Lucas. ☎ *866/234–7350* ⊕ *www.ncl.com.*

Oceania. "Intimate" and "cozy" are terms that get bandied about to describe the ships of Oceania, a relative newcomer to the cruise scene. Before arrival at Cabo San Lucas or any port, you can attend a lecture about its history, culture, and tradition. The *Regatta* stops here on a 16-day cruise out of Miami. ☎ *800/531–5619* ⊕ *www.oceaniacruises.com.*

Princess Cruises. Not so great for small children but good at keeping tweens, teens, and adults occupied, Princess strives to offer luxury at an affordable price. Its cruises may cost a little more than others, but you also get more for the money: large rooms, varied menus, and personalized service. Seven- to 11-day Mexican Riviera cruises aboard the *Sapphire Princess, Grand Princess, Coral Princess, Crown Princess*, or *Star Princess* start in Los Angeles or San Francisco and hit Los Cabos and other Pacific ports. Shorter three- or four-day trips out of Los Angeles call at Ensenada. ☎ *800/774–6237* ⊕ *www.princess.com.*

Regent Seven Seas Cruises. RSSC's luxury liner the *Navigator* offers trips that originate in Miami and San Francisco and call at Cabo San Lucas on select Panama Canal and transpacific itineraries. Some stop here for a half day; others stay in

port longer, making RSSC a rare cruise company that lets you sample Los Cabos' evening diversions. ☎ *877/505–5370* ⊕ *www.rssc.com.*

Royal Caribbean. Royal Caribbean's 14-night Panama Canal cruises on *Jewel of the Seas* or *Legend of the Seas* originate in Fort Lauderdale, Los Angeles, and San Diego and call at Cabo San Lucas, among other Mexican Pacific ports. Striving to appeal to a broad clientele, the line offers lots of activities and services as well as many shore excursions. ☎ *866/562–7625* ⊕ *www.royalcaribbean.com.*

Silversea. Loads of activities, including guest lectures, are the hallmark of a cruise aboard Silversea's luxury liners. Its *Silver Spirit, Silver Shadow*, and *Silver Whisper* call at Cabo San Lucas on 16- to 18-day itineraries from Los Angeles and Fort Lauderdale. ☎ *877/276–6816* ⊕ *www. silversea.com.*

WEDDINGS

Choosing the Perfect Place. Los Cabos is growing in popularity as a Mexican wedding and honeymoon destination. Many couples choose to marry on the beach, often at sunset because it's cooler and more comfortable for everyone; others chuck the whole weather conundrum and marry in an air-conditioned resort ballroom.

The luxury of enjoying your wedding and honeymoon in one place has a cost: you may find it hard to have some alone time with your sweetie with all your family and friends on hand for days before and days after the main event. Consider booking an all-inclusive, which has plenty of meal options and activities to keep your guests busy. This will make it easier for them to respect your privacy and stick to mingling with you and your spouse at planned times.

Wedding Attire. Some women choose a traditional full wedding gown with veil, but more popular and comfortable—especially for an outdoor wedding—is a simple sheath or a white cotton or linen dress that will breathe in the tropical heat. Some brides opt for even less formal attire: anything from a sundress to shorts or a bathing suit.

Weddings on the beach are best done barefoot, even when the bride wears a gown. Choose strappy sandals for a wedding or reception that's not on the sand; forget the notion of stockings: it's usually too hot and humid. Whatever type of attire you choose, purchase it and get any alterations done before leaving home. (There's virtually no place here to do either.) Buy a special garment bag and hand-carry your dress on the plane. Don't let this be the one time in your life that your luggage goes missing.

The groom and any groomsmen can take their what-to-wear cue from the female half of the wedding party, but know that Los Cabos has no place to rent formal attire.

Time of Year. Planning according to the weather can be critical for a successful Los Cabos wedding. If you're getting married in your bathing suit, you might not mind some heat and humidity, but will your venue—and your future mother-in-law—hold up under the summer heat? We recommend substituting the traditional June wedding that's so suitable for New England with one held between November and February. March through June is usually dry but extremely warm and humid.

By July, the heat can be unbearable for an outdoor afternoon wedding. Summer rains, rarely voluminous in Los Cabos, begin to fall here in July. Although hurricanes are rarer along the Pacific than the Caribbean, they can occur August through late October and even early November. For an outdoor wedding, establish a detailed backup plan in case the weather lets you down.

Finding a Wedding Planner. Hiring a wedding planner will minimize stress for all but the simplest of ceremonies. The slogan of one firm here is: "if you have the groom and the dress, we can do the rest." And a planner really can. A year or more in advance, the planner will, among other things, help choose the venue, find a florist, and arrange for a photographer and musicians.

The most obvious place to find a wedding planner is at a resort hotel that becomes wedding central: providing accommodations for you and your guests, the wedding ceremony venue, and the restaurant or ballroom for the reception. But you can

also hire an independent wedding coordinator; just Google "Los Cabos wedding" and you'll get tons of hits. Unless you're fluent in Spanish, make sure the person who will be arranging one of your life's milestones speaks and understands English well. (Most here do.) Ask for references, and check them.

When interviewing a planner, talk about your budget, and ask about costs. Are there hourly fees or one fee for the whole event? How available will the consultant and his or her assistants be? Which vendors are used and why? How long have they been in business? Request a list of the exact services they'll provide, and get a proposal in writing. If you don't feel this is the right person or agency for you, try someone else. Cost permitting, it's helpful to meet the planner in person.

Requirements. Getting a bona fide wedding planner will obviously facilitate completing the required paperwork and negotiating the legal requirements for marrying in Mexico. Blood tests must be done upon your arrival, but not more than 14 days before the ceremony. All documents must be translated by an authorized translator from the destination, and it's important to send these documents certified mail to your wedding coordinator at least a month ahead of the wedding.

You'll also need to submit an application for a marriage license as well as certified birth certificates (bring the original with you to Los Cabos, and send certified copies ahead of time). If either party is divorced or widowed, official death certificate or divorce decree must be supplied, and you must wait one year to remarry after the end of the previous marriage. (There's no way around this archaic requirement, still on the books,

designed to ensure that no lingering pregnancy remains from a former marriage. It doesn't matter whether you're 25 or 75.) The bride, groom, and four witnesses will also need to present passports and tourist cards. Wedding planners can round up witnesses if you don't have enough or any.

Since religious weddings aren't officially recognized in Mexico, a civil ceremony (*matrimonio civil*) is required, thus making your marriage valid in your home country as well. (It's the equivalent of being married in front of a justice of the peace.) Cabo San Lucas and San José del Cabo each have one civil judge who performs marriages, a good reason to start planning months in advance. Often for an extra fee, the judge will attend the site of your wedding if you prefer not to go to an office. Civil proceedings take about 10 minutes, and the wording is fixed in Spanish. Most wedding planners will provide an interpreter if you or your guests don't speak the language. For a Catholic ceremony, a priest here will expect evidence that you've attended the church's required pre-wedding sessions back home. If you're planning a Jewish wedding, you'll need to bring your rabbi with you: Los Cabos has no synagogues. Another option is to be married (secretly?) in your own country and then hold the wedding event without worrying about all the red tape.

Same-sex civil unions are now legal in Mexico City, the northern state of Coahuila, and measures are likely or pending in six other Mexican states. In Los Cabos, unfortunately, it's not. A few Los Cabos wedding planners have organized same-sex commitment ceremonies, but these have no legal standing.

KIDS AND FAMILIES

Los Cabos and Baja don't necessarily leap to mind when planning a vacation with the kids. (This isn't Orlando, after all.) It's not that the region is unfriendly to children, but enjoying time with the kids here does take some advance preparation and research.

Places to Stay

Except those that exclude children entirely, many of Los Cabos' beach hotels and all-inclusive resorts cater to families and have children's programs. A few offer little more than kid's pools, but several of the big hotels and their wealth of activities go way beyond that and make fine options for families with kids. A few of the standouts:

Dreams Los Cabos has an active Explorers Club for children ages 3–12. (The search for a beach treasure is always a crowd-pleaser.) Older kids will appreciate tennis, badminton, volleyball, and soccer.

Hilton's Cabo Kids' Club is geared toward kids 4–12, with cookie decorating, arts and crafts, board games, Spanish classes, cinema under the stars, and even spa treatments for kids at Spa Oasis.

Vacation Rentals: Apartments, condos, and villas are an excellent option for families. You can cook your own food (a big money saver), spread out, and set up a home away from home, which can make everyone feel more comfortable. If you decide to go the apartment- or condo-rental route, be sure to ask about the number and size of the swimming pools and whether outdoor spaces and barbecue areas are available.

Beaches

Ah, here's the rub: if you have visions of you and your kids frolicking in the surf, revise them a bit. Many Los Cabos–area beaches are notoriously unsafe for swimming, making a day at the beach literally a day *on* the beach, rather than in the water.

Even those strands of sand that are regarded as all right for swimming have some "But don't forget" cautions: Playa Palmilla, near San José del Cabo, offers tranquil water most days, with emphasis on "most." Playa Buenos Aires in the Corridor is safest between Hilton and Melia Cabo Real, where a man-made cove serves as a wave breaker. Playa Médano, just outside Cabo San Lucas, is good for swimming, but has some very quick drop-offs. Playa del Amor, at Land's End near Cabo San Lucas, is regarded as OK for swimming on the Sea of Cortez side, but not the Pacific side. (All Pacific beaches here are no-go for swimming.)

After Dark

Nightlife here is mostly geared toward grown-ups, but a few kid-friendly dining spots do exist. Even the restaurants at Cabo Wabo and the Hard Rock Cafe have familiar food that will satisfy the most finicky of eaters, and the U.S. chains are all here, too.

All restaurants in Mexico are nonsmoking (lighting up is permitted only in outdoor-seating areas). Both San José del Cabo and Cabo San Lucas have modern theaters that show Hollywood movies a few weeks after they premiere back home; note, though, that animated films or those rated "G" are often dubbed in Spanish.

Baja Top Five for Kids

Zoológico de Santiago, Santiago: Lions and tigers and bears, oh, my! Yes, they do exist here at this small zoo, an unexpected delight in such a remote locale. The sign shows a picture of an elephant, but don't get your hopes up on that one.

Bucaneer Queen, Cabo San Lucas: Avast ye mateys! Kids of all ages can dress up like pirates and go swashbuckling and hunting for treasure on this, one of several pirate cruises that operate out of Los Cabos. Just practice saying, "Aaaaarrrrrrrr!"

La Bufadora, near Ensenada: Literally "the buffalo snort," this natural tidal-wave phenomenon near Ensenada resembles a whale's blowhole. It sprays water 75 feet into the air, and everyone, no matter how curmudgeonly, delights in getting wet.

Swim with the Dolphins, San Jose del Cabo: Kids can swim and interact with friendly dolphins at the Marina in Puerto Los Cabos near San Jose. A second dolphin center is located at the Marina in Cabo San Lucas.

Whale-Watching, Los Cabos, Ensenada, Guerrero Negro, Loreto, Magdalena Bay: You'll find whale-watching venues up and down the peninsula. The vehicles make Baja whale-watching so special: outfitters here take you out to sea in pangas, small boats that let you get an up-close view of the magnificent beasts. We'd argue that, no matter what your age, Baja has no greater thrill.

Some Legalities

All children over the age of two require a Mexican Tourist Card (FMT card) to venture beyond the U.S. border region. Kids 15 and under require only a birth certificate to return to the United States by land from Mexico. If you fly home, everyone, regardless of age, must hold a passport to get back into the United States.

Don't forget Mexico's well known and stringent laws regarding the entry and exit of children under 18. All minors must be accompanied by both parents. In the absence of that, the parent not present—or parents, plural, in the case of kids

traveling with an organized group—must provide a notarized statement granting permission for the child to travel. Divorce, separation, or remarriage complicate these matters, but do not negate the requirement.

Even if you are traveling as a full family, we recommend erring on the side of caution if anything in your situation varies from that stereotypical 1950s *Leave It to Beaver* image of what a family looks like.

Mexican immigration officials really do know about remarriages, adoptions, blended families, multiethnic families, same-sex parents, and different last names, but copies of relevant documentation never hurt, just in case there are questions.

SNAPSHOT LOS CABOS

Where Desert Meets Sea

A visitor flying into Los Cabos will readily observe the peninsula's stark, brown terrain—indeed, it feels like you're arriving in the middle of nowhere. You'll realize soon after landing that even though the tip of Baja once also resembled the rest of the dry, inhospitable, stark desert, it has been transformed into an inviting desert oasis. The desert topography, where once only cacti and a few hardy palms resided, is now punctuated by posh hotels, manicured golf courses, and brimming swimming pools. As shown by the thousands of sun-worshipping, partying people seemingly oblivious to the fact that true desert lies, literally, across Highway 1 from their beachfront hotel, Los Cabos has successfully beaten back the drylands. Pay some respect to the area's roots by taking a hike or tour around the surrounding desert landscape.

A similar phenomenon exists in the northern sector of the peninsula, with the metro area anchored by Tijuana, in reality just a continuation of U.S. Southern California. Irrigation has turned this desert into one of Mexico's prime agricultural regions.

In between far-northern Baja and Los Cabos—the peninsula logs a distance of just over 1,600 km (1,000 miles), which compares to the north–south length of Italy—expect mostly desert scrubland. Two-thirds of the land mass is desert—a continuation of the Sonora Desert in the southwest United States—and receives about 10 inches of rain per year. The remaining third of the peninsula forms a mountainous spine, technically four mountain ranges. The northernmost of these mountains are pine-forested and might make you think you've taken a wrong turn to Oregon. East of San Felipe,

Baja's highest peak, the Picacho del Diablo ("Devil's Peak"), measures 10,150 feet and is snowcapped in winter.

The Bajacalifornianos

Geography, history, and economics have conspired to give Baja California a different population mix than the rest of Mexico. The country as a whole is the quintessential *mestizo* (mixed indigenous and white-European descent) culture, but only half of *Bajacalifornianos*—the name is a mouthful—can point to any indigenous ancestry. Historically, the peninsula was a land apart, a Wild West where only the intrepid dared to venture to seek their fortunes—many Mexicans still view Baja through that prism—and has drawn a more international population. The indigenous population that does live here is a recent addition of migrants from the poorer southern states of Oaxaca and Chiapas drawn to jobs in the border cities.

Baja's population is over 3 million, but nearly two-thirds of that number lives near the U.S. border. The 1,600-km (1,000-mile) drive from north to south confirms this is a sparsely populated region of Mexico. The state of Baja California Sur, the southern half of the peninsula, is the country's least populous.

U.S. citizens make up around 10% of the population, with retirees, business owners who have set up shop here, or commuters who live in Mexico but work in the San Diego metro area among them.

A Multifaceted Economy

By Mexican standards, the Baja Peninsula is prosperous, but things were not always so. It was only some six decades ago that Mexico even deemed part of the region to be economically viable enough for statehood, creating the state of Baja California north of the 28th parallel in 1953. Baja

California Sur became Mexico's newest state in 1974. Prior to that, the region, once considered far-off and neglected, was administered as a territory directly from Mexico City.

This is Mexico, however, and all is relative, even today. Wages here may be double, triple, or quadruple those in the rest of the country, but you pause when you realize that about $5 a day is still the national average. The presence of the maquiladora economy has brought up the on-paper average level of prosperity to the peninsula. This industry of tariff-free, export-geared manufacturing congregates on the U.S. border with more than 900 factories providing employment for more than 300,000 people, but critics decry the sweatshop conditions. Urban magnet Tijuana—whose population now stands at 1.5 million—attracts people from all over the country looking for jobs.

Agriculture and fishing contribute to Baja's economy, too. Cotton, fruit, flowers, and ornamental plants grow in the irrigated northern region. (Most of the rest of Baja California is too arid and inhospitable to support much agriculture.) Large populations of tuna, sardines, and lobster support the fishing industry.

And it goes without saying that tourism is a huge business in Baja, with an impressive $1 billion flowing into Los Cabos annually. Historically, the border region has tallied those kinds of numbers as well, but fears of drug-cartel violence have greatly eaten into tourism revenues for that area. The U.S. recession—Mexico's northern neighbor provides the bulk of Baja visitors—dampened peninsula-wide figures somewhat, but increased numbers since 2012 have sparked optimism.

Livin' la Vida Buena

Living the good life in Mexico—specifically in and around Los Cabos—seems to get easier year after year. Americans and Canadians are by far the biggest groups of expats, not only at the peninsula's southern tip, but in communities such as Ensenada, Rosarito, Loreto, and La Paz. In addition to those who have relocated to make Mexico their home, many foreigners have part-time retirement or vacation homes here.

Do not fall prey, though, to the dreaded "Sunshine Syndrome" that afflicts countless visitors to Los Cabos and Baja. Pause and take a deep breath if you find yourself on vacation here and starting to utter the words: "Honey, we met that nice real estate agent in the hotel bar. You know, we should buy a house here." Many succumb to the temptation, go back home and sell the farm, and return, only to find that living in Baja bears little resemblance to vacationing here. Experts suggest doing a trial rental for a few months. See if living the day-to-day life here is for you.

The sheer number of foreigners living in Los Cabos and the larger communities of Baja means that contractors and shopkeepers are used to dealing with gringos; most speak good to excellent English. Los Cabos, especially, is rich with English-language publications and opportunities for foreigners to meet up for events or volunteer work.

FLAVORS OF
LOS CABOS

"Me sube el colesterol, mi amorcita," goes the chorus to a bouncy, popular song here. "My cholesterol's going up, my love," laments the singer about the heavy, fried Mexican food he gets at home. We take it he's never been to Baja and seen how innovative chefs here are playing around with traditional Mexican fare. Not too long ago the dining options in the Cape were pretty limited, though tastily so, with mostly tacos *de pescado y cerveza* (fish tacos and beer) or *pollo y cerveza* (chicken and beer). No longer, amigos. Walking the streets of Cabo and San José, travelers will be pleased to find grand, innovative dining experiences. Things will never go completely high-brow here because, some days, nothing beats tacos and beer.

Sibling Rivalry

The friendly inter-Cabo rivalry infuses everything—the dining scene included. Historically, it's been a comparison of quantity vs. quality: Cabo San Lucas wins hands down in sheer volume and variety of dining places. What San José del Cabo lacks in numbers, it makes up for with the finesse and intimacy of its dining experience. The Golden Rule of Cabo San Lucas restaurateurs was once: "As long as you keep the margaritas coming, the customer will be happy." (The mass-market eateries still adhere to this rule.) But a growing number of San Lucas dining spots have followed San José's lead and have begun to offer intimate, cozy dining experiences.

Nuevo Mexican

The terms get bandied about: "Nouveau Mexican," "Contemporary Mexican," *"Nueva Mexicana."* Ask a dozen Los Cabos chefs for a definition of today's Mexican cuisine, and you'll get a dozen different answers. Many prefer the description "Baja chic," to emphasize the peninsula's uncanny ability to find the right mix of fashionable and casual. Major changes have come to Mexican gastronomy in the past decade. Traditionally heavy cuisine is being altered and reinterpreted. The trend is moving toward using quality local, organic ingredients and combining traditional Mexican fare with elements of other cuisines, all the while asserting one's own interpretation. All chefs are quick to point out that they're not abandoning Mexican cooking entirely. "People visit Mexico. They do expect Mexican food," one chef told us. The rise in popularity of north Baja's steadily growing wine region can also be found on many of Los Cabos' menus, so be sure to try some of the quality Mexican varietals that you can't yet obtain in the United States.

Seafood

With 4,025 km (2,500 miles) of coastline and no point more than 110 km (70 miles) from the ocean, seafood figures prominently in Baja's cuisine. Baja's signature dish is the ubiquitous *taco de pescado*, or fish taco: take strips of batter-fried fish (frequently halibut or mahimahi), wrap them, along with shredded cabbage, in a corn tortilla, and top it all off with onions, salsa, lime juice, and a dollop of sour cream or a mayonnaise-based sauce. You'll find as many recipes for Baja-style seafood stew as there are cooks, who refer to the dish as paella or *zarzuela*. (Ensenada is Baja's most famous spot for paella.) Any mix-and-match combination of clams, crab, shrimp, cod, sea bass, red snapper, or mahimahi could find its way into your dish, along with requisite white wine, garlic, and spices. Shellfish is frequently served here as a *coctel*, steamed with sauce and lime juice.

BEACHES

Updated by
Marlise Kast

Along the rocky cliffs of the Pacific Ocean and the Sea of Cortez lie many bays, coves, and some 80-odd km (50-odd miles) of sandy beach. The waters range from translucent green to deep navy (and even a stunning turquoise on some days of the year).

Playa Médano, in Cabo San Lucas, is the most visited and active stretch of sand. Playa del Amor (Lover's Beach) is five minutes across the bay by *panga* (water taxi, $7–$10), and is gorgeous and somewhat secluded, but by no means free of people. It's a great spot for swimming, although the waters can be somewhat busy with all the panga traffic. Just southwest of San José, the most popular beaches are Costa Azul and Playa Palmilla.

Most beaches in the area are seldom crowded, with the one major exception being the 3-km (2-mile) Playa Médano in Cabo San Lucas. Most people on this beach are here for the crowds, though, and there is no better place to people-watch. No other beaches are within walking distance of either Cabo San Lucas or San José del Cabo; some can be accessed by boat, but most require a car ride (unless you're staying at a Corridor hotel nearby). You can reach nearly all the beaches by bus. Taking the local public bus in Los Cabos is a safe and affordable way to access the beaches, but it takes time and it is imperative that you lug extra water if your adventuring is going to take place during the searing summer months.

PLANNING

WHEN TO GO
Nearly 360 warm and sunny days per year, few bugs, and fantastic water temperatures (70s in winter and 80s in summer) allow visitors to enjoy this natural wonderland year-round. The winter holiday season is busy, and people often book months in advance. Spring break is another busy time. Late May through September is when it's hottest, and the least crowded.

SUN AND SAFETY

If swimming in the ocean or the sea is important to you, be sure to research beachside resorts, as most in this region are on stretches of beach where swimming is dangerous or forbidden due to strong currents. Nearly all resorts discourage guests from swimming in the ocean, except for Hilton and Melia Cabo Real where a man-made cove between the two hotels makes for calmer waters. Look for the beach warning flags posted outside resorts: red meaning conditions are dangerous, yellow a symbol to use caution, and green signifying conditions are safe. Barely visible rocks and strong undertows make many of the beaches unsuitable for swimming. Take care when you go swimming—it can be serenely calm or dangerously turbulent, depending on the day or even the hour. The Pacific side is notorious for rogue waves and intense undertows. Also, the sun here is fierce: don't underestimate the need for waterproof sunscreen and a wide-brimmed hat.

BEACH ETIQUETTE

As on most beaches in Mexico, nudity is not permitted on Los Cabos beaches. If you head to a beachside bar, it's appropriate to put on a cover-up, although you'd be hard-pressed to find a strict dress code at any of these places unless you're at one of the more posh resorts. As tempting as it is to pick up seashells from the beach, be advised that U.S. Customs commonly seizes these items upon reentry to the United States. Packing a picnic or cooler for a day at the beach is a great idea, as few of the public beaches have restaurants or food vendors. A few beaches have vendors offering umbrella rentals, but if you're really keen on having one for shelter, it's best to take your own.

BEACH FACILITIES

As a general rule, Los Cabos beaches are no-frills, with very few facilities. There is no established lifeguard program in the entire Los Cabos region. Hotels will often post a red flag on the beach to alert swimmers to strong currents and undertows, but you won't see such warnings on the stretches of public beach along the coasts.

More and more of the public beaches have toilets, but you'll still be hard-pressed to find a shower. The picnic tables, grills or fire pits, playgrounds, and other amenities common at U.S. beaches simply aren't part of the scene in Los Cabos. If you want or need anything for your day at the beach, it's best to pack it yourself. If any of the following facilities are present at a beach, we'll list them: lifeguard, toilets, showers, food concession, picnic tables, grills or fire pits, playground, parking lot, camping.

Mexican beaches are free and open to the public, although some of the resort developments along the Corridor are doing their best to keep everyone but their guests off the beaches in front of the resorts. Resort boundaries are usually very well marked; any beach after that is free for all.

IF YOU LIKE:	IN CABO SAN LUCAS	ALONG THE CORRIDOR	IN SAN JOSÉ DEL CABO OR BEYOND
Crystal clear water	El Médano, Playa del Amor	Bahía Santa María	San José del Cabo's main beach (aka Playa del Sol)
Snorkeling/ Swimming	Playa del Amor (near the Sand Falls area)	Bahía Santa María, Bahía Chileno	For snorkeling, keep going to the East Cape and Cabo Pulmo area
Surfing	Monuments Beach (at eastern end of El Médano Beach)	Costa Azul stretch, Acapulquito Beach (at the Cabo Surf Hotel)	Shipwreck, 14½ km (9 miles) northeast of San José; Nine Palms, just beyond
Beachside or ocean-view bars	The Office, Mango Deck, Billygan's at El Médano Beach	Zipper's at Costa Azul, or Acapulquito Beach at 7 Seas at Cabo Surf Hotel	Buzzard's Bar & Grill (east of La Playita) or El Ganzo Beach Club
Undis-covered beaches	El Faro Viejo Beach is difficult to access, with dangerous waves, but is a gem for sunbathing	A drive along the highway will reveal many "acceso a playa" signs—be wary of waves!	Los Frailes and Cabo Pulmo at Playa Los Arbolitos is distant—a full day's adventure—but pristine for water activities and well worth the time

SAN JOSÉ DEL CABO

Oh, the madness of it all. Here you are in a beach destination with gorgeous weather and miles of clear blue water, yet you dare not dive into the sea. Most of San José's hotels line Playa Hotelera on Paseo Malecón San José, and brochures and websites gleefully mention beach access. But here's the rub—though the long, level stretch of coarse brown sand is beautiful, the currents can be dangerously rough, the drop-offs are steep and close to shore, and the waves often pound brutally up onto the shore. While surfers love this type of water and flock here in droves, it's extremely dangerous for the casual swimmer. Warning signs are posted up and down the beach, just in case you happen to forget. Feel free to walk along the beach to the Estero San José, play some beach

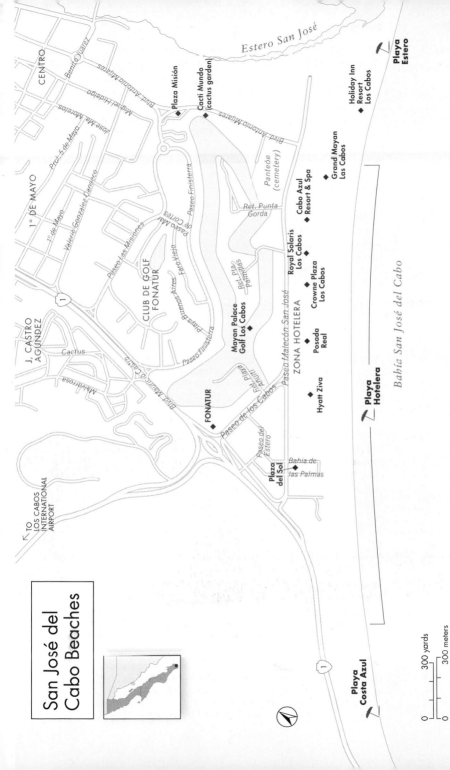

volleyball, or enjoy a horseback ride along the shore. But for swimming, head to protected Playa Palmilla just a few miles west, in the Corridor.

Playa Estero. A sandy beach can be enjoyed at the mouth of the Estero San José, the lush estuary that starts just east of the Holiday Inn hotel. This oasis is home to more than 350 species of wildlife and vegetation (200-plus species of birds alone), and can be explored on foot, or via kayaks rentable at El Ganzo Beach Club. Not recommended for swimming, it is nevertheless a worthwhile trip in an area that is otherwise not known for its lushness. Public parking is available just beyond the Holiday Inn. **Amenities:** parking lot. **Best for:** walking; sunrise. ⊠ *San José del Cabo.*

FAMILY **Playa Hotelera.** The long stretch of beach running in front of the hotels on the coast of San José del Cabo is called Playa Hotelera. This stretch of sand isn't swimmable, but once you step off the hotel property, it is public. You can always duck into one of the hotels for a snack or a sunset drink, or head across the street to Plaza Del Pescador for a meal at one of the restaurants. This beach often has locals with horses to rent for a beachside ride. At the west end of the beach you'll find shade palapas and children's play structures at Plazas Garuffi and Caracol, where there's also public parking. **Amenities:** parking lot. **Best for:** walking. ⊠ *San José del Cabo.*

ALONG THE CORRIDOR

The Corridor's coastline edges the Sea of Cortez, with long, secluded stretches of sand, tranquil bays, golf fairways, and huge resorts. Only a few areas are safe for swimming, but several hotels have man-made rocky breakwaters that create semi-safe swimming areas when the sea is calm. Look for blue-and-white signs along Highway 1 with symbols of a snorkel mask or a swimmer and "*acceso a playa*" ("beach access") written on them to alert you to beach turnoffs. It's worth studying a map ahead of time to get an idea of where your turnoff will be. Don't hesitate to ask around for directions, and don't lose hope if you still need to circle back around once or twice. Facilities are extremely limited and lifeguards are nonexistent, though many of the beaches now have portable toilets. ⚠ The four-lane Highway 1 has more-or-less well-marked turnoffs for hotels. Be alert: signage as a rule appears at the very last minute. Drivers tend to speed along most of the Corridor highway, which makes for a lot of business for the police officers who patrol the Corridor. Slow buses and trucks seem to appear out of nowhere, and confused tourists switch lanes with abandon. If you're driving, wait until you're safely parked to take in Sea of Cortez views.

Bahía Santa María and **Bahía Chileno** are two beautiful strands in the Corridor. Bahía Santa María is the less busy of the two, and both beaches offer fun snorkeling and safe swimming; the docile fish will actually approach you. For some truly secluded gems, drive northeast to the stunning beaches on the dirt road northeast of San José del

Continued on page 42

SURFING
CABO STYLE

by Larry Dunmire

From the gentlest of beginner waves
at Old Man's surf spot to the gnarliest winter
waves at Los Cerritos, Los Cabos has surf for everyone.
The tip of the Baja Peninsula has three key areas: the Pacific
coast (often called "the Pacific side"), the East Cape, and the Cabo
Corridor between them. This means that there are east-, west- and
south-facing beaches taking waves from just about every direction.

There are also warm, crystalline seas and great surf schools.
Friendly instructors make lessons fun and are more than willing to
tailor them to the needs of anyone—from tots to retirees, aspiring
surfers to experts. Schools also offer surf tours so you can benefit from
insider knowledge of the local waves and quirky surf spots before
heading out on your own.

LOS CABOS SURF FINDER

Surfer at a right-hand point break

Gentle waves during summer time.

Pacific Coast

Punta Conejo
Todos Santos
Punta Lobos
Playa San Pedrito
El Pescadero
El Pescadero
Playa Los Cerritos

WEST CAPE

19

PACIFIC SIDE

In winter, the Pacific from Cabo San Lucas town north to Todos Santos, often roils with rough, thundering swells. Surf spots here are only for the most accomplished although Los Cerritos, home to the Costa Azul Surf Shop and school, can have gentle waves in summer. Pacific-side beaches face essentially west and slightly north. Hence, winter swells coming from these directions (thanks to Alaskan storms) make landfall head on, creating great waves.

Punta Conejo: a rocky point break north of Todos Santos; unique in that it's surfable on both north and south swells. Has good right and left breaks. *11 km (7 miles) north of Todos Santos; turn off Hwy. 19 near Km 80.*

Punta Lobos: big point breaks with south swells. *South of Todos Santos; turn off Hwy. 19 at Km 54 onto dirt road, and continue for about 2.5 km (1.5 miles).*

Surfer on the nose of his long-board on a clean wave

Perfect waves in Salsipuedes, Baja California

Playa San Pedrito: a beautiful, broad, curved, sandy beach break, surfable on both west and north swells. *About 5 km (3 miles) south of Todos Santos; turn off Hwy. 19 at CAMPO EXPERIMENTA sign, and continue about 2.5 km (1.5 miles).*

El Pescadero: fast, consistent, right reef and beach breaks; watch out for painful sea urchins in shallow water! *Hwy. 19 at Km 59.*

Playa Los Cerritos: highly versatile beach—in summer, good for beginners, with gentle breaks and a safe, sandy bottom; winter waves are gnarly. Best ones are on northwest swells, though south swells aren't bad. Both left and right beach breaks. Home to Costa Azul Surf Shop; can get crowded. *Less than a km (half a mile) south of Todos Santos; Hwy. 19 at Km 66.*

CABO CORRIDOR

The 20-mile stretch of beautiful beaches and bays between the towns of Cabo San Lucas and San José del Cabo has no less than a dozen surf spots, including some that are hard to find and access. Opportunities range from the expert-only Monuments break just outside of Cabo to the beginner-friendly Old Man's spot. For experts, surfing in the Corridor is generally best in the summer and fall, when storms as far away as New Zealand and Antarctica can send south swells all the way up here.

Playa Monumentos: powerful left point break, offering great gut-wrenching waves on south and west swells. Dangerously shallow at low tide; many sea urchins. Great surf and sunset watching from bluff near parking area. *Far south end of Cabo's El Medano Beach, east of Cabo San Lucas on Hwy 1; pull off at Misiones de Cabo, drive to gate, park at right.*

Playa El Tule: long wide beach with great right reef break in El Tule Arroyo, near highway bridge of same name. One of few places you can still camp; need 4WD to get here. *Midway btw. Cabo San Lucas and San José. East on Hwy. 1, look for EL TULE sign, pull off road and drive toward ocean on soft, sandy road.*

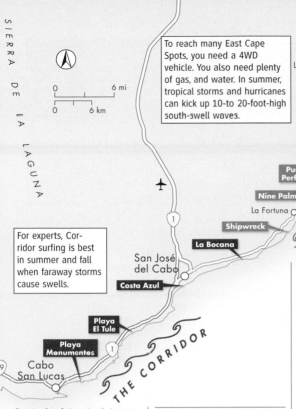

To reach many East Cape Spots, you need a 4WD vehicle. You also need plenty of gas, and water. In summer, tropical storms and hurricanes can kick up 10-to 20-foot-high south-swell waves.

For experts, Corridor surfing is best in summer and fall when faraway storms cause swells.

Costa Azul: beach of choice in summer. World-famous, experts-only Zippers break often tops 12 feet. Has two other popular breaks: Acapulquito (Old Man's) in front of Cabo Surf Hotel—forgiving with a gentle surf break and good for beginners—and The Rock, a more challenging reef break to the east. The rocks are near the surface; quite shallow at low tide. There's a restaurant and a branch of the Costa Azul Surf Shop here. *Hwy. 1.*

La Bocana: freshwater estuary with a river mouth beach break (i.e., giant barrels break upon sand bars created by runoff sand deposited here after powerful summer rains). Both left and right rides. *Hwy. 1, south of Intercontinental hotel.*

EAST CAPE

North and east of San José, up the rough, unpaved East Cape Road, there are many breaks with good waves that are perpetually empty—with good reason. To get here, you need a 4WD vehicle. You also need plenty of gas, sufficient water, an umbrella, and *mucho* sun block. Waves here aren't for beginners, and some of the coast is on private property. Note, too, that locals (both Mexican and gringo) can be protective of their spots. East Cape beaches face south and east, and, in summer, tropical storms and hurricanes can kick up 10-, 15-, and even 20-foot-high south-swell waves—exciting for beginners to watch from the shore.

Shipwreck: fast, right reef break with south swells in summer. Considered the second-best summer surfing spot. Need 4WD to get here. *Off East Cape Rd., about 16 km (10 miles) up a rough, washboard road.*

Nine Palms: right point break with good, long waves and great shape but at least an hour's drive out. *East Cape Rd., near village of Santa Elena and a palm-tree grove.*

Punta Perfecta: right point break; can get big and hollow (i.e., "tubular") during summer's south swells. Out of the way (4WD required) and hard to find; territorial local surfers get testy when asked for directions. *East Cape Rd., near Crossroads Country Club and Vinorama.*

Los Frailes: Waves get big on a south swell. Down a long, dusty, pounding drive (need 4WD). Beautiful white sand beach and tranquil desert surroundings. *East Cape Rd.*

Stand-up paddling: SUPing

LEARNING TO SURF

WHAT TO EXPECT
Expect introductory classes to cover how to lie on the board, paddle properly, pop up into a surf stance, handle wave-riding, and duck incoming waves.

GEARING UP
Both surf shops and schools offer a wide selection of lessons, gear, and boards—sometimes including "skegs," soft, stable beginners's boards with safe rubber fins. Novices will want to use longboards, which offer the most stability. Rash guards (form-fitting polyester vests) protect you from board chafing and sunburn. Booties, rubberized watershoes, protect your feet from rocks, coral and sea urchins.

GETTING OUT THERE
Most agree that the best place for beginners is San José del Cabo's Acapulquito Beach, home to Old Man's surf spot. It has gently breaking, "feathering" (very forgiving) waves and the region's most understanding surfers. Acapulquito Beach is also home to the Cabo Surf Hotel, with a top school. The **Mike Doyle Surf School** (⊕ *www. mikedoylesurfschool.com*) has five full-time teachers, certified by the NSSIA, the National Surf Schools and Instructor's Association (U.S.) and a great selection of more than 100 boards—short, long, "soft" boards for novices, and even a couple of SUP boards. The school shows an informative introductory video in the hotel's air-conditioned viewing room before you hit the beach.

Costa Azul Surf Shop (⊕ *www.costa-azul. com.mx*), with branches in San José del Cabo (near Zipper's Restaurant) and south of Todos Santos, near Los Cerritos Beach, is another option for lessons. Staff here can arrange tours to breaks so far off the path that roads to them aren't always marked on maps, let alone paved. The shop's website also has good interactive surfing maps.

Costa Azul's surf excursions—with guides (one guide for every two students), transportation, equipment, and two-hour lessons—cost US$180 a person.

SURF'S DOWN?

If the surf's flat, *no problema!* The latest craze is SUPing, or Stand-Up Paddling. It's done on flat waters using broad, long, light-weight boards that are comfortable to stand on. You paddle along, alternating sides for balance, using what resembles a single-bladed kayak paddle. SUPing is easy to master, great exercise, and highly enjoyable.

Accomplished surfers have pushed the SUPing envelope, paddling their boards into the surf line (or surf zone) and right into the waves, be they small or large. The paddle is then used to steer, almost like a boat's rudder. One step at a time, though—this type of SUPing is *not* as easy as the masters make it look!

Surf's up: you can really ride the waves in Los Cabos.

BOARD SHAPES

Longboard: Lengthier (about 2.5–3 m/9–10.5 feet), wider, thicker, and more buoyant than the often-miniscule shortboards. Offers more flotation and speedier paddling, which makes it easier to get into waves. Great for beginners and those with relaxed surf styles. **Skill level:** Beginner to Intermediate.

Funboard: A little shorter than the longboard with a slightly more acute nose and blunt tail, the funboard combines the best attributes of the longboards with some similar characteristics of the shorter boards. Good for beginners or surfers looking for a board more maneuverable and faster than a longboard. **Skill level:** Beginner to Intermediate.

Fishboard: A stumpy, blunt-nosed, twin-finned board that features a "V" tail (giving it a "fish" like look, hence the name) and is fast and maneuverable. Good for catching small, steep slow waves and pulling tricks. At one point this was the world's best-selling surfboard. **Skill level:** Intermediate to Expert.

Shortboard: Shortboards came on the scene in the late '60s when the average board length dropped from 9'6" to 6'6" (3m to 2m) and changed wave riding forever. This short, light, high-performance board is designed for carving the wave with a high amount of maneuverability. These boards need a fast steep wave, completely different from a "longboard" break, which tends to be slower with shallower wave faces. **Skill level:** Expert.

Beginner

Expert

Funboards

Fish

Longboards

Shortboards

Shallow wave faces, easiest surfing

Steeper wave faces, difficult surfing

SURF SLANG

By Leland Baxter-Neal
and Larry Dunmire

Barrel: The area created when a wave breaks onto itself in a curl, creating a tube that's the surfer's nirvana. Also called the green room.

Barreled: becoming totally enclosed inside the wave's barrel during a ride. The ultimate "stoke!" Getting "barreled" is also sometimes known as spending time inside the "green room" or getting "tubed."

Beach break: The safest, best type for beginners. Waves break over sandy beaches. Found at Acapulquito (Old Man's), San Pedrito, and Los Cerritos.

Close out: When a wave or a section of a wave breaks all at once, rather than steadily in one direction. A frustrating situation for surfers; there's nowhere to go as the wave crashes down.

Ding: A hole, dent, crack or other damage to a board.

Drop in: To stand up and drop down in the face of a wave. Also used when one surfer cuts another off: "Hey, don't drop in on that guy!"

Duck dive: Maneuver where the surfer first pushes his or her board underwater and then dives with it, ducking under waves that have broken or are about to break. Difficult with a longboard.

Goofy foot: Having a right-foot-forward stance on the surfboard. The opposite is known as regular.

Outside: The area farther out from where waves break most regularly. Surfers line up here, and begin their paddling to catch waves.

Point break: Created as waves hit a point jutting into the ocean. With the right conditions, this can create very consistent waves and very long rides. Punta Lobos, Punta Conejo, and Monuments are examples.

Reef break: Waves break as they pass over reefs and create great (but sometimes dangerous) surf. There's always the chance of being scraped over extremely sharp coral or rocks. Found at El Tule, Shipwreck, and The Rock in Costa Azul.

Right/Left break: Terms for which direction the surfer actually travels on the wave, as seen from his or her perspective. Think of break direction in terms of when you're actually surfing the wave.

Set: waves often come in as sets, or groups of three to seven, sometimes more, in a row.

Stick: A surfboard.

Stoked: really, totally excited—usually about the surf conditions or your fantastic wave ride.

Swells: created by wind currents blowing over the sea's surface. The harder and the longer the winds blow, the larger the waves, and the longer the swell lasts.

Turtle roll: the surfer rolls over on the surfboard, going underwater and holding the board upside down. Used by longboarders and beginners to keep from being swept back toward shore by breaking waves.

Wipeout: a nasty crash off your board, usually having the wave crash down upon you.

(top) A surfer rips it up in Mexico; (bottom) Baja California Sur sunset

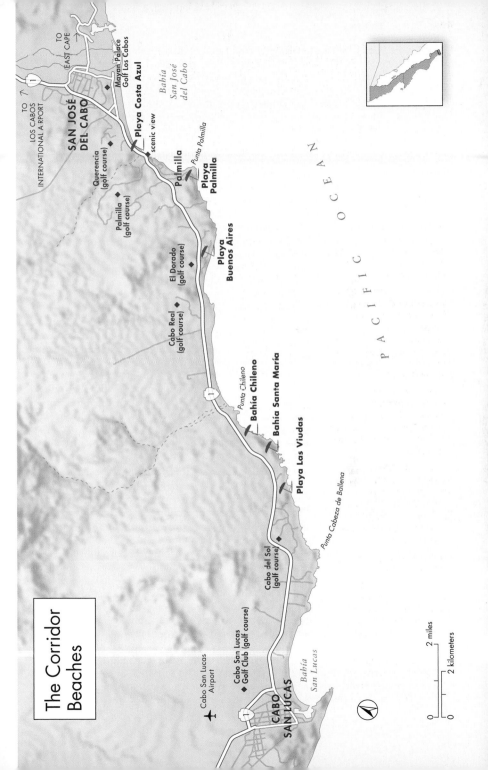

The Corridor Beaches

SAN JOSÉ DEL CABO

TO EAST CAPE

TO LOS CABOS INTERNATIONAL AIRPORT

Mayan Palace Golf Los Cabos

Playa Costa Azul

scenic view

Querencia (golf course)

Palmilla (golf course)

Punta Palmilla

Palmilla

Playa Palmilla

Bahía San José del Cabo

El Dorado (golf course)

Playa Buenos Aires

Cabo Real (golf course)

Punta Chileno

Bahía Chileno

Bahía Santa María

Playa Las Viudas

Punta Cabeza de Ballena

PACIFIC OCEAN

Cabo del Sol (golf course)

Cabo San Lucas Airport

Cabo San Lucas Golf Club (golf course)

CABO SAN LUCAS

Bahía San Lucas

2 miles

2 kilometers

0

Cabo. Soon after leaving San José you'll see mile after mile of gorgeous white sands, dotted with shade palapas and surfers looking for the next big break. Don't be put off by all of the private homes or "no trespassing" signs—beaches are plentiful and public access is clearly marked. The dirt road is well maintained and fine for passenger cars (despite dire-sounding warnings from locals who will tell you that you must have a four-wheel-drive vehicle)—but the dirt roads are best avoided if it's raining.

FAMILY
Fodor'sChoice
★

Bahía Chileno. A private enclave—with golf courses and residences—is being developed at Bahía Chileno, roughly midway between San José and Cabo San Lucas. Consistently ranked one of the cleanest beaches in Mexico, Chileno has been awarded "Blue Flag" certification, meaning 32 criteria for safety, services, water quality and other standards have been met. The beach skirts a small, crescent-shape cove with aquamarine waters and an outside reef that are perfect for snorkeling and swimming (there are even restrooms, showers, and handicap access). To the east are tide pools great for exploring with the kids. Getting here is easy, thanks to the well-marked access ramps on both sides of the road. The Chileno Bay project, a resort community on the rocky cliff at the east end of the beach continues to be developed. Along the western edge of Bahía Chileno, some 200 yards away, are some good-size boulders that you can scramble up. On the trek down you may see some stray wrappers and cans, but the beach itself is clean and usually not too crowded except on Sundays. In winter, this part of the Sea of Cortez gets chilly—refreshing for a dip, but most snorkelers don't spend too much time in the water. On weekends, get to the bay early if you want to claim shade under a palapa. **Amenities:** toilets; showers; parking lot. **Best for:** swimming; snorkeling; tide pools. ⊠ *Bahía Chileno, Corridor* ✛ *The turnoff for the beach is at Km 14.5 on Hwy. 1. Look for the signs whether driving west from San José or at Km 16 when driving east from Cabo San Lucas.*

FAMILY
Fodor'sChoice
★

Bahía Santa María. This wide, sloping, horseshoe-shape beach is surrounded by cactus-covered rocky cliffs; the placid waters here are a protected fish sanctuary. The bay is part of an underwater reserve and is a great place to snorkel: brightly colored fish swarm through chunks of white coral and golden sea fans. Unfortunately, this little slice of paradise offers no shade unless you sit in the shadows at the base of the cliffs, so you may want to bring a beach umbrella. In high season, from November to May, there's usually someone renting snorkeling gear for $10 a day or selling sarongs, straw hats, and soft drinks. It's best to bring your own supplies, though, including lots of drinking water, snacks, and sunscreen. Snorkel and booze-cruise boats from Cabo San Lucas visit the bay in midmorning through about 1 pm. Arrive midafternoon if you want to get that total Robinson Crusoe feel. The parking lot is a quarter mile or so off the highway and is sometimes guarded; be sure to tip the guard. The bay is roughly 19 km (12 miles) west of San José and 13 km (8 miles) east of Cabo San Lucas. Heading east, look for the sign saying "playa santa maría." **Amenities:** toilets; parking lot. **Best for:** snorkeling;

swimming; partiers. ⊠ *19 km (12 miles) west of San José del Cabo, 13 km (8 miles) east of Cabo San Lucas, Corridor.*

Playa Buenos Aires. This wide, lengthy, and accessible stretch of beach is one of the longest along the Cabo Corridor. Reef breaks for surfers can be good, but the beach is also known for its riptides, making it unswimmable. It's a great beach for long, quiet runs or walks, and it's not uncommon to find locals with horses to rent for a beach-side ride. Whales can easily be spotted from the beach from January through March. The section between Hilton and Meliá Cabo Real is best for swimming because of a small man-made cove that keeps waters calmer than exposed beaches. Here you'll find a tiny shack renting boogie boards and other water sports equipment. **Amenities:** toilets; parking lot (exit at Km 22 or 24). **Best for:** surfers; walking. ⊠ *Near the Secrets Marquis Hotel Los Cabos/Hilton and stretching down to Meliá Cabo Real.*

Playa Costa Azul. Cabo's best surfing beach runs 3 km (2 miles) south from San José's hotel zone along Highway 1. The Zipper and La Roca breaks are world famous. Playa Costa Azul connects to neighboring **Playa Acapulquito** in front of Cabo Surf Hotel. Surfers gather at both beaches year-round, but most come in summer, when hurricanes and tropical storms create the year's largest waves, and when the ocean is at its warmest. This condo-lined beach is popular with joggers and walkers, but swimming isn't advised. When getting in and out of the water in front of Cabo Surf Hotel (where surf lessons take place), watch out for the sea urchins that cling to the shallow rocks. Beginner surfers should ask locals to point out the mound of hidden rocks near the break closest to the cliffs; this means it's much safer to take "rights" than "lefts" at this break. Although not overly common, jellyfish can also be a problem here. The turnoff to this beach is sudden and only available to drivers coming from Cabo San Lucas (not from San José del Cabo). It's on the beach side of the highway, at Zipper's restaurant, which is on the sand by the surf breaks. If coming from San José del Cabo, you have to exit at Costa Azul Surf Shop and drive under the highway to the parking area. Food and drinks are available at Zipper's restaurant or at 7 Seas restaurant. **Amenities:** toilets; food concession; picnic tables; parking lot. **Best for:** surfing; walking; partiers. ⊠ *Just over 1 km (½ mile) southwest of San José del Cabo.*

Playa Las Viudas (*Widow's Beach*). Just west of Santa María Bay, this small public beach is often referred to as Twin Dolphin Beach after the Twin Dolphin Hotel, a longtime landmark that was demolished in mid-2007. The reef makes it a great place for snorkeling (bring your own gear), but it is open to the ocean and all the inherent dangers that entails, so swimming is not recommended. Low tides reveal great tidal pools filled with anemone, starfish, and other sea creatures (please leave these creatures in the sea). **Amenities:** toilets; parking lot. **Best for:** snorkeling. ⊠ *Hwy. 1, Km 12, Santa Maria Bay.*

Playa Palmilla. Check out the impressive multimillion-dollar villas on the road to Playa Palmilla, the best swimming beach near San José. Turn off the highway as if you're going to the One&Only Palmilla

Bahía Santa María (Santa Maria Bay) is a popular swimming and snorkeling spot along the Corridor.

and then cross over the highway on an overpass. Continue about half a mile. The entrance is from the side road through the ritzy Palmilla development; take a left before you reach the guardhouse of the One&Only Hotel. There are signs, but they're not exactly large. The beach is protected by a rocky point, and the water is almost always calm, however Punta Palmilla further out is popular with surfers during huge swells (20 ft+). A few thatched-roof palapas on the sand provide shade; there are trash cans but no restrooms. Panga fishermen have long used this beach as a base, and they're still here, after winning lengthy legal battles to ensure their continued access to the beach that provides their livelihood. Guards patrol the beach fronting the hotel, discouraging nonguests from entering the exclusive resort—although the public legally has access to cross the beach in front of the resort property. **Amenities:** parking lot. **Best for:** solitude; walking. ⊠ *Entrance on Hwy. 1, at Km 27, 8 km (5 miles) southwest of San José del Cabo.*

CABO SAN LUCAS

Fodor'sChoice
★
Playa del Amor (*Lover's Beach*). These days, lovers have little chance of finding much romantic solitude here. The azure cove on the Sea of Cortez at the very tip of the Land's End Peninsula may well be the area's most frequently photographed patch of sand. It's a must-see on every first-timer's list. Water taxis, glass-bottom boats, kayaks, and Jet Skis all make the short trip out from Playa Médano to this small beach, which is backed by cliffs. Snorkeling around the base of these

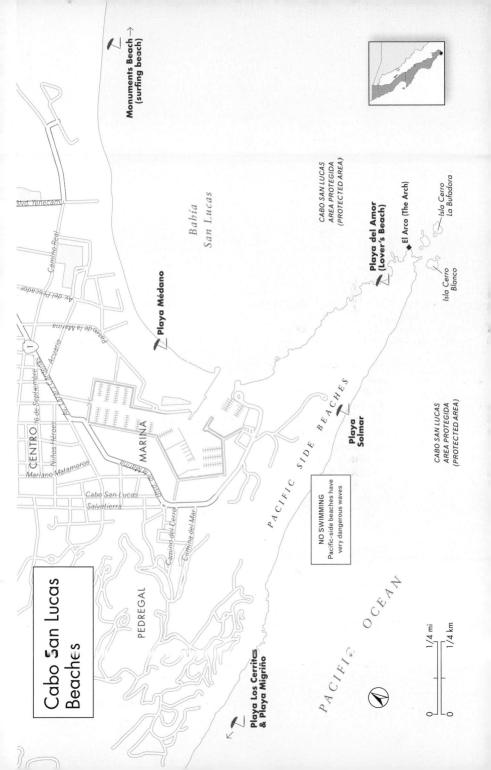

Cabo San Lucas Beaches

Monuments Beach →
(surfing beach)

Bahía San Lucas

Blvd. Yenecamú

Camino Real

Av. del Pescador

Paseo de la Marina

Playa Médano

CENTRO

16 de Septiembre

Niños Héroes

Lázaro Cárdenas

Acuario

MARINA

Mariano Matamoros

Cabo San Lucas

Salvatierra

Camino del Cerro

Camino del Mar

PEDREGAL

CABO SAN LUCAS
AREA PROTEGIDA
(PROTECTED AREA)

**Playa del Amor
(Lover's Beach)**

El Arco (The Arch)

*Isla Cerro
La Bufadora*

*Isla Cerro
Blanco*

P A C I F I C   S I D E   B E A C H E S

**Playa
Solmar**

CABO SAN LUCAS
AREA PROTEGIDA
(PROTECTED AREA)

NO SWIMMING
Pacific-side beaches have
very dangerous waves

P A C I F I C   O C E A N

**Playa Los Cerritos &
Playa Migriño**

1/4 mi

1/4 km

0

0

DID YOU KNOW?

Fascinating rock formations abound along the beaches of Los Cabos. Seismologists say that about 30 million years ago, a major seismic event tore a long finger of land—now called Baja California Peninsula—away from mainland Mexico.

CLOSE UP

Don't Stop the Parade

You've heard the saying "wine, women, and song," right? Well, along the festive Médano Beach it's "*cervezas, chicas, y música*" (beers, babes, and music). A walk along this colorful, pulsating half-mile stretch of beach, on the east side of Cabo San Lucas's harbor, will reveal people checking each other out and local vendors trying to sell something to everyone. Fun-loving crowds sit and sun, and eat and drink, listening to the rock and roll from the beach bars. Teams queue up for impromptu games of soccer and volleyball, Jet Skis roar in the distance, and Cabo's eternally ample sun beats down on it all. El Médano is essentially a daylong parade route, the parade itself fueled by buckets of beer, powerful margaritas, and that carefree feeling of being on vacation. If you don't want to be out on the beach in the thick of it, grab a table at The Office and enjoy it all from the shady haven created by its dozens of blue umbrellas.

rocks is fun when the water is calm; you may spot striped sergeant majors and iridescent green and blue parrot fish. Seals hang out on the rocks a bit farther out, at the base of "El Arco," Cabo's famed arched landmark. Swimming and snorkeling are best on the Sea of Cortez side of Lover's Beach, where the clear, green, almost luminescent water is unquestionably the nicest in Cabo San Lucas. The Pacific side is too turbulent for swimming but ideal for sunbathing. Vendors are usually present, but it's always best to bring your own snacks and plenty of water. The beach is crowded at times, but most people would agree that it's worth seeing, especially if you're a first-timer. To get here, take a five-minute panga water-taxi ride ($7–$10) or the half-hour glass-bottom boat tour. Opt for the latter if you wish to have some time to photograph the arch from the Pacific-side view. Both boats leave with relative frequency from the Cabo San Lucas marina or Playa Médano. **Amenities:** none. **Best for:** swimming; snorkeling; sunrise; sunset. ⊠ *Just outside Cabo San Lucas, at El Arco, Cabo San Lucas.*

Pisces Water Sports. Contact Pisces Water Sports for Hobie Cats, parasail, Waverunners, stand up paddle boards, water jetpacks (the latest craze), and ocean kayaks. ⊠ *Playa Médano next to Pueblo Bonito Rosé Hotel* ☎ *624/143–1288* ⊕ *www.piscessportfishing.com.*

FAMILY **Playa Médano.** Foamy plumes of water shoot from Jet Skis and dozens of water taxis buzz through the calm waters off Médano, a 3-km (2-mile) span of grainy tan sand that's always crowded. When cruise ships are in town, it's mobbed. Bars and restaurants line the sand, waiters deliver ice buckets filled with beer to sunbathers in lounge chairs, and vendors offer everything from silver jewelry to hats, T-shirts, and temporary henna tattoos. You can even have your hair braided into tiny cornrows or get a pedicure. Swimming areas are roped off to prevent accidents, and the water is usually calm enough for small children. But be aware: there are quick shoreline drop-offs, so life preservers are a good idea for the little paddlers in your group. Hotels line Médano, which is just north of downtown off Paseo del

EN ROUTE TO TODOS SANTOS

Playa Los Cerritos. This long, expansive beach on the Pacific Ocean, about 64 km (40 miles) north of Cabo San Lucas and on the way to the town of Todos Santos, is famous among surfers for its wonderful breaking waves in winter. Great for beginners, the waves here are consistent, accessible, and not overly powerful. Boards and lessons are available at the Costa Azul Surf Shop right on shore. This beach works best on northwest swells. Even if you don't ride the waves, you can watch them crash along the shore. The sandy beach is wide, flat, and ideal for wading and swimming close to shore. Swimming farther out is not recommended because of the strong currents. Most of the surfing crowd camps or stays in RVs near the beach. The developing area covers the basics with a few conveniences—including bustling Los Cerritos Club restaurant and two surf shops. Access to the beach is marked on Highway 19 (which connects Cabo San Lucas and Todos Santos) by a sign for Playa Los Cerritos at Km 64 (13 km [8 miles] south of Todos Santos). The graded dirt road to the beach is 2½ km (1½ miles) from Highway 19. **Amenities:** toilets; showers (for restaurant patrons); food concession; parking lot; camping; surfboards. **Best for:** surfing; swimming; snorkeling; walking. ⊠ *64 km (40 miles) north of Cabo San Lucas, 13 km (8 miles) south of Todos Santos.*

Pescador. Construction is constant on nearby streets, and parking is virtually impossible. The most popular spot on the beach is around the Baja Cantina Beach Club, where more than half a dozen bar-restaurants have set up beach chairs and tables. This is a hot spot for people-watching (and for singles). For something a bit more tranquil, grab a bite at Casa Dorada Resort's oceanfront restaurant Maydan, which is open to the public. Be prepared to deal with the many crafts vendors cruising the beach. They're generally not pushy, so a simple head shake and "*no, gracias*" will do. **Amenities:** food concession. **Best for:** partiers; snorkeling; swimming. ⊠ *Paseo del Pescador, Cabo San Lucas.*

Playa Migriño. There is a high probability you'll see whales here in winter. Don't expect peace and quiet here because this is one of the most popular beaches for ATV tours and horseback riding excursions. It's about 30 minutes north of Cabo San Lucas, so you'll find less crowds than Playa Medano but the pounding waves make this spot dangerous for swimming. When the swell is pumping, surfers come here for the hollow waves and the right point break. This is probably one of the best beaches in the area to catch the sunset. **Amenities:** none. **Best for:** horseback riding; surfing; sunset. ⊠ *North of Cabo San Lucas, off Mexico 19, Km 97, Playa Migriño.*

Playa Solmar Huge waves crash onto the sand on the Pacific side of Cabo San Lucas. This wide, beautiful beach stretches from Land's End north to the cliffs of El Pedregal, where mansions perch on steep cliffs. Swimming is impossible here because of the dangerous surf and undertow; stick to sunbathing and strolling. From December to March, you can spot gray whales spouting just offshore; dolphins leap above the waves year-round. The beach is at the end of Avenida Solmar off Boulevard Marina—an easy walk from downtown Cabo San Lucas. Five resorts—Solmar, Grand Solmar, Terrasol, Playa Grande, and Sandos Finisterra—are all on this beach, making it easy to stop for a meal if you get hungry. Crowds are minimal, as guests tend to stick to the hotel pools. **Amenities:** none. **Best for:** walking; solitude. ⊠ *Blvd. Marina to hotel entrances, Cabo San Lucas.*

SPORTS AND
THE OUTDOORS

Updated by
Marlise Kast

Long stretches of coastline along the Sea of Cortez and the Pacific Ocean make Los Cabos a beautiful spot for a beach vacation. However, you must be careful about where you take a dip, because many of those beautiful beaches border sea waters that are too dangerous for swimming due to strong undercurrents. Nearly 360 warm and sunny days per year make Los Cabos a natural wonderland, where outdoor activities—both land- and water-based—can be enjoyed year-round.

Los Cabos has something for everyone in a relatively small area. Whether you want a people-packed beach or a secluded cove, high-speed Jet Ski rides or leisurely fishing trips, deep-sea scuba expeditions or casual snorkeling, the waters off Cabo and the surrounding area offer endless possibilities.

Waterskiing, jet skiing, parasailing, and sailing are found almost exclusively at Cabo San Lucas's Playa Médano, where you can also go kayaking. At least eight good scuba-diving sites are near Playa del Amor. The East Cape, which includes the town of Cabo Pulmo, is a great area for kayaking, fishing, diving, and snorkeling. In fact, Cabo Pulmo has the only coral reef in the Sea of Cortez and there are numerous spots to dive—even just snorkeling right off the beach is amazing. Both the Sea of Cortez and the Pacific provide great waves for year-round surfing whether you're a longboarder or a hotshot on a short board. Still, in the spot known as the "Marlin Capital of the World," sportfishing remains one of the most famous and popular water sports.

If you'd like to mix up your Los Cabos experience with some land-based adventures, the area's desert terrain lends itself to all sorts of possibilities, whether you're a thrill-seeker or a laid-back bird-watcher. You can explore cactus fields, sand dunes, waterfalls, and mountain forests on foot or horseback. Several tall rock faces make for great climbing and rappelling, and zip-lining (sliding across cables with a pulley) is all the rage around Arroyo Azul. Back in town, you can play beach volleyball on Playa Médano, tennis at one of the hotels or at the Fonatur complex, get in a workout at your hotel or one of several gyms, or play a round of golf at one of the many courses available. If you are fortunate enough to be in Los Cabos during the whale migration (December through April)—when the weather is absolutely fantastic—a whale-watching trip with one of the many tour-boat operators is a must.

U.S. OPERATORS

Jig Stop Tours. Jig Stop Tours is located in Southern California and books fishing trips for a number of Los Cabos fleets like Gaviota, Pisces, and La Leona Fleets. It is one of the best, and easiest, one-stop fishing shops in the United States. ⊠ *34186 Coast Hwy., Dana Point, California, United States* ☎ *800/521–2281* ⊕ *www.jigstop.com.*

SAN JOSÉ DEL CABO AND THE CORRIDOR

BIKING

The Bicycle Experience. For those who want to get their blood pumping, but still feel like they're on vacation, this easy 5.3-km (3.3-mile) route circles the Marina at Puerto Los Cabos and to the Wirikuta Cactus Gardens with 1,500 species of cacti and nearly a million plants set in geometric patterns. The trail also passes the Sculpture Gardens where works by Jose Luis Cuevas, Manuel Felguerez, and Gabriel Macotela are on display. The ride conveniently ends at the chic El Ganzo Beach Club, the ideal spot to reward yourself with a margarita. ⊠ *Tiburón S/N, La Playita, El Ganzo Hotel, Marina, San José del Cabo* ☎ *624/104–9000 at El Ganzo* ⊠ *Bikes are available for $20 for 4 hours, which includes the $3 entrance fee to the Wirikuta Cactus Gardens.*

FOUR-WHEELING

Fodor's Choice
★
Sierra Buggies. Anyone apprehensive about off-roading in the desert should definitely experience this tour where safety is the top priority. The fleet of 650cc Sand Spider buggies is well-maintained with excellent suspension, so even at high speeds, you can easily tackle the ruts, rocks, and rugged terrain. Tours explore the dirt trails of Baja's high sierra country and are customized to skill level and comfort. After traversing the Biosphere Reserve north of Cabo San Lucas, you can wash off the dirt during a refreshing swim at a hidden lagoon, followed by a light lunch. The 4½-hour tour starts at 9 and 1. ⊠ *Calle Nopal 19, Colonia Magisterial, Daily departures from Hotel Zone in San Jose del Cabo and Cabo San Lucas, San José del Cabo* ☎ *624/130–7623, 213/426–8790 in U.S.* ⊕ *www.sierrabuggies.com* ☎ *$180 for a single buggy, $230 for a double.*

LOS CABOS GOLF TIPS

■ Make reservations in advance to assure your tee time.

■ The pricing for golf changes frequently and many hotels offer combination promotional packages. Golf here is quite expensive, due, in part, to the cost of the water required to maintain each facility. The fees will typically include range access, the golf cart, and bottled water.

■ Twilight rates can offer significant savings; check ahead if that interests you.

■ Though Cabo is a casual, laid-back area, appropriate golf attire is required at all facilities: no T-shirts,

tank tops, halter tops, cutoffs, swimwear, or denim.

■ During the warm season, be sure to drink plenty of water.

■ Mexican banks have made it increasingly difficult for all businesses, including golf courses, to accept U.S. currency, but all golf courses accept major credit cards.

■ Consider using a reputable golf-tour operator. An experienced operator can be of immense assistance and can provide direct transport to the course that fits your desires and logistics. Refer to **Cabo Golf Tours** (☎ 877/718–4617 ⊕ *www. cabogolftours.net*).

GOLF

Greens fees quoted include off- and high-season rates and are subject to frequent change.

Los Cabos has become one of the world's top golf destinations, thanks to two factors. First came the support of Fonatur, Mexico's government tourism-development agency. In 1988 it expanded Los Cabos' appeal beyond sportfishing by opening a 9-hole course in San José. The second reason is that the Cabo area features some of the best winter weather in North America—Los Cabos doesn't experience even the occasional frigid winter possible in the southern United States. Green fairways dot the arid landscape like multiple oases in the desert. You will encounter many sublime views of the Sea of Cortez, and, on a few courses, play alongside it. Otherwise the motif is desert golf. The other strength of the area is that the overall quality of golf is quite high, with the likes of Tom Nicklaus, Robert Trent Jones II, Tom Weiskopf, Roy Dye, Greg Norman, and now Tiger Woods applying their design talents here.

Cabo Real Golf Course. This visually attractive layout features spectacular views of the mountains and sea, as well as a challenging test. Designed by Robert Trent Jones Jr., Cabo Real has straight and narrow fairways, difficult slopes, and strategically placed bunkers. The first six holes are in mountainous terrain, working their way up to 500 feet above sea level. The course then heads back to the water and eventually descends down to the Sea of Cortez by the 14th hole. Recovering from mistakes here can be quite difficult. In 2012, the back nine was redesigned by Jones with a new green on the 14th repositioned closer to the sea and the old 15th removed. Greens fee includes cart (walking is not permitted), water, practice balls, and towel. Taylormade clubs available to rent for $55. ⊠ *Hwy. 1, Km 19.5, San José del Cabo* ☎ 624/173 9400, 877/795–8727 ⊕ *www.questrogolf.com* ⊠ *$235; $165 after 1:30 pm. Taylormade rental clubs, $55* ⚡ *18 holes, 6848 yards, par 71.* ☞ *Facilities: Practice range, putting green, snack bar, restaurant, golf carts.*

Camp Campestre San José Golf Course. Here you are greeted by panoramic views stretching to the Sea of Cortez, canyons, and mountains on a Jack Nicklaus-design. This semiprivate course also features dramatic elevation changes and undulating tricky multilevel putting surfaces. Attractive bunkering requires well-placed tee shots and very accurate iron play. They have used paspalum grass throughout the course that sets Camp Campestre among the best manicured in the region. The only downfall is that there are no holes on the water. ⊠ *Km. 119, Libramiento Aeropuerto, San José del Cabo* ☎ *877/795–8727 from U.S., 624/173–9400* ⊕ *www.questrogolf.com* ⊠ *$140–$180* ⚡ *18 holes, 7055 yards, par 71* ☞ *Facilities: Carts, practice range, putting green, short-game area, restaurant, snack bar, rental clubs.*

Fodor's Choice **One&Only Palmilla Golf Course.** Here you will encounter 27 holes of some
★ of the best resort golf that Mexico has to offer. Crafted by Jack Nicklaus, it was his first work here. The Mountain and Arroyo Nines came first, with the Ocean Nine finished later. Generous target-style fairways wind their way through rugged mountainous desert terrain that is beautifully landscaped. The Ocean Nine drops 600 feet in elevation as you visit the edge of the Sea of Cortez, while the Mountain and Arroyo Nines are positioned higher and farther back from the water. Many will remark that the stretch of 6 to 8 holes on the Arroyo Course is one of the best anywhere, while the 3rd through 5th holes really get your attention on the Mountain Course. No matter the combination of Nines, you won't feel cheated and the conditioning is usually excellent though expensive. Five sets of tees on every hole accommodate various skill levels. ⊠ *Hwy. 1, Km 7.5, San José del Cabo* ☎ *624/144–5250* ⊕ *www.palmillagc.com* ⊠ *$135–$210* ⚡ *27 holes. Mountain Nine, 3602 yards; Ocean Nine, 3527 yards; Arroyo Nine, 3337 yards. All nines are par 36.* ☞ *Facilities: Practice range, putting green, lessons, beverage cart, limited restaurant, Callaway rental clubs.*

Puerto Los Cabos Golf Course. This course features an unusual combination of one 9 designed by Jack Nicklaus and the other by Greg Norman. Eventually each will build a second line to make this into two separate courses. This does not detract from its appeal as this is one of the area's most popular courses for visitors. Nicklaus's 9 features more expansive driving areas whereas the Norman 9 puts more of a premium on driving accuracy. Both 9s feature attractive bunkering and paspalum putting surfaces. ⊠ *Paseo de los Pescadores, San José del Cabo* ☎ *624/173–9400, 877/795–8727* ⊕ *www.questrogolf.com* ⊠ *$175–$250* ⚡ *18 holes, 7461 yards, par 73.* ☞ *Facilities: Practice range, putting green, short game area, snack bar, restaurant, rental clubs.*

Punta Sur Golf Course. Los Cabos' original course opened in 1987. Of all the golf courses in the area, this one would be the "starter" golf course. The layout has wide fairways and few obstacles or slopes. It's fairly flat and good for beginners or as a warm-up. The 9-hole course is lined with residential properties (broken windows are not unusual). Some holes (particularly the 7th) have nice ocean views. Beware, you will find the three par-3's to be long and testing. The conditioning is average and this heavily played course does not take reservations as it is played on a first-come, first-served basis. It was designed by Mario Schjtanan and Joe Finger. Greens fees include cart. There's a swimming pool, tennis, and gym on-site. ⊠ *Paseao Finisterra, No.1, San José del Cabo* ☎ *624/142–0905* ⊕ *www.vidantagolf.com* ⊠ *$59 for 9 holes or $89 for 18* ⚑. *9 holes, 3153 yards, par 35* ⊙ *6 am–6:30 pm* ☞ *Facilities: Putting green, short game area, hitting nets, carts, pull carts, men's and women's rental clubs ($30), shoe rentals, pro shop, golf lessons, bag storage, restaurant, bar, snack bar, swimming pool, tennis, gym.*

GUIDED ADVENTURE TOURS

FAMILY

Fodor's Choice

★

Baja Outback. Baja Outback offers a variety of guided tours that range from four hours to several days long. The routes run through Baja backcountry, where you have the opportunity to explore the Cape's rarely seen back roads while learning desert lore from a knowledgeable guide-cum-biologist. One option takes you to a remote mountain ranch before lunching and snorkeling at Cabo Pulmo. Day trips may include anything from hiking and snorkeling to city tours and turtle release programs (August to November). Baja Outback also offers multiday tour packages especially designed for kids with boogie boarding and sand castle building. For adventure-driven vacationers, tours include kayaking, surfing, and stand-up paddle boarding. ⊠ *San José del Cabo* ☎ *624/142–9215* ⊕ *www.bajaoutback.com* ⊠ *From $185 per person.*

Baja Wild. Baja Wild has a number of adventure packages including the "Six Day Inn-to-Inn Hiking, Biking, Kayaking, Snorkeling, Surfing, and Whale-Watching Adventure." You'll see the natural side of Cabo, with hikes to canyons, hot springs, fossil beds, and caves with rock paintings. They offer backcountry jeep tours, full-day kayak tours at Cabo Pulmo, and ATV tours in the desert. Private tours are available. ⊠ *Plaza Costa Azul, Hwy. 1, Km 28, San José del Cabo* ☎ *624/172–6300* ⊕ *www. bajawild.com* ⊠ *Backcountry jeep tours from $420 per vehicle; full-day kayak tours at Cabo Pulmo, $140; half-day ATV tours, $80. Private tours are available for double price.*

FAMILY

Wild Canyon Adventures. It's all in the name at this outdoor adventure company that offers zip-lining, camel rides, bungee jumping, ATV tours, a giant swing, and a glass-bottom gondola—all of which enter the vast El Tule Canyon. ATV tours (and brave hikers) can cross the Los Cabos Canyon Bridge, the longest wooden pedestrian bridge in the world measuring 1,082 feet long. Free transportation is offered from your hotel, but be sure to time your activities properly since the shuttle only runs every 3½ hours. ⊠ *El Tule Bridge, The Corridor* ☎ *624/144–4433* ⊕ *www.wildcanyon.com.mx.*

HORSEBACK RIDING

FAMILY **Cuadra San Francisco Equestrian Center.** The Cuadra San Francisco Equestrian Center offers trail rides and lessons on 50 beautiful and extremely well-trained horses. Trail rides go into the hills overlooking the Cabo Real property or to the San Carlos arroyo; both focus on the flora as much as the riding. Trips are limited to 20 people, with one guide for every six or seven people. Cuadra also specializes in private trail rides. Reserve at least a day in advance and request an English-speaking guide. Note that you must query them for rates, but expect to pay close to $50 per hour. ⊠ *Hwy. 1, Km 19.5, across from Casa del Mar and Las Ventanas al Paraíso hotels, San José del Cabo* ☎ *624/144–0160* ⊕ *www. loscaboshorses.com.*

KAYAKING

One of the most popular, practical, and eco-friendly ways to explore the pristine coves that dot Los Cabos' western shoreline is by kayak. Daylong package tours that combine kayaking with snorkeling cost anywhere from $70 to $150. Single or double kayaks can be rented by the hour for $15 to $20.

Baja Wild. For a combined kayak and snorkeling trip, try Baja Wild. Daylong outdoor trips include surfing; hiking; ATV; and whale-watching trips (November through April), as well as baby sea turtle release excursions (September through November). All trips include transportation, equipment, and lunch; you can substitute scuba diving for snorkeling. ⊠ *Plaza Costa Azul, Hwy. 1, Km 28, s/n Local 5, San José del Cabo* ☎ *624/172–6300* ⊕ *www.bajawild.com* ▰ *$140.*

SCUBA DIVING

Expert divers head to the **Gordo Banks** (100–130 feet; also known as the Wahoo Banks), which are 13 km (8 miles) off the coast of San José. The currents here are too strong for less experienced divers. This is the spot for hammerhead sharks—which are not generally aggressive with divers—plus many species of tropical fish and rays, and, if you're lucky, dolphins. Fall is the best time to go.

The Corridor has several popular diving sites. **Bahía Santa Maria** (20–60 feet) has water clear enough to see hard and soft corals, octopuses, eels, and many tropical fish. **Chileno Reef** (10–80 feet) is a protected finger reef 1 km (½ mile) from Chileno Bay, with many invertebrates, including starfish, flower urchins, and hydroids. The **Blowhole** (60–100 feet) is known for diverse terrain—massive boulders, rugged tunnels, shallow caverns, and deep rock cuts—which house manta rays, sea turtles, and large schools of amberjacks and grouper.

SPORTFISHING

The waters off Los Cabos are home to more than 800 species of fish—a good number of which bite all year-round. It's easy to arrange charters online, through hotels, and directly with sportfishing companies along the docks at Marina Cabo San Lucas. Indeed, to select a company yourself, consider hanging out at the marina between 1 pm and 4 pm when the boats come in, and asking the passengers about their experiences. Rather than book through an independent agent roaming the marina, it's best to reserve through a reputable company in an actual office. ⚠ Do not give a deposit to any agent walking along the marina since there is no guarantee someone will be there the next day to follow through. Cheaper boats often have engine trouble at sea, resulting in passengers switching to a lower category vessel without financial compensation. Yes, you might get an incredible deal from an independent agent, but you get what you pay for.

Prices range from $200 or $250 a day for a *panga* (small skiff) to $500 to $2,700 a day for a larger cruiser with a bathroom, a sunbathing deck, air conditioning, and possibly a few other amenities. The sky's the limit with the larger private yachts (think 80 feet); it's not unheard of for such vessels to cost $5,000 or $7,000 a day. No matter what you pay, rates should include a captain and crew, tackle, bait, drinks, and—sometimes—lunch. If you plan to spend a full day at sea, it's best to purchase an all-inclusive package rather than a bare bones trip lacking in services. Factor in the cost of a fishing license (about $16), required for all passengers over 18 years of age regardless if he or she is fishing. Slightly more affordable fishing licenses can be purchase through the CONAPESCA website (⊕ *www.conapescasandiego. org*). Most hotels in San José will arrange fishing trips. All of the Corridor hotels work with fishing fleets anchored at the Cabo San Lucas marina and a few with boats in Puerto Los Cabos, so any one of them can help you set up your fishing trips. Note that some hotels send customers to the company with the highest commission, so double-check recommendations and do your research. The major drawback of arranging a fishing trip from one of the Corridor hotels is the travel time involved in getting down to the water. It takes up to half an hour or more to reach the docks from Corridor hotels, and most boats depart at 6:30 am.

Gordo Banks Pangas. The pangas of Gordo Banks Pangas are near some of the hottest fishing spots in the Sea of Cortez: the Outer and Inner Gordo banks. The pangas accommodate up to three. Their cruisers

FLUTTER BY

Walk amid hundreds of butterflies at Sia Tikuva, a butterfly farm. Learn about the life of the flitting mariposas, and the magnificent flight of the monarchs here in the Baja Peninsula and Mexico. Move slowly and relax and you'll have dozens of these magical creatures landing on you in no time. ✉ *Ocotillo 1701, near the San José hotel beaches* ☎ *624/120-6233 or 624/154-5888* ⊕ *www. siatikuva.com.*

SPORTFISHING CONSERVATION

For decades, anglers wanted their trophies, a photo of themselves with their fish, and a sign showing the weight of the vanquished. Then came the realization that the fish didn't need to be killed, and the conservation movement began encouraging a "catch-and-release" program, returning to the water whatever wasn't to be eaten. In recent years, the world's sportfishing factions have been battling Mexico's powerful commercial union because the Mexican government enacted a law that would enable Mexico's many commercial longliners, as well as gillnet and seiner boats, to fish very close to Mexico's coast, practices that would quickly decimate the fragile fish stocks off Mexico's west coast and into the Sea of Cortez. For more information, go to ⊕ *www.seawatch.org*. The Billfish Foundation is leading the fight against the newest Mexican shark regulation, which would allow boats within 24 km (15 miles) of the Sea of Cortez and 32 km (20 miles) of Baja's west coast, and does not restrict by catch. It supports a bill in Mexico's congress at this writing that would roll the no-commercial-fishing zones back to 80 km (50 miles) offshore, and to 161 km (100 miles) off the coast of Los Cabos. A 2009 study conducted by the foundation concluded that sportfishing provides, directly or indirectly, 24,000 jobs and an annual $630 million to Los Cabos' economy. More info can be found at ⊕ *www.billfish.org*.

accommodate up to five. ⊠ *La Playa near San José del Cabo, San José del Cabo* ☎ *624/142–1147, 619/488–1859 in U.S.* ⊕ *www.gordobanks. com* ⊠ *Pangas from $210; cruisers from $380 per day.*

La Leona Fleet. Long a favorite for its great selection of pangas and superpangas, La Leona Fleet has boats available at both Playa Palmilla in the Corridor and La Playita in the San José del Cabo area. It has seven comfortable and speedy little rides; it's solely represented by the Jig Stop in Dana Point, California, who also represents the Abaroa, Gaviota, and Ana Mar fleets and a total of about 30 boats. ⊠ *The Puerto Nuevo Marina, Marina, San José del Cabo* ☎ *624/142–1152, 800/521–2281* ⊕ *www.jigstop.com* ⊠ *From $220 per day, not including fishing licenses, food, or drinks; cruisers range up to $560 per day.*

Minerva's Baja Tackle. Fishing gear and line are available at Minerva's Baja Tackle, which has nearly 40 years of experience fishing in Los Cabos. ⊠ *Francisco Madero just off of Blvd. Paseo de Marina, Marina, Cabos San Lucas* ☎ *624/143–1282* ⊕ *www.minervas.com*.

Santi Sport Fishing. Captain Victor at Santi Sport Fishing has a fleet of pangas near Cabo Adventures. Rates start at $175. ⊠ *Blvd Paseo de la Marina, Dock #2, near Cabo Adventures, Marina, Cabo San Lucas* ☎ *624/157–1499 cell* ⊕ *www.santisportfishing.com*,

Continued on page 67

SPORTFISHING

By Larry Dunmire

Cabo San Lucas is called both the Marlin Mecca and Marlin Capital of the World for good reason. Thanks to the warm waters of the Sea of Cortez, the tip of the Baja Peninsula has one of the world's largest concentrations of billfish. And, no matter what time of year you visit, there's a great chance— some locals say a 90% one—you'll make a catch, too.

More than 800 species of fish swim off Los Cabos, but anglers pursue only about half a dozen types. The most sought-after are the huge blue or black marlin, which have been known to fight for hours. The largest of these fish—the so-called granders—weigh in at 1,000 pounds or more. The more numerous, though smaller (up to 200 pounds), striped marlin are also popular catches.

Those interested in putting the catch-of-the-day on their table aim for the iridescent green and yellow dorado (also called mahi-mahi), tuna, yellowtail, and wahoo (also known as ono)—the latter a relative of the barracuda that can speed along at up to 50 mph. Also gaining popularity is light-tackle fly-fishing for roosterfish, jack crevalle, and pargo from small boats near the shore.

Something's always biting, but the greatest diversity of species inhabit Cabo's waters from June through November, when sea temperatures climb into the high 80s.

(above) A billfish catch in progress

WHAT TO EXPECT

You don't need to be experienced or physically strong to sportfish. Your boat's captain and crew will happily help you along, guiding you on how to properly handle the equipment.

Some of the larger boats have the so-called fighting chairs, which resemble a dentist's chair, firmly mounted to the deck. These rotate smoothly allowing you to follow the movement of a hooked fish and giving you the support you need to fight with a large black or blue marlin for an extended period of time.

Experienced fishermen sometimes forego chairs for the stand-up technique using a padded harness/fighting belt that has a heavy-duty plastic-and-metal rod holder connected to it. Though physically demanding—especially on the arms and lower back—this technique often speeds up the fight and is impressive to watch.

FISHING TWO WAYS

Most of Cabo's boats are equipped for the more traditional heavy-duty sportfishing using large, often cumbersome rods and reels and beautiful, colorful plastic lures with hooks. A modified form of fly-fishing is gaining popularity. This requires a finessed fly-casting technique and spot-on timing between crew and the fisherman. It utilizes ultra-lightweight rods and reels, relatively miniscule line, and a technique known as bait and switch.

You attract fish as near to the back of a boat as possible with hook-less lures. As the crew pulls in the lures, you cast your fly (with hooks) to the marlin. Fights with the lighter equipment—and with circle hooks rather than regular ones—are usually less harmful, enabling more fish to be released.

(top) Sportfishing in Los Cabos—one man's catch

CONSERVATION IN CABO

You're strongly encouraged to use the less-harmful circle hooks (shaped like an "O"), as opposed to straight hooks (resemble an L), which do terrible internal damage. It's now common to release all billfish, as well as any dorado, wahoo, or tuna that you don't plan to eat. Folks have frowned on trophy fishing unless it takes place during an official tournament. Instead, quickly take your photos with the fish, then release it.

The Cabo Sportfishing Association has a fleet-wide agreement that no more than one marlin per boat be taken per day. Usually all are released, denoted by the "T" flags flown from a boat's bridge as it enters the marina.

The few marlin that are brought in are hoisted and weighed, photographed, and then put to good use—taken to be smoked or given to needy locals. You can ask the crew to fillet the tastier species right on your boat, and you can usually arrange for the fish to be smoked or vacuum-packed and frozen to take home. Many restaurants, especially those found marina-side in Cabo San Lucas, will gladly prepare your catch any way you like. You hook it, they cook it.

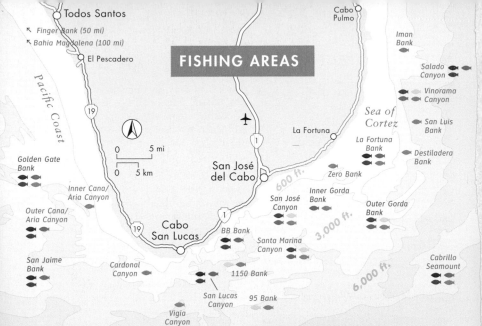

FISHING AREAS

Todos Santos

Finger Bank (50 mi)

Bahia Magdalena (100 mi)

El Pescadero

Pacific Coast

19

Golden Gate Bank

Inner Cana/ Aria Canyon

Outer Cana/ Aria Canyon

San Jaime Bank

Cardonal Canyon

19

Cabo San Lucas

BB Bank

Santa Marina Canyon

1150 Bank

San Lucas Canyon

95 Bank

Vigia Canyon

San José del Cabo

San José Canyon

Inner Gorda Bank

Outer Gorda Bank

Cabrillo Seamount

Sea of Cortez

La Fortuna

La Fortuna Bank

Zero Bank

Destiladera Bank

San Luis Bank

Vinorama Canyon

Salado Canyon

Iman Bank

Cabo Pulmo

600 ft.

3,000 ft.

6,000 ft.

0   5 mi

0   5 km

	FISH	AVAILABILITY
	Billfish*	Year around
	Yellowfin Tuna	Year around
	Dorado	July–December
	Wahoo	Year around
	Yellowtail	January–May
	Reef fish**	March–December

*Billfish include marlin, sailfish, and swordfish.

**Reef fish include roosterfish, cabrilla, sierra, pargo, and dog snapper.

For more information on fishing locations, check out BajaDirections.com.

Although there are many great fishing areas amid the underwater canyons and seamounts off the Baja coast, there are four major spots within 40 to 50 km (25 to 30 miles) of Cabo. From north to south these banks are the Golden Gate, San Jaime, the Gordo Banks (outer and inner), and the San José Canyon. All are within an hour or so of the Marina Cabo San Lucas, if you've chartered one of the faster boats. Farther north, about 80 km (50 miles) on the Pacific side above Todos Santos, is the Finger Bank. Also on the Pacific side, more 160 km (100

miles) north of Cabo, is Bahia Magdalena (Mag Bay), where the waters teem with marlin and game fish, and experienced anglers have been known to catch and release as many as 67 billfish in one day.

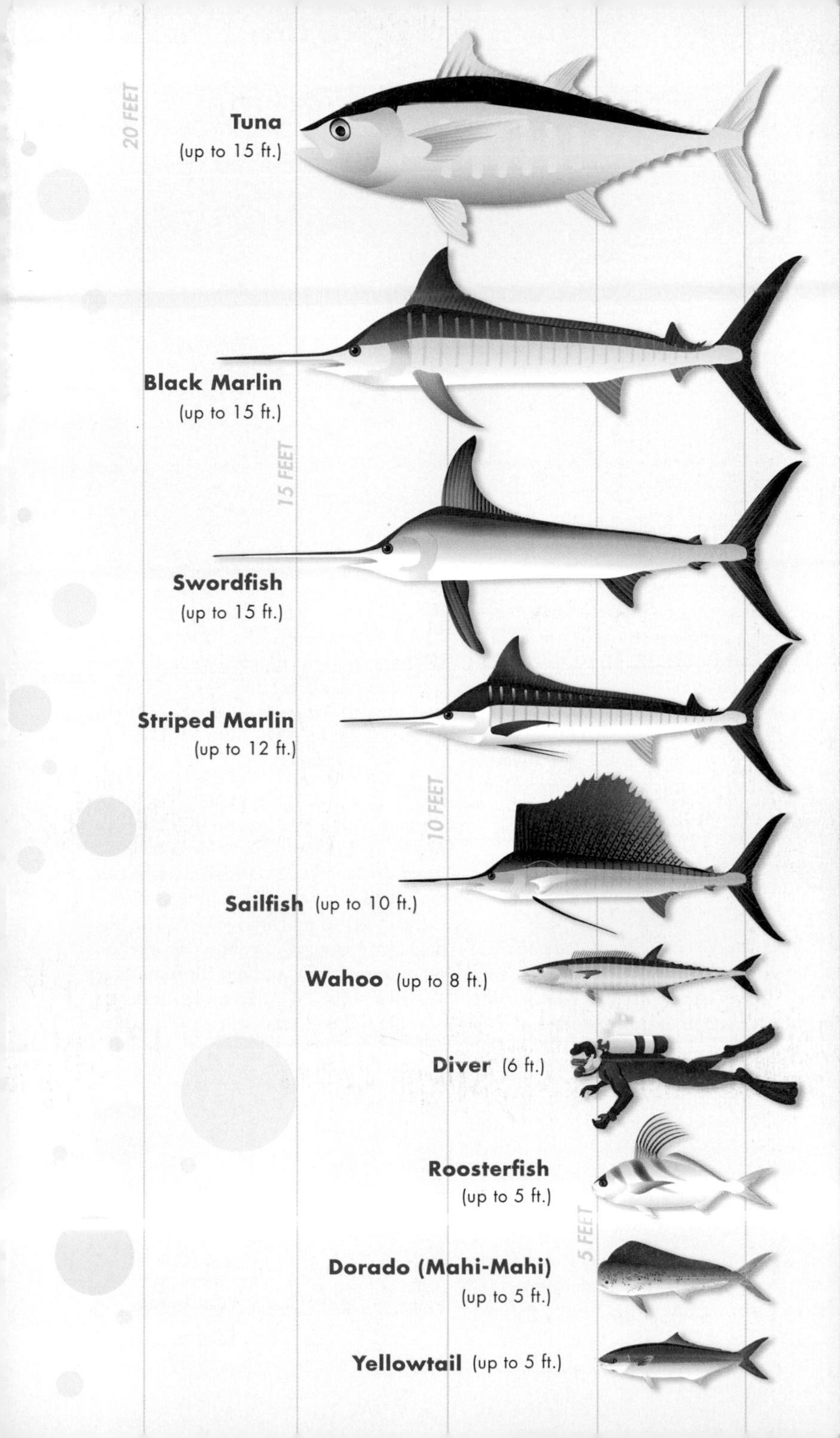

Tuna
(up to 15 ft.)

Black Marlin
(up to 15 ft.)

15 FEET

Swordfish
(up to 15 ft.)

Striped Marlin
(up to 12 ft.)

10 FEET

Sailfish (up to 10 ft.)

Wahoo (up to 8 ft.)

Diver (6 ft.)

Roosterfish
(up to 5 ft.)

5 FEET

Dorado (Mahi-Mahi)
(up to 5 ft.)

Yellowtail (up to 5 ft.)

CHARTERING A BOAT

You can arrange charters at hotels—through a concierge or a charter desk—at Los Cabos tackle shops, or directly through charter companies. It's also possible to make arrangements online before you arrive. Indeed, it's good to do this up to three months in advance for the busiest months of October and November. ■TIP➔ Don't arrange charters through time-share companies. They aren't always reliable and sometimes work with boats that aren't that well equipped.

Rates usually include a captain and crew, tackle, bait, fishing licenses, and soft drinks. You often need to bring your own lunch; if it is included, it usually costs extra, as do alcoholic drinks. Unless you're quoted an all-inclusive charter price, confirm what is and isn't included. Also, a tip of 15% of the cost of the charter will be appreciated. Note, too, that some charter companies will try to help solo anglers hook up with a group to share a boat.

A walk along the perimeter of the Marina Cabo San Lucas demonstrates that Cabo really is all about fishing.

Indeed, this is where most vendors are based and where most yachts set sail. (Departures are generally predawn—between 6 and 6:30 AM—so it's not a bad idea to locate your dock and boat ahead of time, in the light of day.)

It seems as if every yacht tied to the docks is a sport fisher, and you'll see different colored flags flying from the boats' outriggers. These designate the numbers and types of fish caught during the previous day of fishing as well as the number of marlin released. The blue flags are for marlin, yellow for dorado, white for wahoo, and red for tuna. Each red and white "T"-flag means a billfish was tagged and released.

(top) A cruiser out to sea; (bottom) Back to the marina

SURFING

You can rent a board right at the beach at Costa Azul in San José del Cabo, or at the Cabo Surf Hotel, and paddle right into the gentle, feathering waves at the Old Man's surf spot. If you're at the intermediate level or above, walk a short distance eastward to La Roca (The Rock) break. Big waves are best left to the experts up north, in Todos Santos.

Fodor's Choice
★

Costa Azul Surf Shop. For epic surfing tips, rentals, and lessons, head to Costa Azul Surf Shop. They have the best quiver in Los Cabos with over 150 hand-shaped boards from their popular Olea line. They also offer paddleboards, boogie boards, and snorkel gear. Lessons include transportation, the surfboard rental, a rash guard, and bottled water. All instructors are CPR certified and have 25 years of surfing experience. ⊠ *Hwy. 1, Km 28, San José del Cabo* ☎ *624/142–2771, 624/142–4454* ⊕ *www.costa-azul.com.mx* ⊠ *Rentals, $20 per day, $15 per day for four days or more; lessons, $85.*

Mike Doyle Surf School. The Mike Doyle Surf School is the top "surfer-friendly" location in all of Los Cabos. If you stay at the Cabo Surf Hotel where Mike Doyle's is located, you can check the surf conditions from the restaurant, bar, pool, or even from your balcony. The school has over 100 rental boards, from foam boards and short boards to long boards and stand up paddleboards. There are five surf instructors available at the shop for lessons. ⊠ *Cabo Surf Hotel, on the beach at the bottom of the steps, just below the 7 Seas restaurant, San José del Cabo* ☎ *624/172–6188, 858/964–5117 in U.S.* ⊕ *www.mikedoylesurfschool. com* ⊠ *From $30 for two-hour rentals. $79 group rate lessons; $99 for private instruction.*

WALKING TOURS

Land's End Tours. One of the best ways to experience Los Cabos in a single day is through Land's End photo city tour. The outing covers the top attractions of Cabos San Lucas, the Corridor, and San Jose del Cabo; photographs of your adventure are captured throughout the tour and sent to you within one week by email. Tour highlights include San José's historical center, a boat trip to the Arch, a visit to a glass-blowing factory, tequila tasting, shopping, and snorkeling. The six-hour tour begins at 8:15, and the price includes entrance fees, a tour guide, lunch, transportation, and photographs. Tours are offered every day except Wednesday and Sunday. Land's End hosts city tours of Todos Santos on Wednesday and Saturday. ⊠ *San José del Cabo* ☎ *624/123–4962* ⊕ *www.landsendtours.com* ⊠ *$75.*

DID YOU KNOW?

Visiting El Arco, a gorgeous rock formation at the southernmost tip of the Baja Peninsula, makes for a thrilling day trip from Cabo San Lucas.

CABO SAN LUCAS

BOATING

The themes of Los Cabos boat tours vary, but all tours follow essentially the same route: through Bahía Cabo San Lucas, past El Arco and the sea-lion colony, around Land's End into the Pacific Ocean, and then eastward through the Sea of Cortez along the Corridor. Costs run about $75 per person; all tours include an open bar and some offer lunch and snorkel tours. Many of these operators offer whale-watching trips as well.

Cabo Adventures. Cabo Adventures has a three-hour sailing trip on deluxe Beneteau sailboats, during which the crew will teach you some basic sailing maneuvers, or you can simply sit back and enjoy the scenery—the boats pass Lover's Arch. The four-hour trip includes food, drinks, snorkel gear, and stand-up paddleboards. ⊠ *Blvd. Paseo de la Marina, Lot 7, Marina, Cabos San Lucas* ☎ *624/173–9500, 866/393–5255* ⊕ *www.cabo-adventures.com* ⊠ *$109.*

Oceanus. The double-decker party boat *Oceanus* has four-hour snorkel cruises from 10:30 am to 3 pm and a sunset cruise with a live band that leaves at 5 pm (6 pm in summer) from the main dock in Cabo San Lucas. You can rent the *Oceanus* for birthdays, weddings, and other special occasions. Deep discounts can be found when booking online. ⊠ *Blvd. Marina, Marina, Cabo San Lucas* ☎ *624/143–1059, 624/143–3929* ⊕ *www.oceanusloscabos.com.mx* ⊠ *$65.*

Pisces Luxury Yachts. Pisces Luxury Yachts has charters starting at $1,750 for 2½-hour sunset excursions on their smallest 60-foot yacht, *It's All Good,* which holds up to 10 passengers. The full-day, all-inclusive rate runs about $3,300 and climbs to $15,000 for a full day on their 156-foot mega yacht. Photos and descriptions of the six yachts in their luxury fleet are available on their website. ⊠ *Barcos Piscis, S.A. de C.V., Cabo Maritime Center Marina 8-6, Marina, Cabo San Lucas* ☎ *624/143–1288* ⊕ *www.piscesyachts.com.*

FOUR-WHEELING

Riding an ATV across the desert is a thrill, but it is one of the more dangerous things you can do in this area. As fun as these tours may be, it is worth thinking about the destruction these vehicles cause to the fragile desert terrain. Additionally, many of the companies do not have insurance, and will make you sign explicit release-of-liability forms before going. They do issue helmets, goggles, and handkerchiefs to protect you from the sand and dust.

When ATV trips are properly conducted, they can be safe and fun. The most popular trip passes first through Cabo San Lucas, continues through desert cactus fields, and arrives at a big play area of large sand dunes with open expanses and specially carved trails, at the foot of **El Faro Viejo**, the old lighthouse. You can reach frighteningly high speeds as you descend the tall dunes. Navigating the narrow trails in the cactus fields is exciting but not for the fainthearted or steering-impaired. Another favorite trek travels past interesting rock formations, little creeks, and the beach on the way to a small mountain village called **La Candelaria.**

A three-hour trip costs about $100 for a single or $130 for a double (two people sharing an ATV) and includes boxed lunches and drinks. Trips to La Candelaria include lunch and cost about $120 for a single and $150 for a double. Wear tennis shoes, clothes you don't mind getting dirty, and a long-sleeve shirt or sweatshirt for afternoon tours in winter.

GOLF

Greens fee prices quoted include off- and high-season rates and are subject to frequent change.

Cabo del Sol Desert Course. The sister to the Ocean Course, the Desert Course designed by Tom Weiskopf sits on the other side of the Corridor away from the water and features an inland desert motif complete with artistic bunkering. Don't be fooled; the layout here is still very good. The Desert Course is very playable, yet from the back tees it may be even harder than the Ocean Course. The attractive layout includes one of the area's longest par-5 holes at 625 yards. Taylormade rental clubs are available for $65. Special rates are available if you play both this and the Cabo del Sol Ocean Course. ⊠ *Hwy. 1, Km 10.3, Cabo San Lucas* 🕾 *624/145–8200* ⊕ *www.cabodelsol.com* ✉ *$220–$365. Taylormade rental clubs, $65* 🏌 *18 holes, 7049 yards, par 72* ⚑ *Facilities: Practice range, putting green, short game area, golf carts, men's and women's lounges with showers, golf shop, beverage cart, snack bar, restaurant, lessons, club storage.*

Fodor's Choice **Cabo del Sol Ocean Course.** The Ocean Course has been named one
★ of the top courses in the world by numerous publications as it combines the best of ocean and desert golf. Designer Jack Nicklaus brags that it has the best three finishing holes in the world. On the par-3 17th hole, you drive over an ocean inlet with waves crashing below. The par-4 18th hole is a mirror image of the 18th at Pebble Beach, California. Seven holes are seaside, with the 5th and 17th named as one of the "Top 500 Holes in the World" by *Golf World.* Taylormade clubs are available to rent for $65. The Ocean Course is easily the priciest public-access course in the region, but is generally considered to be the best. ⊠ *Hwy 1, Km 10.3, Cabo San Lucas* 🕾 *624/145–8200* ⊕ *www.cabodelsol.com.* ✉ *$255–$365. Taylormade rental clubs, $65* 🏌 *18 holes, 7091 yards, par 72* ⚑ *Facilities: practice range, putting green, short game area, golf carts, men's and women's lounges with showers, golf shop, beverage cart, snack bar, restaurant, lessons, club storage.*

Cabo San Lucas Country Club. Designed by Pete Dye's late brother Roy, this course has lots of length along with seven lakes. It has smallish greens for the approaches, which makes for a real challenge. Routed through avenues of blanco trees, cardon cacti, and bougainvillea, its primary attraction may be the views, which include the famed landmark

Horseback riding along stretches of desolate Los Cabos beaches is a treat not to be missed.

"the Arch at Land's End." It's the golf course that's most convenient to downtown. Upgrades in 2014 have greatly improved the course, and with the addition of two new holes, it is both challenging and fun to play. ⊠ *Hwy. 1, Km 3.7, Cabo San Lucas* ☏ *624/143–4653, 888/239–7951* ⊕ *www.cabosanlucascountryclub.com* ⟋ *$99–$165* ♟ *18 holes, 7220 yards, par 72* ⟋ *Facilities: Pro shop, practice range, putting green, golf carts, rental clubs, bar, snack bar.*

GUIDED TOURS

Cabo Adventures. With a wide variety of unusual activities Cabo Adventures is unique adventure operator. Along with its popular Cabo Dolphins program are the four-hour Desert Safaris, which take you into the Sierra Mountains by Swiss-made Unimog to commune with camels, of all things! They also offer zip-lining, mountain biking, whale shark tours, and flyboards (like water jetpacks). ⊠ *Blvd. Paseo de la Marina, Marina, Cabo San Lucas* ☏ *624/173–9500, 888/526–2238* ⊕ *www. cabo-adventures.com* ⟋ *$109 per person.*

HORSEBACK RIDING

Cantering down an isolated beach or up a desert trail is one of the great pleasures of Los Cabos (as long as the sun isn't beating down too heavily). The following company has well-fed and well-trained horses. One-hour trips generally cost about $50 per person; two-hour trips about $80.

KAYAKING

In Cabo San Lucas, Playa Médano is the beach for kayaking. A number of companies located along El Médano near the Baja Cantina Beachside, at the bottom of Cabo Villas, offer kayak rentals, and there are guided tours that go out to Lover's Beach to view El Arco, and around the Land's End Rocks. Rates are pretty uniform from one operator to the other; you don't need to waste precious time by trying to comparison shop.

Omega Sports. Omega Sports has good rates on single and double kayaks. They also offer jet-skis. ⊠ *Playa Médano, on beach in front of Hotel Casa Dorada, next to Mango Deck, Cabo San Lucas.*

Tio Sports. Tio Sports was one of the original water-sports companies on El Médano Beach about 20 years ago and it's still a major operator with a sports palapa located on the beach at the ME Cabo Resort, plus stands and offices throughout Los Cabos. It provides aquatic tours, kayak rentals, stand-up paddleboards, and packages that include scuba and snorkeling. ⊠ *Playa Médano, Marina, Cabo San Lucas* ☎ *624/143–3399* ⊕ *www.tiosports.com.*

SCUBA DIVING

Generally, diving costs about $70 for one tank and $95 for two, including transportation. Equipment rental, dives in the Corridor, and night dives typically cost extra. Full-day trips to Gordo Banks and Cabo Pulmo cost about $200, including transportation, food, equipment, and two tanks. Most operators offer two- to four-day package deals.

Most dive shops have courses for noncertified divers; some may be offered through your hotel. Newly certified divers may go on local dives no more than 30 to 40 feet deep. Divers must show their C-card (diver certification card) before going on dives with reputable shops. Many operators offer widely recognized Professional Association of Diving Instructors (PADI) certification courses, which usually take place in hotel pools for the first couple of lessons.

At sites in **Bahía San Lucas** near El Arco you're likely to see colorful tropical fish traveling confidently in large schools. Yellow angelfish, green and blue parrot fish, red snappers, perfectly camouflaged stonefish, and long, slender needlefish share these waters. Divers regularly see stingrays, manta rays, and moray eels. The only problem with this location is the amount of boat traffic. The sound of motors penetrates deep into the water and can slightly mar the experience. **Neptune's Fingers** (60–120 feet) is a long rock formation with abundant fish. About 150 feet off Playa del Amor, **Pelican Rock** (25–100 feet) is a calm, protected spot where you can look down on Sand Falls (underwater cascades that drop into a 1,200 foot canyon) discovered by none other than Jacques Cousteau. The Point (15–80 feet) is a good spot for beginners who aren't ready to get too deep. The Shipwreck (40–60 feet), an old Japanese fishing boat, is close to Cabo San Lucas, near the Misiones del Cabo Hotel.

OPERATORS

Amigos del Mar. The oldest and most complete dive shop in Los Cabos area is Amigos del Mar. Its dive boats range from a 22-foot *panga* (a small, open-air skiff) to a 25-foot runabout and a 31-foot custom dive boat. The staff is courteous and knowledgeable, and all the guides speak English. ✉ *Blvd. Marina, Plaza Galicota, across from Finisterra Hotel, Marina, Cabo San Lucas* ☎ *624/143–0505, 513/898–0547 in U.S.* ⊕ *www.amigosdelmar.com* ✎ *Two-tank dives from $90; equipment rental, $35.*

Manta Scuba. This centrally located PADI 5-star outfit makes trips locally in the Corridor, as well as to Cabo Pulmo, Gordo Banks, and East Cape. ✉ *Plaza Gali, Blvd. Marina #7D Local 37 Int., Marina, Cabo San Lucas* ☎ *877/287–1120, 624/144–3871* ⊕ *www.caboscuba.com* ✎ *Two-tank dives from $95; equipment rental, $30.*

Solmar V. Find luxury on the über-comfortable live-aboard dive boat *Solmar V*, which takes nine-day remote diving trips to the islands of Socorro (November–June) and Guadalupe (August–October) for great-white shark cage diving. There are also five-day trips out of Ensenada, northern Baja. Twelve cabins with private baths serve a maximum of 24 passengers. This is one of Cabo's top diving experiences, so book well in advance. ✉ *Cabo San Lucas* ☎ *866/591–4906 toll free, 310/455–3600 in U.S.* ⊕ *www.solmar5.com* ✎ *From $3,450 to $4,175.*

SNORKELING

Many of the best dive spots are also good for snorkeling. Prime areas include the waters surrounding **Playa del Amor, Bahía Santa María, Bahía Chileno,** and **Cabo Pulmo.** Nearly all scuba operators also offer snorkel rentals and trips. Equipment rentals generally cost $10 per hour ($20 for the day). Two-hour guided trips to Playa del Amor are about $70; day trips to Cabo Pulmo cost about $150. Most of the snorkeling and excursion boats are based in the Cabo San Lucas harbor and the best place to make reservations is along the marina walkway, near the Wyndham Hotel or at the beach palapas along El Médano Beach.

If you're willing to plan ahead, booking online will often bring you significant discounts on these tours.

SPORTFISHING

Most vendors are at the Marina Cabo San Lucas. Ships tend to depart from sportfishing docks at the south end of the marina, near the Puerto Paraíso Mall, or from the docks at the Wyndham Hotel. It's very important to get specific directions and departure times, since it's hard to find your spot at 6:30 in the morning.

Gaviota Fleet. The Gaviota Fleet currently holds the record for the largest marlin caught in Cabo San Lucas's waters. The company has charter cruisers and super-pangas from 23 feet to 36 feet. ✉ *Docked between Gates 2 and 3 across from the Marina Fiesta Hotel, office at Villa Serena RV Park, Marina, Cabo San Lucas* ☎ *888/522–2442*

⊕ *www.gaviotasportfishing.com*
✉ *Egg Harbor yachts from $480.*

Minerva's Baja Tackle. Renowned
tackle store, Minerva's Baja Tackle
and Sportfishing Charters, has been
around for nearly 40 years and has
its own fleet with four sportfishing charter boats from 31 feet to
33 feet. ✉ *Madero between Blvd.*
Marina and Guerrero, Marina,
Cabo San Lucas ☎ *624/143–1282*
⊕ *www.minervas.com* ✉ *From*
$764, all-inclusive.

MATANCITAS MAN

The remains of pre-Hispanic
Indians, found in the giant sand
dune region near the current
Cabo San Lucas Lighthouse, were
given the name of Matancitas Man
by archaeologists. These people
were precursors to the Pericú
Indians that lived in the Cape
when explorer Hernán Cortés
arrived in 1535.

Fodor's Choice
★ **Picante Fleet.** One of the top sport-
fishing fleets, Picante Fleet, offers a wide selection of 20 well-equipped,
top-of-the-line, 31-foot to 68-foot Cabo sport fishers. If you prefer
smaller boats, there's the Picantito fleet, with a trio of 24-foot Sham-
rock walk-around boats. These are primarily used for fishing close
to shore. Picante offers trips and boats that vary in size and price.
✉ *Puerto Paraíso Mall Local 39-A, near Harley-Davidson Store,*
Cabo San Lucas ☎ *624/143–2474, 714/442–0644 in U.S.* ⊕ *www.*
picantesportfishing.com ✉ *From $325; up to $3,850 for 8 hours.*

Fodor's Choice
★ **Pisces Sportfishing Fleet.** Some of Cabo's top hotels use the extensive range
of yachts from Pisces Sportfishing Fleet. The fleet includes the usual
31-foot Bertrams, but also has a sizable fleet of 50- to 70-foot Viking,
Mikelson, Hatteras, and Ocean Alexander yachts with tuna towers,
air-conditioning, and multiple staterooms. Pisces also has luxury yachts
up to 156 feet in length. Chartering a 31-foot Bertram is all-inclusive
for up to six people, and trips last for around seven or eight hours.
✉ *Blvd. Marina, Marina, Cabo San Lucas* ☎ *624/143–1288, 877/286–*
7938 toll free in U.S. ⊕ *www.piscessportfishing.com* ✉ *From $445;*
Bertram charter, $695, all-inclusive.

Solmar Fleet. Once the largest fleet in Cabo San Lucas, the long-estab-
lished Solmar Fleet has been subdivided into several parts and its fleet
representatives are now located in both the Solmar Hotel and Playa
Grande Hotel. Solmar offers 13 sportfishing boats, from super-pangas
to 26- and 36-footers. Solmar boats and tackle are always in good
shape, and its longtime regulars wouldn't fish with anyone else. ✉ *Sol-*
mar Resort, Blvd. Marina, Marina, Cabo San Lucas ☎ *624/145–7575,*
800/344–3349 ⊕ *www.solmar.com* ✉ *From $400.*

WHALE-WATCHING

The gray-whale migration doesn't end at Baja's Pacific lagoons. Plenty
of whales of all sizes make it down to the warmer waters off Los Cabos
and into the Mar de Cortés. To watch whales from shore, go to the
beach at the Solmar Suites, The Grand Solmar, Sandos Finisterra, or
any Corridor hotel, or the lookout points along the Corridor highway.

Continued on page 78

A WHALE'S TALE   by Kelly Lack and Larry Dunmire

Seeing the gray whales off Baja's western coast needs to be on your list of things to do before you die. "But I've *gone* whale watching," you say. Chances are, though, that you were in a big boat and might have spotted the flip of a tail 100 yards out. In Baja your vessel will be a tiny panga, smaller than the whales themselves; they'll swim up, mamas with their babies, coming so close that you can smell the fishiness of their spouts.

Grey Whales Guerrero Negro

WHEN TO GO

Gray whales and tourists both head south to Baja around December—the whales in pods, the snowbirds in RV caravans—staying put through to April to shake off the chill of winter. So the beaches, hotels, restaurants, and bars during whale-watching season will be bustling. Book your room five to six months ahead to ensure a place to stay. The intense experience that awaits you at Magdalena Bay, San Ignacio, or Scammion's Lagoon is worth traveling in high season.

Though the average life span of a gray whale is 50 years, one individual was reported to reach 77 years of age—a real old-timer.

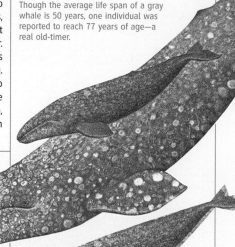

THE GRAY WHALE:
Migrating Leviathan

Yearly, gray whales endure the longest migration of any mammal on earth—some travel 5,000 miles one way between their feeding grounds in Alaska's frigid Bering Sea and their mating/birthing lagoons in sunny Baja California. The whales are bottom-feeders, unique among cetaceans, and stir up sediment on the sea floor, then use their baleen—long, stiff plates covered with hair-like fibers inside their mouths—to filter out the sediment and trap small marine creatures such as crustaceanlike Gammarid amphipods.

DID YOU KNOW?

Gray whales' easygoing demeanor and predilection for near-shore regions makes for frequent, friendly human/whale interactions. Whalers, however, would disagree. They dubbed mother grays "devilfish" for the fierce manner in which they protect their young.

WHALE ADVENTURES

Cabo Expeditions (*www.caboexpeditions.com.mx*) was the first with whale watching tours more than a dozen years ago. The staff is well-trained, and owner Oscar Ortiz believes not only in seeing the whales, but also saving them. Last year his Zodiacs rescued two grays from entanglement in giant fishing nets. Boats depart from the Cabo San Lucas Marina, near Dock M.

You've seen whales, but how about swimming with them? **Baja AirVentures** (*www.bajaairventures.com*) arranges weeklong trips to Bahia de los Angeles where you can swim with whale sharks daily. (Don't worry—the toothless plankton eaters are much more like whales than sharks.)

You fly from San Diego to the secluded Sea of Cortez fishing village, then take pangas out to Las Animas Wilderness Lodge, where you stay in spacious, comfortable yurts.

WHALE NURSERIES: THE BEST SPOTS FOR VIEWING

If you want an up-close encounter, head to one of these three protected spots where the whales gather to mate or give birth; the lagoons are like training wheels to prep the youngsters for the open ocean.

Laguna Ojo de Liebre (Scammon's Lagoon). Near Guerrero Negro, this lagoon is an L-shaped cut out of Baja's landmass, protected to the west by the jut of a peninsula.

Laguna San Ignacio. To reach the San Ignacio Lagoon, farther south than Scammon's, base yourself in the charming town of San Ignacio, 35 miles away. This lagoon is the smallest of the three, and along with Scammon's, has been designated a U.N. World Heritage site.

Bahía de Magdalena. This stretch of ocean, the farthest south, is kept calm by small, low-lying islands (really just humps of sand) that take the brunt of the ocean's waves. Very few people overnight in nearby San Carlos; most day-trip in from La Paz or Loreto.

WHAT TO EXPECT

The experience at the three lagoons is pretty standard: tours push off in the mornings, in *pangas* (tiny, low-lying skiffs) that seat about eight. Wear a water-resistant windbreaker—it will be a little chilly, and you're bound to be splashed once or twice.

The captain will drive around slowly, cutting the motor if he nears a whale (they'll never chase whales). Often the whales will approach you, sometimes showing off their babies. They'll gently nudge the boat, at times sinking completely under it and then raising it up a bit to get a good, long scratch.

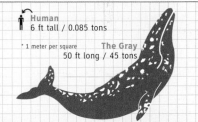

Human
6 ft tall / 0.085 tons

1 meter per square   The Gray
50 ft long / 45 tons

Baja whale watching, gray whale

3

IN FOCUS A WHALE'S TALE

Mutual curiosity between a scuba diver and a gentle whale shark (*Rhincodon typus*).

Virtually all of the companies listed in "Boating" offer whale-watching tours (about $60–$90 depending on size of boat and length of tour) from Cabo San Lucas.

EAST CAPE

If you have your own transportation, it is well worth driving out to Cabo Pulmo, where you can rent snorkel gear and a kayak or arrange a dive or fishing trip with one of the operators in this tiny, super-*tranquilo* village. In these incredible waters, you'll be able to check out everything from the smallest sea horse to a giant black sea bass.

Getting Here: To reach Cabo Pulmo from the airport in San Jose (SJD), follow Highway 1 north past Caduano, Mira Flores, and Santiago turn-offs. Upon reaching the village of Las Cuevas, turn right toward La Ribera/Cabo Pulmo (if you cross the bridge, you've gone too far). Follow the road and turn right just prior to entering La Ribera. Continue along the Cabo Pulmo road south until the pavement ends, and drive another 10 km (6 miles) on the dirt road to the village of Cabo Pulmo. You know you've arrived once you reach the Cabo Pulmo Dive Center housed in a two-story blue building.

KAYAKING

Cabo Pulmo Sport Center. Cabo Pulmo Sport Center has the gregarious César at the ready. He is a wellspring of knowledge and will happily advise you on the best spot to paddle your kayak, depending on the

CLOSE UP

An Underwater Paradise

One of Baja's true gems is Cabo Pulmo, the raw, unspoiled national marine preserve along the Sea of Cortez. More than 8 km (5 miles) of nearly deserted rocky beach border the only living coral-reef system on the Sea of Cortez. Several dive sites reveal hundreds of species of tropical fish, large schools of manta rays, and a sea-lion colony. This is a nearly perfect place for scuba diving and snorkeling.

The village of Cabo Pulmo has 100 or so residents, depending on the season. Power comes from solar panels, and drinking water is trucked in over dirt roads.

The town has two small general stores and three restaurants. Cabo Pulmo is a magnet for serious divers, kayakers, and windsurfers and remains one of southern Baja's natural treasures.

3

conditions of the day. He's also an expert birder. The center has a couple of very clean, simple casitas for rent ($95 per night) should you decide to extend your stay. ⊠ *Hwy. 1 at La Ribera turnoff, at the end of the road in the waterside palapa, Cabo Pulmo* ☎ *624/130–0235* ⊕ *www. cabopulmosportcenter.com* ⊠ *$60.*

SCUBA DIVING

Fodor'sChoice **Parque Nacional Marino Cabo Pulmo.** This 25,000-year-old coral reef has
★ been legally protected since 1995 and is home to more than 2,000 different kinds of marine organisms—including more than 230 species of tropical fish and a dozen kinds of petrified coral. The area is renowned among diving aficionados, whose favorite months to visit are June and July, when visibility is highest. The park isn't difficult to access. Head southwest from La Ribera and it's just 8 km (5 miles) from the end of the paved road; it's bordered by Playa Las Barracas in the north and Bahía Los Frailes to the south. It can also be reached by the well-maintained dirt road running along the coast from San José del Cabo. It'll take you three hours or more this way, but the coast along this route is unmatched. (Though, if it's raining, stick to the paved route.) There are two main dive centers, **Cabo Pulmo Dive Center** and **Cabo Pulmo Divers,** offering full gear rentals, kayaks, snorkel gear, and sportfishing tours. ⊠ *Hwy. 1, Km. 31, Cabo Pulmo* ⊕ *www.cabopulmopark.com* ⊠ *$5.*

OPERATORS

Cabo Pulmo Divers. Cabo Pulmo provides some of the more exceptional dives in the area, and Cabo Pulmo Divers has everything you need, including certification classes (multiday). This 5-star PADI certified outfit is a local family-run shop. It's right on the beach and offers full diving services, as well as cheap rooms from $79 to $129 per night. ⊠ *Hwy. 1 at La Ribera turnoff, at the end of the road, in the palapa right by the water on the beach, Cabo Pulmo* ☎ *624/141–0726* ⊕ *www. cabopulmo.com.*

WHERE TO EAT

THE SCENE

Updated by
Marlise Kast &
Chris Sands

Prepare yourself for a gourmand's delight. The competition, creativity, selection, and, yes, even the prices are utterly beyond comprehension. From elegant dining rooms to casual seafood cafés to simple *taquerías,* Los Cabos serves up anything from standard to thrilling fare.

Seafood is the true highlight here. Fresh catches that land on the menus include dorado (mahimahi), *lenguado* (halibut), *cabrilla* (sea bass), *jurel* (yellowtail), wahoo, and marlin. Local lobster, shrimp, and octopus are particularly good. Fish grilled over a mesquite wood fire is perhaps the most indigenous and tasty seafood dish, while the most popular may be the tacos *de pescado* (fish tacos): traditionally a deep-fried fillet wrapped in a handmade corn tortilla, served with shredded cabbage, cilantro, and salsas. Beef and pork—commonly served marinated and grilled—are also delicious. Many restaurants import their steak, lamb, duck, and quail from the state of Sonora, Mexico's prime pastureland, and also from the United States, though many of the high-end spots are only using local ingredients.

In San José, international chefs prepare excellent Continental, French, Asian, and Mexican dishes in lovely, intimate restaurants, and it's where the major portion of the area's explosion in new eateries has occurred. Following in the footsteps of Northern Baja's Valle de Guadalupe, several restaurants on the outskirts of San José del Cabo are offering farm-to-table cuisine, as well as cooking courses and tours. This organic movement has spread from the Farmer's Market in San José del Cabo to the luxury resorts along the coast that rely on the farms for their daily menu. The Corridor is the place to go for exceptional (and expensive) hotel restaurants, while intense competition for business in Los Cabos means many restaurants go through periodic remodels and reinvention, the Corridor restaurants included. With San José emerging as the hotbed of culinary activity, it's fair to say that Cabos San Lucas lags somewhat behind. But Cabo has comfort food covered, with franchise eateries from McDonald's, Subway, Johnny Rocket's, Domino's, and Ruth's Chris Steak House.

PLANNING

EATING OUT STRATEGY

Although Mexicans often prefer dining late into the evening, be warned that if you arrive at restaurants in Los Cabos after 10 pm, you're taking your chances. Most places are open year-round, sometimes closing for a month in the middle of the hot Baja summer, and many Los Cabos restaurants close one night a week, typically Sunday or Monday.

PRICES

Restaurants in Los Cabos tend to be pricey, even by U.S. standards. Some add a fee for credit card usage. If you wander off the beaten path—often only a few blocks from the touristy areas—you can find inexpensive, authentic Mexican fare (though still more expensive than elsewhere in Mexico), although many of these spots may not accept credit cards. It has been stated in reviews where this applies.

WHAT IT COSTS IN DOLLARS				
	$	**$$**	**$$$**	**$$$$**
At Dinner	Under $12	$12–$20	$21–$30	over $30

Restaurant prices are the average cost of a main course at dinner or, if dinner is not served, at lunch.

Use the coordinate (✛ 1:B2) at the end of each listing to locate a site on the corresponding Where to Eat maps.

RESERVATIONS

Reservations are mentioned when essential, but are a good idea during high season (mid-November to May). Restaurant websites are common, and many let you make online reservations.

SMOKING AND DRINKING

Mexican law prohibits smoking in all enclosed businesses, including restaurants. The drinking age here is 18. Establishments do ask for IDs.

TIPPING

You won't find much consistency in tipping expectations among Los Cabos restaurants. Some upscale places automatically add a 15% service charge (or even up to 18%) to the bill—look for the word "*servicio*"—but no one will object if you leave a few pesos more for good service. If a service charge is not included in your bill, a tip of 15% is common.

WHAT TO WEAR

Dress is often casual. Collared shirts and nice slacks are fine at even the most upscale places. In formal restaurants, men must wear closed toe shoes, so leave the flip-flops behind. Shirts and shoes (or sandals) should be worn any time you're away from the beach.

4

SAN JOSÉ DEL CABO

Updated by
Marlise Kast

San José's downtown is lovely, with adobe houses fronted by jacaranda trees. Entrepreneurs have converted many of the old homes into stylish restaurants, and new and inventive cuisine abounds—fitting for a town with an art district that is burgeoning as well. Boulevard Mijares is San José's Restaurant Row, so simply meander down the main boulevard to find one that will thrill your taste buds and delight your senses. New, organic-focused restaurants are pushing the culinary scene to the outskirts of San José del Cabo. These farm-to-table finds are tucked into green valleys, creating an oasis just beyond the cactus-lined dusty roads of Puerto Los Cabos.

$$
AMERICAN

✕ **Baja Brewing Company.** Baja's popular brewery is right in the middle of San José del Cabo. Fun and upbeat, this brewpub has great music and serves up filling pub meals. Burgers, shepherd's pie, soups, salads, and pizza—and more elegant entrées such as panko crusted sea bass and coffee-rubbed filet mignon—should be accompanied with a pint of any of eight special San José cervezas, along with seasonal offerings, all brewed within sight of the bar and restaurant. Two other branches can be found in Cabo San Lucas. $ *Average main: $15* ⊠ *Morelos 1277, Comonfort and Obregón, Centro* ☎ *624/146–9995* ⊕ *www. bajabrewingcompany.com* ✛ *1:C2.*

$
AMERICAN

✕ **Buzzard's Bar & Grill.** Fronted by miles of secluded beach, this casual seaside cantina (with cheap cervezas) gets rave reviews from locals who make the slightly involved drive out of San José del Cabo. Former Southern California restaurant owners Denny and Judie Jones serve up hefty, reasonably priced New York steaks; seafood entrées, such as coconut shrimp; "burritos like bombs"; hefty burgers; and, without a doubt, *lo mas grande* (the biggest in the world) flan. Indeed, this custardlike dessert could easily be enough for two or three—try it with a shot of Kahlúa poured over the top. Also, Sunday breakfast is a big hit. To get here, turn off Boulevard Mijares at the signs for Puerto Los Cabos and follow the road up the hill, around the small traffic circle, and continue out into the desert, toward the sea. You'll find the restaurant about 5 km (3 miles), about a 10-minute drive, from San José in the Laguna Hills neighborhood. Check out the website for more detailed directions before you head out. $ *Average main: $9* ⊠ *Old East Cape Rd., Laguna Hills* ☎ *624/113–6368* ⊕ *www.buzzardsbar.com* ▭ *No credit cards* ⊘ *Closed Aug. and Sep. No dinner Sun.* ✛ *1:D4.*

$$$$
ECLECTIC
Fodor's Choice
★

✕ **Casiano's.** "No menu, no rules" is the way chef Casiano Reyes describes the spontaneous cuisine at this gem in a tranquil location above Alegranza luxury condominiums. If you're open-minded, you'll relish this creative spot where a changing palette of local ingredients appears on a free-form menu. Once you're seated in the bi-level, indoor-outdoor space, you'll be presented with a little tablet in a bowl that impressively morphs into a hand towel once your waiter adds water. Your server will offer a list of the day's ingredients, which can include anything from goat cheese, heirloom tomatoes, and lobster, to scallops, fillet of beef, and foie gras. Advise the kitchen of your preferences, and the talented, Oaxacan-born Reyes will whip up a three-to-five course

BEST BETS FOR LOS CABOS DINING

With hundreds of restaurants to choose from, how will you decide where to eat? Fodor's writers and editors have selected their favorite restaurants by price, cuisine, and experience in the Best Bets lists below. In the first column, Fodor's Choice properties represent the "best of the best" in every price category. You can also search by neighborhood for excellent eats—just peruse our reviews on the following pages.

Fodor's Choice★

Casiano's, $$$$, p. 84
El Farallon, $$$$, p. 99
Flora's Field Kitchen, $$, p. 87
Lolita Cafe, $, p. 89
Los Tres Gallos, $$, p. 101
Market, $$$$, p. 93
Nick-San–Cabo, $$$, p. 102

Best By Price

$

Crazy Lobster's Bar and Grill, p. 99
El Marinero Borracho, p. 87
Las Guacamayas Taqueria, p. 89
Lolita Café, p. 89
Mariscos Mazatlán, p. 101
Taqueria Rossy, p. 90

$$

Flora's Field Kitchen, p. 87
Los Tres Gallos, p. 101
Nick-San–Palmilla, p. 93

$$$

7 Seas Restaurant, p. 91
Mi Cocina, p. 90
Nick-San–Cabo, p. 102
Sunset Da Mona Lisa, p. 94

$$$$

Bar Esquina, p. 98
Casiano's, p. 84
El Farallon, p. 99
Market, p. 93
The Restaurant at Las Ventanas, p. 94

Best By Cuisine

BEST ASIAN

Market, $$$$, p. 93

Nick-San (both locations), $$, pp. 93, $$$, 102

BEST ITALIAN

La Dolce, $$, p. 88
Sunset Da Mona Lisa, $$$, p. 94

BEST MEXICAN

Edith's Restaurant, $$$$, p. 99
Habanero's, $$, p. 88
Los Tres Gallos, $$, p. 101
Mi Casa, $$, p. 101

BEST SEAFOOD

Crazy Lobster Bar & Grill, $, p. 99
El Farallon, $$$$, p. 99
Lorenzillo's, $$$$, p. 100
Mariscos Mazatlán, $, p. 101
Mariscos Mocambo, $$, p. 101
Nick-San–Cabo, $$$, p. 102

Nick-San–Palmilla, $$, p. 93

BEST ECLECTIC

Casiano's, $$$$, p. 84
Flora's Field Kitchen, $$, p. 87
Los Tamarindos, $$, p. 89

Best By Experience

BEST FOR ROMANCE

El Farallon, $$$$, p. 99
Flora's Field Kitchen, $$, p. 87
Mi Cocina, $$$, p. 90
Sunset Da Mona Lisa, $$$, p. 94

BEST FOR MAKING THE SCENE

Bar Esquina, $$$$, p. 98
Nick-San–Cabo, $$$, p. 102
Nick-San–Palmilla, $$, p. 93
Nikki Beach, $$, p. 102

BEST LOCAL FLAVOR

El Ahorcado, $, p. 87
Gordo Lele's Tacos & Tortas, $, p. 100
Las Guacamayas Taqueria, $, p. 89
Taqueria Rossy, $, p. 90

4

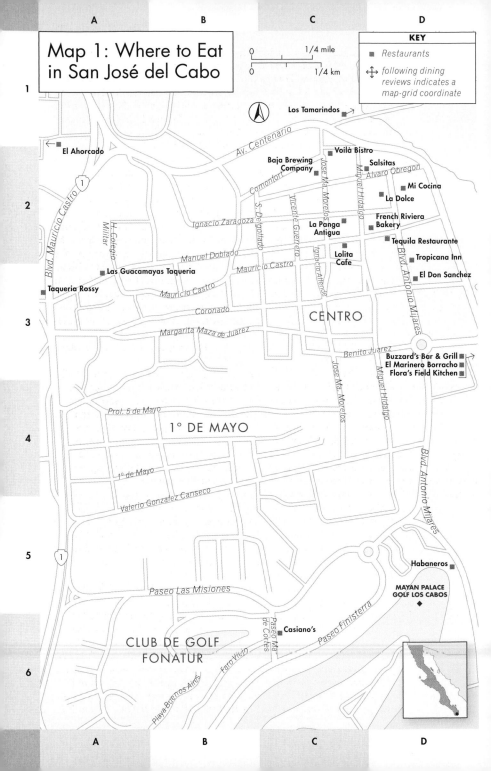

tasting menu. Standouts include the seasonal Mexican specialty *chiles en nogada*, New York steak with sweet corn puree, jumbo shrimp with mushroom sauce, and sea bass with lentils. Wine pairings are pricier, but worth it, especially since the number of courses usually doubles by the end of the meal, thanks to the generous and talented chef. $ Average main: $75 ⊠ *Paseo de Las Misiones 927, Col. Club de Golf Fonatur, at Alegranza Condos, Fonatur* ☎ *624/142–5928* ⊕ *www.casianos.com* ⌂ *Reservations essential* ⊘ *No lunch. Closed Sun.* ✛ *1:C6.*

$ ✕ **El Ahorcado.** By day it looks like a hole-in-the-wall, but when the

MEXICAN sun goes down, the rummage-sale-meets-taco-stand atmosphere of this open-air local favorite truly comes to life. Get beyond the ghoulish silhouette logo—*ahorcado* means "hangman" in Spanish—and you'll find out that the food is pretty good. One of the few area restaurants open late, it's packed until closing, usually around midnight. Old pots, baskets, antique irons, sombreros, and other tchotchkes hang from the walls and rafters. Quesadillas come with vegetarian fillers such as *flor de calabaza* (squash blossom), *nopales* (cactus), and *rajas* (poblano chilies), while meatier house specialties include beef tongue tacos in mustard sauce, *cochinita pibil* tacos, Cantonese-style beef rib tacos, and *cuchiviriachis*—a tostada filled with cheese and meat and roasted for a perfect melt. This is the place to get a chilled Corona for a handful of pesos. $ *Average main: $5* ⊠ *Paseo Pescadores and Marinos* ☎ *624/172–2093, 624/125–7264* ▭ *No credit cards* ⊘ *Closed Mon. No lunch.* ✛ *1:A2.*

$ ✕ **El Marinero Borracho.** This two-story palapa restaurant, named "The

MEXICAN FUSION Drunken Sailor," is always packed with locals and tourists alike. It's no wonder; the location across from the marina is the perfect spot to watch the sunset while enjoying a ginger mint mojito or tamarind margarita. Inspired by the head chef's international upbringing, several dishes feature unexpected Vietnamese and Costa Rican influences, such as the panko-crusted fish taco with ginger cream and the shrimp enchilada with coconut pineapple sauce and fried plantains. The shrimp burger on homemade ciabatta comes with chili lime fries and pairs well with an ice cold *michelada* (salt-rimmed Mexican beer with lime, spices, and hot sauce). Timid palates must overcome any hesitation and try the best dessert in Los Cabos: the avocado-lime chocolate cream pie on graham cracker crust. $ *Average main: $9* ⊠ *Near Hotel El Ganzo, Calle Cabrilla, on dirt road next to Jansens Bait and Tackle, Marina* ☎ *624/105–6464* ⊕ *www.ohnicnic.wix.com/the-drunken-sailor* ▭ *No credit cards* ⊘ *Closed Mon. and Tues.* ✛ *1:D4.*

$$ ✕ **Flora's Field Kitchen.** Gloria and Patrick Greene's Flora's Field Kitchen

AMERICAN is an alfresco dining experience that exemplifies farm to table. Flora's

Fodor'sChoice is built right in the center of the self-sustaining "Flora Farm." It's a

★ charming oasis featuring a restaurant, gift shop, cooking school, organic market, and culinary cottages (private homes), all under the Flora Farm brand. Meals are homemade including produce and meat (chicken and pork) grown on the property and bread baked on-site. Wholly organic meals are served family style at communal tables, and the generous portions include favorites like fried chicken with mashed potatoes and gravy, massive pork chops fired in the wood-burning oven, beet

4

carpaccio laced with *fromage blanc*, radish ravioli, and a selection of pizzas and seasonal salads. Even the sausages served with sweet potato chips are homemade. The adjacent Farm Bar serves unique takes on classic cocktails delivered in mason jars, like the Farm Julep (watermelon juice with basil, mint, and rum). Flora's is a wonderful learning experience for family by day and a romantic spot for couples by night. There's live music nightly at 6:30 and cooking classes Tuesday and Friday from 10:30 to 1:30 pm (cost $50 includes lunch). $ *Average main: $18* ✉ *Flora Farms, Las Animas Bajas* ☎ *624/355–4564* ⊕ *www. flora-farms.com* ☉ *Closed Mon. and Oct. No breakfast or lunch in Sept.* ✦ *1:D4.*

$$ ✕ **French Riviera Bakery.** We challenge you to try to ignore the smell of
CAFÉ   fresh baked French baguettes, or the picture-perfect display of croissants and éclairs, or the selection of colorful candies and refreshing ice creams at this café-bistro just off San José del Cabo's main square. In the creperie area, the cook tucks delicate crepes around eggs and cheese, ground beef and onions, or shrimp and pesto. If you choose to sit down, salads, quesadillas, and other standard fare are offered. The patisserie has a well-designed drink menu of fine wines and tequilas and a full list of coffee and tea-based drinks. $ *Average main: $12* ✉ *Manuel Doblado at Av. Hidalgo, Centro* ☎ *624/130–7864* ⊕ *www. frenchrivieraloscabos.com* ✦ *1:D2.*

$$ ✕ **Habanero's.** The latest restaurant in the culinary empire of celeb-
MEXICAN FUSION   rity Chef Tadd Chapman, this gastro grill and tequila bar features a menu created by Tadd and his mother. Opt for lunch specialties of ginger ahi ceviche and portobello burgers, and for dinner, try the fish-fillet wrapped shrimp with squid ink risotto or the panko-crusted rice cakes, topped with pulled pork. Don't miss the innovative cocktails with infused tequila; there are more than 130 types lining the bar, which is adorned with photos of Don Julio. As a certified "tequilier" (tequila sommelier), Tadd offers tequila pairing courses and tastings upon request. Exceptional breakfasts—ranging from stuffed French toast to eggs Benedict prepared five ways—are served from 8 to 12 for a fixed price just over $8. Leave the baking to mom, who makes the best key lime pie you've ever had—fresh, tart, and not overly sweet. $ *Average main: $18* ✉ *Blvd. Mijares s/n, Int. 4, Plaza Las Misiones, Centro* ☎ *624/142–2626* ⊕ *www.habanerosgastrogrill.com* ✦ *1:D5.*

$$ ✕ **La Dolce.** This popular Italian restaurant, right in the center of San
ITALIAN   José on the town's *zócalo* (square), is known for authentic and afford-able Italian fare. Locals and visitors alike flock to this reasonably priced perennial favorite for antipasti and wood-fired-oven pizzas, a never-ending selection of pastas, and steaks and seafood dishes. The home-made beef ravioli with four-cheese sauce is to die for. Reservations are necessary on Thursday after the Art Walk. Another outpost can be found in Cabo San Lucas. $ *Average main: $12* ✉ *Av. Zaragoza and Av. Hidalgo, Plaza Jardin Mijares, Centro* ☎ *624/142–6621* ⊕ *www. ladolcerestaurant.com* ☉ *Closed Mon.* ✦ *1:D2.*

$$$ ✕ **La Panga Antigua.** A 170-year-old wooden *panga* (small skiff) hangs
MEXICAN   above the door at this seafood-heavy, atmospheric restaurant, just across from San José's historical mission. The setting is a series of

tropical patios, one with a faded mural, another with a burbling fountain, romantically lit by dim fixtures, and a view of the stars above. Chili-infused olive oil accompanies the bread basket that starts the meal, while a roving mariachi band unobtrusively entertains diners with song. Menu highlights focus on seafood; the catch of the day is baked with lemon and served with smoked peppers and risotto, while dishes like lobster tail with chipotle butter and quinoa round out the list. The baked chicken with lemon and sage is also exceptional. ⑤ *Average main: $30* ✉ *Av. Zaragoza 20, Centro* ☏ *624/142–4041* ⊕ *www.lapanga.com* ✛ *1:C2.*

$ ✗ **Las Guacamayas Taqueria.** The outdoor-garden setting of Las Gua-
MEXICAN   camayas is a bit kitschy, with trees sprouting up from the floor, and Christmas lights strung from branch to branch. Painted murals run along the walls, and wooden chairs surround tables with plastic coverings. Massive globes of 15 types of margaritas and a Mexican guitarist singing American covers makes this a magnet for tourists, but, surprisingly, it also draws locals—a good sign. If you're looking for cheap, good Mexican food, you've come to the right place. Tacos stuffed with chorizo, marinated pork, and flank steak pervade the menu, though it's the quesadillas, with fillings like pumpkin flower, poblano pepper and onion, and pork skin, that shine. *Chilangas*, or fried, folded-over quesadillas with melted cheese, also merit the trip, while the volcanoes (hard-shell taco cups filled with cheese and your choice of meat) are not to be missed. Only cash and Visa are accepted here. ⑤ *Average main: $8* ✉ *Calle Paseo de los Marinos, near corner of Pescadores, Centro* ☏ *624/109–5473, 624/109–5993 cell* ⊕ *www.lasguacamayasrestaurant.com* ✛ *1:A3.*

$ ✗ **Lolita Café.** In a relaxing garden filled with retro-styled decor, wait-
CAFÉ   ers in mesh trucker hats and pearl button shirts deliver remarkable
Fodor's Choice   urban Mexican cuisine, spiced up by a dash of grandma's secret recipes.
★   Under the shade of a mango tree, start with the trio of salsas infused with orange and chipotle, served with a basket of freshly fried tortilla chips. Local breakfast favorites are the French toast and Costa Azul (baked eggs with a Dijon cream sauce). You may find yourself debating if you should go straight to the lunch menu, featuring the pork shoulder sandwich, jicama mango salad with grapefruit cream dressing, and a cheese-and-vegetable stuffed poblano sandwich. All pastries are crafted in-house, including the chocolate coconut brownies and sinfully divine churros, served with sweet milk. ⑤ *Average main: $8* ✉ *Manuel Doblado, between Hidalgo and Morelos, Centro* ☏ *624/130–7786* ☺ *Closed Mon. No dinner* ✛ *1:C2.*

$$ ✗ **Los Tamarindos.** A former sugarcane mill dating back to 1888, this
MEXICAN FUSION   quaint restaurant is surrounded by farmland that provides organic fruits and vegetables to many of Cabo's top eateries. Wildflowers in mason jars and hand-painted clay dishes set the scene at this rustic spot where the menu is based on the season's harvest. Start with heirloom tomato soup and a micro-green salad with tamarind vinaigrette. For something fresh and innovative, try the shrimp tacos on thinly sliced jicama (instead of tortillas) topped with a pineapple salsa. A selection of pizzas, and slow roasted meats like the pork shank with green mole and

baked eggplant, are cooked in a wood fire oven. One of the secrets to the fine flavors is the house made herbal oil that is dribbled on breads and meats. A cooking class takes place at 10 and 4, by reservation only. Be sure to visit the small gift shop selling salsas, mole, chocolate, jewelry, and other locally made products. $ *Average main: $20 ⊠ Calle Animas Baja, Las Animas Bajas* ☎ *624/105–6031* ⊕ *www.huertalostamarindos. com* ⊘ *Closed Tues.* ✛ *1:C1.*

$$$
ECLECTIC

✕ **Mi Cocina.** At this outdoor restaurant at Casa Natalia boutique hotel, fire bowls glow on the dining terrace, which is surrounded by palm trees and gentle waterfalls, blending the four elements: earth, wind, fire, and water. Tables are spaced far enough apart so that you don't have to share your whispered sweet nothings with neighbors. Chef-owner Loic Tenoux experiments with his ingredients, calling his approach "Euro-Mexican Bistro." He serves catch-of-the-day with ginger lemongrass salsa, grills vegetables and steak for sizzling fajitas on jalapeño tortillas, and prepares an exceptional free-range "chicken chocolate" with caramelized apples and a dark chocolate pepper salsa. The seafood-infused risotto is always a hit. A generous wine list pairs well with the menu, while the hotel's adjoining martini bar offers more colorful drink selections. $ *Average main: $25 ⊠ Casa Natalia, Blvd. Mijares 4, Centro* ☎ *624/146–7100* ⊕ *www.casanatalia.com* ⊘ *Closed Tues. during summer season* ✛ *1:D2.*

$$
MEXICAN

✕ **Salsitas.** This Mexican cantina-style bar and restaurant is well positioned for people-watching along San José's main drag. Decorated with cozy stone-and-stucco walls, the fare is standard but consistent, and reasonably priced. Choose from chicken tostadas, enchiladas, enormous burritos, or shrimp and fish tacos on jicama tortillas. To wet your whistle, there's a full bar, but you might consider washing down your meal with a refreshing *agua de Jamaïca* (hibiscus-flavored drink) or *horchata* (rice milk and cinnamon drink). Be sure to factor in the 16% sales tax that is tacked onto your bill at the end of your meal. $ *Average main: $15 ⊠ Obregón 1732, Centro* ☎ *624/142–6787* ✛ *1:C2.*

$
MEXICAN

✕ **Taqueria Rossy.** Don't be fooled by the bare-bones atmosphere: Taqueria Rossy serves some of the best tacos in San José. Fish tacos are the thing at this no-frills joint brimming with local families who munch on everything from peel-and-eat shrimp to ceviche and chocolate clams. Served breaded and fried, the shrimp, scallop, and fish (flounder) tacos here are cheap and delicious. Dress them up however you like at a condiment bar that offers avocados, chilies, cabbage slaw, onions, and an assortment of sauces from tomatillo to habanero. $ *Average main: $5 ⊠ Hwy. 1, Km 33, Centro* ☎ *624/142–6755* ✛ *1:A3.*

$$$
ECLECTIC

✕ **Tequila Restaurante.** A beautifully redone adobe home sets the stage for this classy dining experience on an open courtyard under the stars. A lengthy tequila list tempts diners to savor the finer brands of Mexico's national drink, and an extensive wine cellar will give you plenty of choices for what to sip as you sup. The menu is a blend of Mediterranean and Mexican influences; select from excellent regional salads made from produce grown on the restaurant's organic farm, then move on to seafood choices like mussels, shrimp soaked in the restaurant's namesake tequila, or catch of the day in fresh herbs. Another wonderful dish is the beef tenderloin or lamb in Cabernet sauce. The garden setting attracts mosquitoes so come prepared. $ *Average main: $25* ⊠ *Manuel Doblado 1011, Centro* 📞 *624/142–1155* ⊕ *www. tequilarestaurant.com* ⊹ *1:D2.*

$$
INTERNATIONAL

✕ **Tropicana Inn.** Start the day with coffee and French toast at this enduringly popular restaurant set in central San José hotel of the same name. The back garden patio quickly fills up with a loyal clientele for every meal; the front sidewalk seating is a great place to survey the world going by. The menu includes U.S. cuts of beef along with fajitas, chiles rellenos, a variety of seafood platters and lobster—always in demand. Latin bands and other musicians play nightly between October and May. Service can be slow at times, so be prepared to be patient, especially when you're trying to get the bill. $ *Average main: $20* ⊠ *Blvd. Mijares 30, Centro* 📞 *624/142–4146* ⊕ *www.tropicanainn.com.mx* ⊹ *1:D2.*

> **MORE ON TEQUILA**
>
> The real stuff comes from the Tequila region in mainland Mexico, but there's nothing stopping local Los Cabos folks from putting their labels on the bottles. Cabo Surf Hotel now offers its own Cabo Surf Hotel tequila, available only at the hotel. Other tequila brands offered with Los Cabos labels are Cabo Wabo, Hotel California tequila, Mexita, and Las Varitas brand.

4

THE CORRIDOR

Updated by
Marlise Kast

Dining along the Corridor between San José del Cabo and Cabo San Lucas used to be restricted to the ever-improving hotel restaurants. But with the addition of the Tiendas de Palmilla shopping center, just across from the One&Only Palmilla resort, top-notch eateries are establishing a new dining energy along this stretch of highway, giving drivers along the Corridor a tasty reason to slow down, and maybe even stop.

$$$
ECLECTIC

✕ **7 Seas Restaurant.** It's quite soothing to sit in this restaurant at Cabo Surf Hotel, at the ocean's edge under the shade of a palapa while watching the surfers. For breakfast munch on their *machaca con huevos* (eggs scrambled with shredded beef) washed down with a fresh-fruit smoothie. Later in the day, grab some fish tacos, or a Mediterranean tuna wrap with a blueberry mojito. Burgers are piled high with jalapeños and caramelized onions. For something light, try the crab cakes on a bed of tomato chutney with arugula. Drop in to watch the sunset and dine on fresh fish with a flavorful mango sauce. With a focus on healthy cuisine, the kitchen uses all local organic ingredients, cooks with olive oil (instead of butter), uses soybean oil for deep-frying, and will not serve marlin, mahimahi, or parrot fish due to commercial overfishing. Your entertainment is simple: a wonderful view that never stops changing. $ *Average main: $22* ⊠ *Cabo Surf Hotel, Acapulquito Beach, Km. 28* 📞 *624/142–2666* ⊕ *www.7seasrestaurant.com* ⊹ *2:B6.*

$$$$
SEAFOOD

✕ **Cocina del Mar.** Argentinean chef Gonzalo Cerda is changing things up at Cocina del Mar, the elegant restaurant in the exquisite Esperanza Resort. Using daily market ingredients and focusing on simple seafood and lush presentation, Cerda reinterprets classics like tortilla soup, here

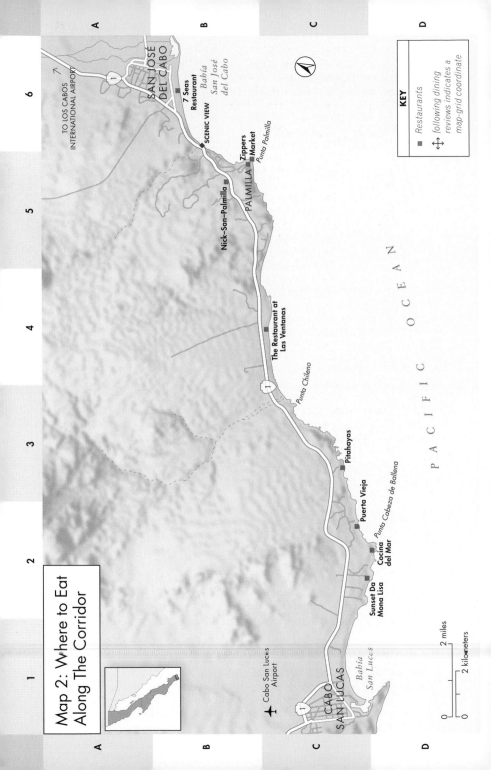

Map 2: Where to Eat Along The Corridor

KEY

■ Restaurants

↔ following dining reviews indicates a map-grid coordinate

TO LOS CABOS INTERNATIONAL AIRPORT

SAN JOSÉ DEL CABO

7 Seas Restaurant

Bahía San José del Cabo

SCENIC VIEW

Zippers Market

PALMILLA

Punta Palmilla

Nick-San-Palmilla

The Restaurant at Las Ventanas

Punta Chileno

PACIFIC OCEAN

Pitahayas

Puerta Vieja

Punta Cabeza de Ballena

Cocina del Mar

Sunset Da Mona Lisa

Cabo San Lucas Airport

CABO SAN LUCAS

Bahía San Lucas

0   2 miles

0   2 kilometers

made with seafood, and presents inventive dishes such as sea scallops with foie gras sauce, or spinach ravioli stuffed with corn, ricotta, and Parmesan. Grilled Angus is accompanied with creamy risotto and a porcini mushroom foam. Just when you thought it couldn't get any better, the waiter delivers a Grand Marnier soufflé. The dining room is under a thatched-roof palapa overlooking the Pacific, but opt for a table on the cliffs where waves crash so close, you can feel the spray. When you're finished with your meal, retire to The Lounge for either a cigar, a nightcap, or a flight of some very fine tequila. $ *Average main: $35* ⌂ *Hwy. 1, Km 7, at Esperanza Resort, Punta Ballena* ☎ *624/145–6400* ⊕ *www. esperanzaresort.com* ⌧ *Reservations essential* ☉ *No lunch* ✛ *2:D2.*

$$$$
ECLECTIC
Fodor's Choice
★

✕ **Market.** The first Latin American restaurant opened by three-star Michelin chef Jean-Georges Vongerichten resides in the One&Only Palmilla. It's one of the priciest spots in Los Cabos, but it's also one of the best. Described as Eurasian with Mexican influences, the elegant yet comfortable restaurant is accented with deep red and rich burgundy details, and original artwork. Appetizers like caramelized foie gras or caviar atop a lemon gelatin will make you swoon. Entrées include thoughtful presentations of almond-crusted duck, sautéed grouper with sweet chili, and corn ravioli with cherry tomatoes and basil fondue. For a sweet finish, try the corn soufflé with chipotle ice cream. You can bring your bill down slightly by opting for a fine Baja wine from the extensive wine list rather than a European one. Feeling more casual? Adjacent to Market, also overseen by Jean-Georges, is Suviche Bar, which offers fresh sushi and Mexican ceviches incorporating both local and Asian flavors, and chic cocktails. $ *Average main: $40* ⌂ *One&Only Palmilla, Hwy. 1, Km 27.5* ☎ *624/146–7000* ⊕ *www. oneandonlyresorts.com* ⌧ *Reservations essential* ✛ *2:B5.*

$$
SUSHI

✕ **Nick-San–Palmilla.** For fresh, inventive sushi, there's no question that the Nick-San franchise corners the market, and this outpost in the Tiendas de Palmilla shopping mall wins the prize. Pair each of your selections with wine or sake, and let chef Eddie Carvajal help you make the best choices from the vast menu. Favorites include the lobster roll (with cilantro, mango, mustard, and curry oil), lobster *sambal* (marinated in sake with soy, ginger, and garlic), and the tuna tostadas served on rice crackers with avocado. The gyozas stuffed with shrimp and scallops— also find their way on most of the tables. Hot dishes like the *chile age*, a California chili stuffed with spicy crab and sesame sauce, and a sea bass in miso and white mushroom sauce, offer even the most fickle diners plenty to marvel at. For an after-dinner drink, head next door to their chic nightclub, Privé. $ *Average main: $18* ⌂ *The Shoppes at Palmilla, Hwy. 1, Km. 27.5* ☎ *624/144–6262* ⊕ *www.nicksan.com* ✛ *2:B5.*

$$$
ASIAN FUSION

✕ **Pitahayas.** Chef Volker Romeike blends Asian and Polynesian ingredients with local products for a menu that showcases well-executed Pacific Rim fusion. Above the beach in the Sheraton's Hacienda del Mar resort in Cabo del Sol, Pitahayas is set under a soaring palapa overlooking the rollicking surf. Seafood-heavy dishes are the specialty. Try the blackened catch of the day accompanied with mango-papaya relish, or the famous coconut shrimp with lilikoi horseradish sauce and chipotle cilantro cream. For an impressive presentation and fresh flavor, the ahi tuna comes with avocado, pineapple, and tobiko. Also on offer is one of the largest wine selections in all of Mexico with nearly 3,000 bottles, as well as private dining in the wine cellar for 8 to 10 people. ⑤ *Average main: $30* ✉ *Sheraton Hacienda del Mar, Hwy. 1, Km 10* ☎ *624/145–8010* ⊕ *www.pitahayas.com* ✛ *2:C3.*

$$$ ✕ **Puerta Vieja.** Puerta Vieja translates into "Old Door" and the beauti-
INTERNATIONAL ful door you walk through to enter this restaurant is actually 150 years old and was imported from India. Though Puerta Vieja serves lunch, we suggest dinner at sunset, when the view of El Arco is the most impressive. The cuisine pulls from Continental, Latin, and Mexican traditions, with a touch of Asian flavorings. Entrées feature lobster, shrimp, and Sonoran cuts of meat. There's live music on Wednesday, Friday, Saturday and Sunday from 6:30 to 10 pm. ⑤ *Average main: $30* ✉ *Hwy. 1, Km 6.5* ☎ *624/104–3252, 624/104–3334* ⊕ *www.puertavieja.com* ✛ *2:C2.*

$$$$ ✕ **The Restaurant at Las Ventanas.** It's well known that Las Ventanas is
MEXICAN one of the best hotels in Mexico, and The Restaurant on the property does not disappoint. Chef Fabrice Guisset has unveiled a new Mexican menu that pays homage to the country's culinary traditions. With a focus on local ingredients and traditional recipes, highlights include Ensenada-sourced mussels cooked in dark Negra Modelo beer, chipotle, tomatillo, and *acuyo* (an herb that tastes like anise); and braised beef ribs in *pascalito* sauce (mole made from roasted pumpkin seeds and serrano chilies) and *epazote* (a Mexican herb)—with homemade tortillas. Also recommended are the lamb chops with black bean puree, the grilled octopus, and the suckling pig presented in an updated interpretation of the classic Mayan *cochinita pibil*. The desserts are as varied as the main courses, so save room for The Restaurant's version of *tres leches* cake, churros, flan, and an excellent house-made tequila ice cream. There's live music Monday through Saturday and private cooking demonstrations are hosted by Chef Fabrice Guisset in the Rosewood herb garden (by reservation). ⑤ *Average main: $35* ✉ *Hwy. 1, Km 19.5* ☎ *624/144–2800* ⊕ *www.rosewoodhotels.com/en/lasventanas* ⚑ *Reservations essential* ✛ *2:C4.*

$$$ ✕ **Sunset Da Mona Lisa.** Stunning views of El Arco from cocktail tables
ITALIAN along the cliffs make this restaurant just outside of Cabo San Lucas the best place to toast the sunset. If the breeze is still, stay outside and enjoy dining alfresco; if not, move into the candlelit dining room under a palapa. Italian chef Paolo Della Corte's menu offers seafood lime risotto or shrimp wrapped in a phyllo dough stuffed with mozzarella and sun-dried tomatoes. If you can't decide, go for the three-pasta sampler. The beef tenderloin is delivered on a hot stone and grilled tableside. Portions are on the smaller side, so it's worth splurging for the Mona Lisa tasting menu, which includes five or seven courses, respectively. If you arrive without a reservation, you can always head upstairs to the more casual Sunset Point, a wine and pizza lounge with daily tapas specials from 5 to 6 pm. ⑤ *Average main: $26* ✉ *Hwy. 1, Km 5.5* ☎ *624/145–8160* ⊕ *www.sunsetmonalisa.com* ⚑ *Reservations essential* ✛ *2:C2.*

$$ ✕ **Zippers.** Popular with the surfing crowd this palapa-covered joint is on
AMERICAN Cabo Azul beach, just south of San Jose del Cabo. Though their burger
FAMILY is the reason to come, the aroma of grilling lobster and tacos, and a

soundtrack of surf tunes are good reasons to return. Casual doesn't begin to describe the crowd, which can get downright rowdy. But hey, have fun, *amigo*, you've entered the Los Cabos Surf Zone! There's no question that owner "Big Tony" feeds you well for your pesos. With half-pound burgers, slabs of prime rib, or steak and lobster for two at under $40, you'll leave the beach a glutton, albeit a jolly one. Bring the kids in the daytime; they'll enjoy running from the dining table to the sand between every couple of bites. Sporting events sometimes blare on the TV, and live music is offered nightly. ⑤ *Average main: $12* ✉ *Hwy. 1, Km 28.5* ☎ *624/172–6162* ✛ *2:B5.*

CABO SAN LUCAS

Updated by Chris Sands

Cabo San Lucas is known for its rowdy nightlife, and, though much of the fine-dining scene has moved to the Corridor and San José, there are still some solid choices in Cabo. A pedestrian walkway lined with restaurants, bars, and shops anchored by the sleek Puerto Paraíso mall curves around Cabo San Lucas harbor, itself packed with yachts. The most popular restaurants, clubs, and shops are along Avenida Cárdenas (the extension of Highway 1 from the Corridor) and Boulevard Marina, paralleling the waterfront.

$$
ITALIAN

✕ **Alcaravea.** From its humble beginnings as "the parking-lot restaurant," Alcaravea has come a long way and is now considered one of Cabo's top stops for Italian and Mediterranean-style cuisine. Enter through a flower and vine garlanded opening into an intimate dining area and the pleasures of Chef Enrique Diaz's menu, which features salads, fresh pastas, chicken, seafood like *pescado con champiñones*—fresh catch of the day with mushrooms, garlic, herbs, lemon and a touch of Parmesan—and meat dishes such as rib-eye steak and scalloped beef with prosciutto. The wine list is modest, but includes nice selections from Mexico, Italy, Argentina, and the U.S. ⑤ *Average main: $18* ✉ *Zaragoza and 16 de Septiembre, Centro* ☎ *624/143–3730* ⊕ *www. alcaraveagourmet.com* ✛ *3:B4.*

$$
EUROPEAN

✕ **Alexander Restaurant.** Ideally located along Cabo San Lucas's busy marina walkway, Alexander's is where Switzerland meets Mexico. Pull up a chair at one of the sidewalk tables and start with a meat-and-cheese fondue, a treat for which Swiss chef and owner Alex Brulhart is known. You could finish with the chateaubriand in béarnaise sauce or tempura prawns served in a half coconut—but it's the flambéed tequila shrimp and duck à l'orange that draw other diners' eyes in wonder and awe. ⑤ *Average main: $22* ✉ *Plaza Bonita, Cabo San Lucas Marina, Marina* ☎ *624/143–2022* ⊕ *www.alexandercabo.com* ✛ *3:B4.*

$$
AMERICAN

✕ **Baja Brewing Company.** This branch of the established San José del Cabo microbrewery features the same menu—burgers, soups, salads, and pizza—same prices, and the same tasty selection of freshly brewed beers as the locations in San José del Cabo and Cabo Marina. The beers are still brewed in San José, meaning what you get here is "20 minutes fresh." No quibbles with the system; the eight house brews and seasonal additions are a flavorful change from the ubiquitous Tecate. The location of this outpost on the rooftop of the Cabos Villas hotel on Médano

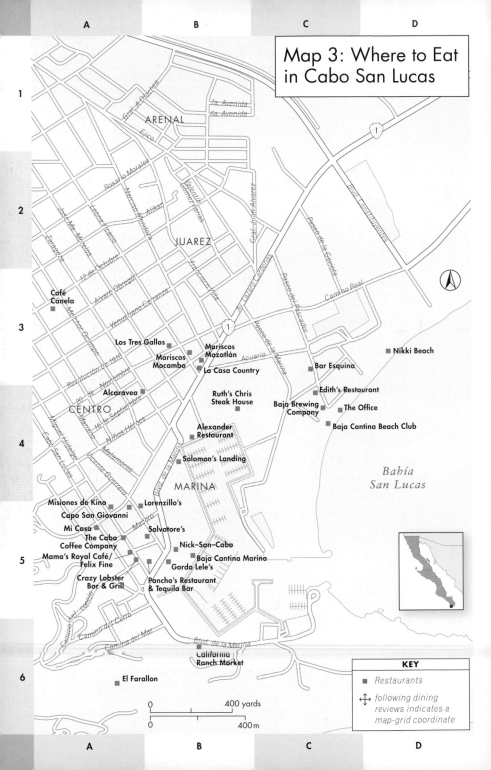

Map 3: Where to Eat in Cabo San Lucas

ARENAL

7a. Avenida
6a. Avenida

JUAREZ

Café Canela

CENTRO

Los Tres Gallos
Mariscos Mocambo
Mariscos Mazatlán
La Casa Country
Alcaravea
Ruth's Chris Steak House
Bar Esquina
Nikki Beach
Edith's Restaurant
Baja Brewing Company
The Office
Baja Cantina Beach Club

Alexander Restaurant
Solomon's Landing

MARINA

Bahía San Lucas

Misiones de Kino
Capo San Giovanni
Mi Casa
The Cabo Coffee Company
Mama's Royal Café/Felix Fine
Crazy Lobster Bar & Grill
Lorenzillo's
Salvatore's
Nick–San–Cabo
Baja Cantina Marina
Gordo Lele's
Pancho's Restaurant & Tequila Bar

California Ranch Market

El Farallon

Blvd. de la Marina

0   400 yards
0   400 m

KEY

■ Restaurants

⟨⊕⟩ following dining reviews indicates a map-grid coordinate

Budget Bites

Street stands offer low-cost, often fine local food. These places usually cook to order, so you can tell if something has been sitting out too long or hasn't been cooked well. If there's a crowd of locals, the food is probably fresh and well prepared. Safe bets include quesadillas, fish tacos, corn on the cob, and *tortas* (sandwiches). Some restaurants have a *comida corrida* (prepared lunch special), a three-course meal that consists of soup or salad, an entrée with rice and vegetables, coffee, and a small dessert. It's not gourmet, but you'll be sated, and at a reasonable price.

In Cabo San Lucas, head for the taco stands in the couple of blocks behind Squid Roe and Avenida Cárdenas, and the backstreets inland from the marina.

The best tacos in Cabo can be found off Highway 1, just outside Cabo San Lucas between Cabo Cielo and the Go-Kart track, at **Asi y Asado** (⊠ *Hwy 1, Km. 3.8* ☎ *624/105–9500* ⊕ *www. asiyasado.com* ⊹ *2:C1*). There are more than 20 types of tacos, including marinated skirt steak, grilled octopus, and smoked tuna, but it's the Vampiros, served in a hard corn shell and filled with cheese and the meat of your choice, that takes the prize. Pair with made-to-order juices, such as watermelon or lime with pineapple or cucumber.

Open for lunch only, **Los Micho-acanos** (⊠ *Leona Vicario between Carranza and Obregon* ☎ *624/146–3714* ⊕ *www.losmichoacanos.com*) sells savory roasted pork served in tacos or tortas for about $3 each and is beloved by locals and tourists in the know.

With branches in both San José and Cabo San Lucas, **Los Claros** (⊠ *Zaragoza at 16 de Septembre in Cabo San lucas and at Blvd Antoinio Mijares in San José* ☎ *624/355–8278*) is the place for a quick taco fix; $2 (fish and shrimp) or $5 (lobster) gets you some serious tacos, while $6 will buy you a killer breakfast. Two for one margaritas are served all day and five beers (Corona or Pacifico) can be had for $10.

At **Pollo de Oro** (⊠ *Morelos at Av. Cárdenas* ☎ *624/143–0310*), a half-chicken meal costs about $8.

For inexpensive Mexican eateries close to the marina and hotels, try the juice stands.

Rico Suave (⊠ *Av. Cárdenas between Av. Hidalgo and Calle Guerrero* ☎ *624/143–1043*) makes great smoothies with yogurt, as well as cheese tortas.

In San José del Cabo, there are at least a dozen stands at the **Mercado Municipal** (⊠ *Calle Coronado at Vicente Ibarra*), a couple of blocks west of the heart of San José. You may be the only gringo at the tables— a great way to practice your Spanish. Stock up on fresh papayas, mangoes, melons, and other fruits.

Look for reasonably priced restaurants on Zaragoza and Doblado by the market. Good taco stands line streets on the inland side of Highway 1. **Super Tacos Indios** has filling baked potatoes. **Las Ranas**, a *taquería* (taco eatery), has a full bar, and **Los Claros** has a few locations serving fish tacos and all-day-margarita and Mexican beer specials.

Beach, however, ups the ante with a semi-open-air venue and view of the ocean. $ *Average main: $18* ⊠ *Cabo Villas Hotel, Callejon del Pescador, Playa El Médano* ☎ 624/143–9199 ⊕ *www.bajabrewingcompany. com* ⊕ *3:C4.*

$$$ ✕**Baja Cantina Beach Club.** Lit by torches at night with a killer view
SEAFOOD of Land's End, this restaurant on busy Médano Beach (with another outpost on the Cabo San Lucas Marina) is barefoot casual and quite romantic. Featuring fresh local seafood, USDA cuts of meats, Mexican staples from fajitas to chile rellenos, and "dinner for two" specials, it's calmest during breakfast, and most festive on Wednesday night when it hosts a Fiesta Mexicana with live mariachi music, folk dances, and fireworks. The shaded bar features tropical cocktails and a full sushi menu. Multicourse tasting menus with wine pairing options from Baja's Valle de Guadalupe are available in a special dining area. $ *Average main: $25* ⊠ *Av. El Pescador, in front of Cabo Villas, Playa El Médano* ☎ 624/143–1111 ⊕ *www.bajacantinabeachclub.com* ⊕ *3:C4.*

$$ ✕**Baja Cantina Marina.** This large, casual, sportfishing-oriented cantina,
MEXICAN just around the corner from the Wyndham Hotel, draws a lot of guys who come for the all-day drink specials. Boasting a top marina location near M Dock, an excellent view of the sportfishing and megayachts, $2.50 cervezas all day, affordable eats, and American sports on multiple TVs, it's a favorite of the sportfishing deckhands and boat captains for the affordable prices. You can enjoy a Captain's breakfast special for $5, a budget-friendly afternoon appetizer menu, or splurge a bit more for daily seafood and steak specials. Most meals can be had for under $13. Friday night is Ladies' Night —ladies drink free from 9:30 to 11:30 pm—and if you stay late, you'll catch the live DJ and dancing. Free Wi-Fi is accessible throughout the restaurant. $ *Average main: $12* ⊠ *Cabo Marina, Dock L-M, Marina* ☎ 624/143–1111 ⊕ *www. bajacantinamarina.com* ⊕ *3:B5.*

$$$$ ✕**Bar Esquina.** Set in Cabo San Lucas's boutique Bahia Hotel, Bar
ECLECTIC Esquina is making a name for itself as Medano Beach's best new restaurant. Whether you're craving eggs Benedict in the morning to help you absorb last night's party; pizza or ceviche; or a burger while you lie by the pool, La Esquina is the spot to fit your mood. For dinner try the highly recommended tuna tartare, spicy shrimp, or lamb chops. With tall cocktail tables in the bar, an open-air dining room, chalkboard menus written on columns that front an open kitchen, and live music five days a week, this very cool spot is where it's at on Medano Beach. For a quick refuel, there's Esquina Coffee Shop right next door. Open at 7 am, it sells muffins, coffee, and bagels for takeaway. $ *Average main: $35* ⊠ *Av. El Pescador, Playa El Médano* ☎ 624/143–1890 ⊕ *www. bahiacabo.mx, www.baresquina.com* ⊕ *3:C3.*

$ ✕**The Cabo Coffee Company.** If you're impressed with the quality of local
CAFÉ coffee, it's probably because many of the area's best restaurants source their blends from Cabo Coffee Company. Their café just off the town square, Plaza Amelia Wilkes, serves up a wide array of espresso-style coffee drinks made from organic beans grown in Oaxaca's cloud forest. The café is a popular meeting place for locals, who appreciate the comfortable couches and complimentary Wi-Fi, as well as the fresh pastries

and medium, dark, and decaf roasts. $ *Average main: $2* ✉ *Hidalgo at Madero, Centro* ☎ *624/105–1754* ⊕ *www.cabocoffee.com* ✛ *3:A5.*

$$ ✕ **Café Canela.** Café Canela offers contemporary Mexican fare, as well MEXICAN as a generous selection of soups, salads, sandwiches and pastas. The bi-level space near the marina is filled with traditional arts and crafts, and its walls are lined with tequila bottles. Inexpensive breakfasts are $3 to $5; quick appetizers include Baja-style fish tacos and Caribe peppers stuffed with shrimp. Dinners such as the oven-roasted pork short ribs, baked in smoked chili and tamarind adobo, will delight your taste buds. This spot is also great for just a quick cocktail while shopping in downtown Cabo, and it's a favorite with the cruise ship crowd. $ *Average main: $14* ✉ *Plaza del Sol shopping center, Francisco Madero and Blvd. Marina, Marina* ☎ *624/143–7577* ⊕ *www.micasagroupcabo.com* ✛ *3:A3.*

$ ✕ **California Ranch Market.** With a great selection of beer and wines, as MEXICAN well as organic and frozen foods, healthy and low-calorie offerings, and cheese, California Ranch Market also has prices that can be even lower than those at Costco. This corner shop carries familiar products and brands from the U.S. $ *Average main: $5* ✉ *Blvd. Marina and Camino del Cerro, at the western end of Marina San Lucas* ☎ *624/143–1947* ☾ *Closed Sun.* ✛ *3:B6.*

$ ✕ **Crazy Lobster Bar & Grill.** Lobster's the thing here, but daily specials like MEXICAN surf-and-turf combos round out the list. Open for breakfast, lunch, and dinner, this typical Mexican sit-down locale has a happy hour that runs from 8 am to 6 pm—and prices are supercheap. You can get a lobster tail with rice and beans for less than 11 bucks; Cuervo tequila shots are a mere 70¢; and Don Julio tequila shots are less than $3! As you sit under the open-air palapa enjoying this feast fit for a king, strolling mariachis will pass by, providing your dining sound track. $ *Average main: $10* ✉ *Hidalgo and Zapata, Centro* ☎ *624/143–6535* ⊕ *www.facebook.com/TheCrazyLobster* ☾ *Closed Sept.* ✛ *3:A5.*

$$$$ ✕ **Edith's Restaurant.** One of the more upscale choices near hectic Médano MEXICAN Beach, Edith's is the sister restaurant to the popular The Office on the FAMILY Beach. The Caesar salad and flambéed banana crepes are prepared tableside at this colorful and popular restaurant. Wally's Special, including with lobster, shrimp, and fish is also a hit with the tourist set that tends to dine here. The focus here is on Mexican ingredients—quesadillas feature Oaxacan cheese and are filled with seasonal zucchini flowers; meat and fish dishes are doused in local chili or tropical fruit sauces. Edith's air-conditioned wine cellar offers a large selection of domestic and imported wines and is ideal for hosting small intimate dinner parties of up to 10. Families dine in early evening, so come in later if you're looking for a less crowded experience. $ *Average main: $60* ✉ *Paseo del Pescador, Playa El Médano* ☎ *624/143–0801* ⊕ *www.edithscabo.com* ☾ *Closed Sept.* ✛ *3:C4.*

$$$$ ✕ **El Farallon.** Atop a bluff in the Capella Pedregal hotel, El Farallon pro-SEAFOOD vides one of the most breathtaking vantage points from which to have **Fodor's**Choice a meal in Cabo San Lucas. Chef Yvan Mucharraz presents a seafood-★ heavy menu with a "fresh fish market" displaying the catch of the day. Customize your dish from an array of fish and meats—from yellowtail,

parrot fish, spiny lobster, rib-eye
steak, and sea bass to the irresistible
local chocolate clams. All dishes
come with a tasting of the day's
three appetizers, which can include
anything from tuna ceviche to crab-
and-chipotle soup, as well as two
sides that range from asparagus to
grilled corn to cilantro-infused rice.

> **FRUITY FLAN**
>
> Flan is usually sinfully, sweetly, caramel flavored. But guava? Guava flan is *delicioso*, and can be found at hot spot La Fonda restaurant, in Cabo San Lucas.

Fish and meats are simply prepared on a flat grill with fine herbs and a drop of butter. They're so well executed that you may forego the accompanying sauces. It's challenging, but save room for desserts like Mexican doughnuts, then digest over an after-dinner drink while you ogle the view. ⑤ *Average main: $80* ✉ *Capella Pedregal Hotel, Camino Del Mar 1, Pedregal* ☎ *624/163–4300* ⊕ *www.capellahotels.com/cabosanlucas* ⌫ *Reservations essential* ✛ *3:A6.*

$
MEXICAN

✕ **Gordo Lele's Tacos & Tortas.** Ready for a floor show along with your tacos or *tortas*? Listen for the blaring Beatles' tunes, then watch owner Javier Reynoso don his Beatles wig and sing along to "I Wanna Hold Your Hand" or "Let it Be." The walls here are filled with Fab Four photos and album covers. Javier's tacos and *tortas* (sandwiches) are made with loving care, and his fans can have two or three ham-and-cheese tortas for the price of one anywhere else, plus an assortment of generously sized tacos. ⑤ *Average main: $4* ✉ *Matamoros, between Lázaro Cárdenas and Niños Héroes, Centro* ☎ *624/134–3677* ▭ *No credit cards* ✛ *3:B5.*

$$$
STEAKHOUSE

✕ **La Casa Country.** For a good steak in a rustic atmosphere accented by wood tables and leather stools, head to La Casa Country. Serving breakfast, lunch, and dinner, complete with sports games on oversize TVs, La Casa is the spot for some toothsome *carne* at reasonable prices and a wide variety of Mexican fare, against the bustling backdrop of the Marina's many boats. ⑤ *Average main: $21* ✉ *Cabo San Lucas Marina, Next to Puerto Paraiso, Marina* ☎ *624/105–1999* ⊕ *lacasacountry.com* ✛ *3:B3.*

$$$$
SEAFOOD

✕ **Lorenzillo's.** Gleaming hardwood floors and polished brass give a nautical flair to this second-floor dining room, where fresh lobster is king. Lorenzillo's has long been a fixture in Cancún, where lobster is raised on the company's farm. That Caribbean lobster is shipped to Los Cabos and served in nearly a dozen styles (the simpler preparations—steamed or grilled with lots of melted butter—are best). Menu items are named after pirates and Caribbean marine history, so Sir Francis Drake is the rib-eye steak, Henry Morgan is broiled yellowfin tuna served with cognac and pink pepper sauce, and *El Comodoro* is a filet of Angus beef and lobster tail. The dessert list is lengthy and mouthwatering, and if you're in the mood for a less formal meal, an oyster bar with a limited selection of the same menu sits on the pier near the entrance. Flaming coffee cocktails are another specialty of the house. Try the Xtabentun, which showcases a Mayan liqueur made from run, anise, and fermented honey. ⑤ *Average main: $50* ✉ *Av. Cárdenas at Marina, Marina* ☎ *624/105–0212* ⊕ *www.lorenzillos.com.mx* ✛ *3:A5.*

$$ ✕ **Los Tres Gallos.** A romantic courtyard shaded by fruit trees, clas-
MEXICAN sic *rancheras* (Mexican folk music), and traditional preparations of
Fodor'sChoice regional Mexican specialty dishes are the hallmarks at Los Tres Gallos.
★ Discover their delicious heritage dishes such as *cochinita pibil* (slow-
roasted pork) and *cecina de Yecapixtla* (a specially prepared beef). The
downtown eatery's name pays tribute to three of the greatest stars of
Mexico's golden age of cinema. Photographs of Jorge Negrete, Pedro
Infante, and Javier Solís—collectively referred to as "the three roost-
ers"—line the walls of one of the rear dining areas, and their music often
plays softly in the background, adding to the restaurant's old-fashioned
charm. For dessert, try the flan or the *pastel de tres leches con tequila.*
⑤ *Average main: $17* ⊠ *20 de Noviembre at Leona Vicario, Centro*
☎ *624/130–7709* ⊕ *www.lostresgallos.com* ✛ *3:B3.*

$$ ✕ **Mama's Royal Café/Felix Fine Mexican & Seafood Restaurant.** Claiming
MEXICAN to have "the best damn breakfast restaurant in the entire country,"
Mama's is a casual, lively, indoor-outdoor spot in Cabo San Lucas
that serves up bountiful plates of omelets and poached eggs with avocado and ham, and finger-licking fried potatoes. Mama's also claims,
and might actually have, the "World's Best French Toast"—a treasure
stuffed with cream cheese, strawberries, mangoes, bananas, pecans, and
topped with orange liqueur. At night, the colorful restaurant morphs
into Felix and serves traditional dishes like *chiles en nogada* (chilies in
walnut sauce) and *pozole* (pork soup with hominy, onion, garlic, dried
chilies, and cilantro), as well as Mexican-style jambalaya. Signature
fresh fruit cocktails include a sweet watermelon mojito, and refreshing
cucumber and mango mint margaritas. ⑤ *Average main: $14* ⊠ *Hidalgo
at Zapata, Centro* ☎ *624/143–4290* ⊕ *www.mamasroyalcafeloscabos.
com* ☾ *Closed Sun. Closed Sept.* ✛ *3:A5.*

$ ✕ **Mariscos Mazatlán.** Ask a local where he or she goes for dinner, and
SEAFOOD they inevitably mention Mariscos Mazatlán, and the crowds of Mexicans lunching at this simple seafood restaurant lend credibility to the
claim. Huge glass cases packed with fresh shrimp, ceviche, and other
seafood cocktails abound. You can dine inexpensively and quickly on
wonderful seafood soup, or spend a bit more for tender *pulpo ajillo*
(marinated octopus with garlic, chilies, onion, and celery) and enjoy
some great people-watching as you eat. ⑤ *Average main: $12* ⊠ *Nar-
ciso Mendoza at 20 de Noviembre, Arenal* ☎ *624/143–8565* ✛ *3:B3.*

$$ ✕ **Mariscos Mocambo.** Veracruz—a region known for its seafood prepa-
SEAFOOD rations—meets Los Cabos in an enormous dining room packed with
appreciative locals. The menu has such regional dishes as shrimp *chil-
pachole*, crab and fish empanadas, and a *tumbada*-style seafood platter
that includes crab, clams, octopus, squid, and shrimp. Musicians stroll
among the tables and the chatter is somewhat cacophonous beneath the
huge palapa roof, but you're sure to have a great local dining experi-
ence here. ⑤ *Average main: $16* ⊠ *Leona Vicario at 20 de Noviembre,
Centro* ☎ *624/143–2122* ✛ *3:B3.*

$$ ✕ **Mi Casa.** One of Cabo San Lucas's top restaurants is in a cobalt-blue
MEXICAN adobe building painted with murals. Interior decorations range from
FAMILY Day of the Dead statues and silver crosses and hearts, to T-shirts and
tequilas. The place seats up to 450 and is often full of tourists, but

the menu is *muy auténtico* and filled with regional Mexican specialty dishes. Standouts include the *mole poblano* with chicken topped in a sauce made from dried peppers, seeds, spices and chocolate, and *chiles en nogada*, poblano chilies stuffed with a meat-and-fruit mixture and covered with white walnut sauce and sherry cream sauce. The tortilla soup is also recommended, as is the oven-roasted spare rib in chili and tamarind adobo. Mi Casa offers a variety of different fruit-flavored margaritas, and a wine list focused on Mexican, California, and South American wines. The large back courtyard glows with candlelight at night, and mariachis provide entertainment. $ *Average main: $20 ⊠ Av. Cabo San Lucas at Lazaro Cardenas, Centro* ☎ *624/143–1933* ⊕ *www. micasarestaurant.com.mx* ☉ *No lunch on Sun.* ✢ *3:A5.*

$$ ✕**Misiones de Kino.** You may feel like you've discovered a well-kept
MEXICAN   secret when you find, and enter, this palapa-roof house with adobe walls, just a few blocks off the main strip and around the corner from the Mar de Cortez Hotel. Sit on the front patio or in a backyard hut strung with weathered lanterns and photographs of the Mexican Revolution. Menu highlights include *cabrilla con salsa de frambuesa* (sea bass with raspberry sauce), *camarón coco* (coconut shrimp with mango sauce), and the crab or fish with garlic sauce. A second menu, called Pasta Bella, offers a wide range of pastas and Italian dishes. $ *Average main: $20 ⊠ Calle Vicente Guerrero at 5 de Mayo, Centro* ☎ *624/105– 1408* ⊕ *www.misionesdekino.com* ☉ *Closed Sun.* ✢ *3:A5.*

$$$ ✕**Nick-San–Cabo.** Dare we make such a claim: Nick-San may very well
SUSHI   be Cabo San Lucas's top restaurant. Owner Angel Carbajal is an artist
Fodor's Choice   behind the sushi counter (he also has his own fishing boats that collect
★   fish each day), and his creative fusion menu of Japanese and Mexican cuisines truly sets his masterpieces apart. The sauce on the cilantro sashimi is so divine that some say diners sneak in bread to sop up the sauce (rice isn't the same), while all of the tuna specialties—from seared sashimi with sesame seeds to tuna tostadas—are exquisite. Beware: you can run up a stiff tab ordering sushi here, though it's worth the splurge. The mahogany bar and minimalist dining room are packed most nights, but the vibe is upbeat. If you're staying in the Corridor, you're in luck; there's also a second Nick-San in Las Tiendas de Palmilla shopping center. Reservations are recommended, especially on weekend nights and during high season. Otherwise, be prepared for a wait. $ *Average main: $22 ⊠ Blvd. Marina, next to Wyndham Hotel, Marina* ☎ *624/143–2491* ⊕ *www.nicksan.com* ✢ *3:B5.*

$$ ✕**Nikki Beach.** Undoubtedly one of the hippest places in Cabo, by day
ECLECTIC   or by night, this restaurant by the pool of the ME Cabo Hotel is really more than a place to eat—it's a scene in and of itself. Surrounded by sometimes chill, sometimes pulsing music and many scantily-clad revelers, you'll be tempted by appetizers such as tuna sashimi, an assortment of ceviches, calamari rings, and tomato bruschetta. Kobe beef sliders, tacos, chicken sandwiches, and quesadillas are offered at lunchtime. At dinner you can choose from chicken satay, an assortment of fajitas, surf and turf, and Pacific salmon. Those who want to eat light will find an additional sushi menu. This is not, however, a quiet spot for dinner; the restaurant becomes a full-blown club as the evening wears on.

⑤ *Average main: $20* ⊠ *Playa Médano, in ME Cabo Hotel, Playa El Médano* ☎ *624/145–7800* ⊕ *www.nikkibeachcabo.com* ✢ *3:D3.*

$$$
MEXICAN

✗ **The Office.** At least once during your visit to Los Cabos, you should visit The Office, the original breakfast spot on Médano Beach's sandy shore. The Office screams "tourist-trap," bedecked with tiki torches and colorful rainbow tablecloths, but it's all in good fun, and it's always packed with revelers enjoying the near-perfect views of El Arco. Start your morning with a lobster omelet, fresh-fruit smoothie, and powerful cup of Mexican coffee. The French toast is another favorite. Service is super-friendly but the menu is a bit expensive. Later in the day, decent, if not stellar, ceviche, nachos, fish tacos, seafood, and burgers are served in large portions that justify the high prices. Dinners of grilled shrimp or fish with garlic, and steaks are popular, especially when paired alongside cold beers and goblet-sized margaritas. Connoisseurs of the suds will want to sample the bottled options from Rámuri, a downtown brew pub managed by the same ownership group. ⑤ *Average main: $28* ⊠ *Playa El Médano, Playa El Médano* ☎ *624/143–3464* ⊕ *www.theofficeonthebeach.com* ⚤ *Reservations essential* ✢ *3:C4.*

$$
MEXICAN
FAMILY

✗ **Pancho's Restaurant & Tequila Bar.** Owner John Bragg has an enormous collection of tequilas, and an encyclopedic knowledge of the stuff. His restaurant is something of a tequila museum, with a colorful array of hundreds of the world's top tequilas—many no longer available—displayed behind the bar. Sample one or two of the nearly 560 labels available, and you'll appreciate the rainbow-colored Oaxacan tablecloths, murals, painted chairs, and streamers even more than you did when you first arrived. Hungry, too? Try fresh local seafood and regional specialties like tortilla soup, chiles rellenos, or *chamorro* (pork shank in wine sauce). For larger appetites, the Pancho's combo, which includes steak, quesadilla, chile relleno, and a chicken enchilada, is the way to go. Pancho's offers special and private tequila tastings, which will give you a greater appreciation of this piquant liquor from Jalisco. ⑤ *Average main: $20* ⊠ *Calle Hidalgo, between Zapata and Camino del Conejo, Centro* ☎ *624/143–2891, 624/143–0973* ⊕ *www.panchos.com* ⊘ *No lunch Jun.–Sept.* ✢ *3:A5.*

$$$$
STEAKHOUSE

✗ **Ruth's Chris Steak House.** If you've eaten enough fish tacos for a while, and are hankering for a steak like they cook 'em back home, then Ruth's Chris at the Puerto Paraíso mall, facing the Marina, is your best bet. It's known for its wide range of meaty cuts from filets to porterhouse, and also serves veal, chicken, fish, and lamb. Not finished yet? There's crème brûlée and key lime pie, both freshly baked, and specialty cocktails from martinis to Manhattans. Lunch isn't served until 1 pm. ⑤ *Average main: $75* ⊠ *Puerto Paraíso, 1st floor, Marina* ☎ *624/144–3232* ⊕ *www.ruthschris.com* ✢ *3:B4.*

$$
ITALIAN

✗ **Salvatore's.** The local gringo cadre has nothing but *bueno* things to say about this affordable and dependable little Italian spot, located by the pool at the Siesta Suites Hotel in downtown Cabo San Lucas. Baked rigatoni, osso buco, chicken parmigiana, lasagna, and lamb ravioli are just some of the many Italian staples offered at this funky little spot. Portions are large and prices are reasonable. Finish dinner off with tiramisu before hitting the main drag for some serious nightlife.

$ *Average main: $15* ✉ *Zapata between Guerrero and Hidalgo, Centro* ☎ *624/105–1044* ☉ *No lunch Sun.* ✛ *3:A5.*

$$
SEAFOOD
FAMILY

✕ **Solomon's Landing.** Chef and owner Brian Solomon runs one of the most popular restaurants on the Cabo San Lucas Marina, supplementing great seaside views with first-class service and an enormous range of quality food and beverage. There are seven separate menus—breakfast, bar, kids, lunch, sushi, dinner, and dessert—each with enough variety to satisfy the pickiest of eaters. Fresh local seafood is the specialty of the house, but pastas, steaks, and traditional Mexican favorites are also staples of the lunch and dinner menus. For dinner, start with a traditional tortilla or five bean soup, enjoy a Caesar salad prepared tableside, then try the fresh catch of the day prepared in your choice of the restaurant's seven signature styles. Live music and dancing are featured on Friday night, and visiting oenophiles should ask about monthly food and wine pairing events. $ *Average main: $20* ✉ *Cabo San Lucas Marina, behind Wyndham Cabo San Lucas Resort, Marina* ☎ *624/143–3050* ⊕ *www. solomonslandingcabo.com* ✛ *3:B4.*

5

WHERE TO STAY

THE SCENE

Updated by
Marlise Kast

Expect high-quality accommodations wherever you stay in Los Cabos—whether at a huge resort or a small bed-and-breakfast. Much of the area's beaches are now backed by major properties, all vying to create the most desirable stretch on the sand. For the privilege of staying in these hot properties, you'll pay top dollar—and more for oceanfront rooms with incredible views.

Prices at accommodations off the beach reflect the popularity of the area and may surprise travelers used to spending much less in other areas of Mexico—even in the hot summer months which are, technically, the low season.

Sprawling Mediterranean-style resorts of generally 200 to 400 rooms dominate the coastline of Los Cabos, especially on the 29-km-long (18-mile-long) Corridor, but also on the beaches in Cabo San Lucas and San José (the town of San José is not on the coast, but inland just a bit). Near the marina in San José del Cabo, the area of Puerto Los Cabos has become a hot spot of development, with the 2014 Grand Opening of Secrets Puerto Los Cabos and a 2015 unveiling of JW Marriott. This upscale community is also home to Hotel El Ganzo, Wirikuta Cactus Gardens, Dolphin Discovery, and the Puerto Los Cabos Golf Course. There are rumors that a Ritz Carlton and Montage will follow suit along the coast.

Los Cabos resorts are known for their lavish pools and lush grounds in addition to their beachfront access, although the majority of beaches on the densely developed coastline, with the notable exception of Playa Médano in Cabo San Lucas, can have an oddly deserted appearance because of the dangerous currents in the water and the predominance of luxurious pools.

Many of the resorts along the Corridor offer all-inclusive plans if you want to check into your hotel and stay put for the duration of your stay. Choosing that option means you'll have little reason to venture out and taste some of the diverse and remarkable food available in this region. These huge resorts offer high-quality facilities and pleasant service, to be sure, but guests looking to get a feel for the local culture may find the generic, chain-hotel atmosphere frustrating. For those wanting less Westernized slickness, and a more intimate experience of Mexican hospitality, checking into one of the many excellent smaller properties is the way to go.

If you're inclined to go beyond the beach-and-party vibe of Cabo San Lucas, it's well worth spending time in Todos Santos (⇨ *see Los Cabos Side Trips chapter*) and San José del Cabo. Both towns offer exceptional independent hotels and inns, as well as burgeoning art scenes, great restaurants, and ambience you won't find elsewhere.

PLANNING

5

WHEN TO GO
With its growing popularity, Los Cabos has a high season that seems to keep gaining months. It's been said that high season is now mid-November through May, though the crowds are a bit more manageable in October and after mid-April. Summers can be scorchers in this desert landscape, reaching temperatures in the 90s and above. Book early—as many as six months in advance for top holidays such as Thanksgiving, Christmas, New Year's, and Easter, and at least three months in advance for other high-season stays.

WHAT TO EXPECT
Bargains here are few; rooms generally start at $200 a night and can climb into the thousands. For groups of six or more planning an extended stay, condos or villas can be a convenient and economical option, though you should always book early.

Hotel rates in Baja California Sur are subject to a 10% Value-Added Tax and a 2% hotel tax for tourism promotion. Service charges (at least 12%) and meals generally aren't included in hotel rates, except at some all-inclusive resorts. Several of the high-end properties include a daily service charge in your bill; be sure you know the policy before tipping (though additional tips are always welcome). We always list the available facilities, but we don't specify extra costs; so always ask about what's included.

CHOOSING THE RIGHT REGION
San José del Cabo is the closest to the international airport, and it's here that you'll be farthest from the crowds that gravitate toward downtown Cabo San Lucas's fiesta atmosphere. These towns have retained their Mexican colonial roots and are the most charming of Los Cabos region. Some boutique hotels and bed-and-breakfasts lie in or near the town centers of these very walkable towns, and others are more remote. For high-season stays, try to make reservations at least three months in advance, and six months in advance for holidays. Precious few lodgings serve travelers on a budget.

The Corridor—the stretch that connects San José with Cabo San Lucas—has seen the growth of several megaresorts. These microcosms contain two or more hotels, throughout which golf courses, private villas, and upscale condo projects are interspersed. ⚠ **If you are planning a vacation in Los Cabos, do keep in mind that most of the beaches at the resorts along the Corridor are not swimmable.**

Cabo San Lucas continues its meteoric climb into the 5-star stratosphere. Nearly every hotel in Cabo has undergone some kind of renovation, from minor to complete makeovers. The ME Cabo by Meliá is one such example. When Casa Dorada Resort opened, smack in the middle of busy El Médano Beach, it raised the bar in regards to rooms, services, and pampering, and Capella Pedregal and Grand Solmar Land's End have set a new high standard.

The rate of development in the area is astonishing, and begs the question of sustainability. As developable space in Los Cabos region diminishes and becomes prohibitively expensive, the newest expansions are moving beyond the Sea of Cortez coastline north of San José del Cabo, known as the "East Cape," and north of Cabo San Lucas along the Pacific coast. For years, building restrictions have been discussed, but money talks in every language. The only "restrictions" seem to be how much actual land is left.

ALL ABOUT ALL-INCLUSIVES

All-inclusives are like all-you-can-eat buffets—with all the positive and negative aspects included. You fork over the cash and just have at it, from the food and drink to an expansive pool complex and often water sports and excursions, too. You might consider this as one way for first-time visitors (especially families) to experience Los Cabos and not break the bank. The all-inclusive concept has come a long way since Club Med launched the concept decades ago. These days, all-inclusive properties are becoming more and more sophisticated, offering an impressive array of restaurants, bars, activities, and entertainment—and often striving to keep some local flavor present in the process. Note that while some all-inclusives offer endless complimentary amenities, others have a list (in fine print) of what you'll be billed for in the end.

WEDDINGS

If you decide to get married in Los Cabos, you'll be able to enjoy nuptials with friends and family in a gorgeous setting, and there'll be no worries about heading out for the honeymoon the morning after—you're already there. Los Cabos has a bevy of choices, and prices, for dream destination weddings. If money is no object, look into the big-name properties such as One&Only Palmilla, Las Ventanas al Paraíso, Esperanza, Capella Pedregal, and the Secrets Marquis Los Cabos, where celebs often say "I do." Palmilla even has an official Director of Celebrations to assist. At Las Ventanas, the Romance Director has an entire program dedicated to dream weddings, offering everything from a fireworks display to a ring bearer on horseback. But the true champion of weddings has got to be the Dreams Los Cabos property, where as many as five couples get hitched each week. Let anyone concerned about the legitimacy of a Mexican wedding know that as long as you satisfy a few easy requirements, the ceremony will be legally binding.

WHAT IT COSTS IN DOLLARS				
	$	$$	$$$	$$$$
Hotels	Under $200	$200–$299	$300–$399	over $399

Hotel prices are the lowest cost of a standard double room in high season.

CABOS WITH KIDS
If you're heading down to Los Cabos with the little ones in tow, you're in luck, because many properties are kid-friendly. Unless they are adults-only properties, most of them welcome children with Kids' Clubs. *The properties that go out of their way to provide entertainment for kids are marked with "family" in this chapter.* Many of the independent hotels listed don't restrict children, but their size and arrangement suggest more adult-oriented accommodations. We've mentioned these factors in our reviews.

CABO CONDOS
If you're planning to stay a week or more, renting a condo can be more economical and convenient than a hotel. Los Cabos has countless condominium properties, ranging from modest homes to ultra-luxurious villas in such exclusive areas as Palmilla near San José del Cabo and the hill-clinging Pedregal neighborhood above Cabo San Lucas and its marina. Many private owners rent out their condos, either through the development's rental pool or property management companies. The price is the same for both, but with the latter you might get a better selection.

Nearly all condos are furnished and have a fully equipped kitchen, a television, bed and bath linens, laundry facilities, and maid service. Most are seaside and range from studios to three-bedroom units. A minimum stay of one week is typically required, though rules can vary by property. Start the booking process at least four months in advance, especially for high-season rentals.

CONTACTS
Cabo Homes and Condos ☎ 866/321–CABO(2226) *from U.S.* ⊕ *www.cabohomesandcondos.com.*

Cabo Villas. Offering private villa vacation rentals, Cabo Villas represents several high-end homes at 5-star properties throughout Los Cabos. ☎ 855/745–2226 *in U.S./Canada* ⊕ *www.cabovillas.com.*

OUR REVIEWS
Hotel reviews have been shortened. For full information, visit Fodors.com.

Use the coordinate (✛ 1:B2) at the end of each listing to locate a site on the corresponding maps.

SAN JOSÉ DEL CABO

If being in Mexico (and not in the thick of a hopping resort scene) is more your speed, Cabo San Lucas's sister city San José del Cabo is the place to base your stay. Its downtown, with century-old buildings and many elevated sidewalks, is a delight to explore on foot. Plaza Mijares, the open and popular *zócalo*, is graced by a "dancing waters" fountain, lighted at night, and a stage where live music takes place frequently for the crowds who gather to stroll, enjoy ice cream, and relax after the heat of the day has let up. Several streets fronting the square are pedestrian-only, giving this historic downtown a lush and leisurely feel. Just beyond the center of town, and a bit farther south, is the ever-expanding Zona Hotelera, where a dozen or so new hotels, time-shares, and condo projects face the long stretch of beach (also referred to as Playa Hotelera) on the usually placid Sea of Cortez. Closer to the marina at Puerto los Cabos, the boutique El Ganzo Hotel and chain resorts like Secrets and JW Marriott are staking their claim, with plans for further development past La Playita.

$$
ALL-INCLUSIVE
FAMILY

Barceló Grand Faro Los Cabos. On Playa del Sol, along San José del Cabo's hotel zone, this five-story hotel caters to both business and fun, with four restaurants, three pools, four bars, and massive meeting rooms. **Pros:** friendly service and reasonable rates for the beach; La Tortuga kids' club keeps tots busy; no time-share salespeople. **Cons:** food is standard; beach not safe for swimming; $15 daily fee for Internet access. $ *Rooms from: $232* ⊠ *Paseo Malecón, Blvd. San Jose s/n Lote 9, Zona Hotelera* ☎ *624/142–9292, 866/400–2692 in U.S.* ⊕ *www. barcelo.com* ⤳ *333 rooms, 22 suites* ⦿ *All-inclusive* ✛ *1:C5.*

$$$$
RESORT
Fodor's Choice
★

Cabo Azul Resort. On the beach in San José del Cabo, this chic, white-washed property is peaceful from the moment you walk through the 20-foot antique door marking the entrance. **Pros:** huge villas; sophisticated and elegant property; well-maintained amenities. **Cons:** spotty Internet; beach not safe for swimming; not all rooms have ocean views; time-share focused; some lackadaisical staff. $ *Rooms from: $400* ⊠ *Paseo Malecón, Zona Hotelera* ☎ *624/163–5100, 877/216–2226 in U.S.* ⊕ *www.caboazulresort.com* ⤳ *145 villas* ⦿ *No meals* ✛ *1:C5.*

$
HOTEL
Fodor's Choice
★

Casa Natalia. An intimate, graceful boutique hotel, Casa Natalia is in the heart of San José's downtown and opens onto the Zócalo. **Pros:** oasis in the heart of downtown; fantastic complimentary breakfast for superior rooms; lovely pool area. **Cons:** no bathtubs in the standard rooms; occasional noise from music and fiestas on Plaza Mijares. $ *Rooms from: $185* ⊠ *Blvd. Mijares 4, Centro* ☎ *624/146–7100* ⊕ *www.casanatalia.com* ⤳ *16 rooms, 3 suites* ⦿ *Breakfast* ✛ *1:C2.*

$
B&B/INN

El Delfin Blanco. Offering the culture and charm of Mexico, this is an affordable alternative for independent travelers who don't want all the hoopla of a highly developed, all-inclusive-style resort. **Pros:** natural surroundings make this a great place to get away from it all; shared kitchen for cooking catch of the day; wonderfully attentive innkeepers; a few restaurants are within walking distance. **Cons:** 10-minute drive to San José del Cabo; basic rooms; property closes if there are no bookings, meaning drop-ins are not recommended. $ *Rooms from: $67* ⊠ *Pueblo La Playita, end of Calle Delfins, near the lighthouse,*

BEST BETS FOR LOS CABOS LODGING

Fodor's offers a selective listing of quality lodging experiences in every price range, from the city's best budget beds to its most sophisticated luxury hotels. Here, we've compiled our top recommendations by price and experience. The very best properties — in other words, those that provide a particularly remarkable experience in their price range — are designated in the listings with the Fodor's Choice logo.

La Playita ☎ 624/142–1212 ⊕ *www.eldelfinblanco.net* ⌁ 4 *casitas, 1 cabana* ❘○❘ *No meals* ✛ *1:D2.*

$ 🎬 **El Encanto Inn.** In the heart of San José's Historic Arts District, this
HOTEL   gorgeous and comfortable inn has two separate buildings—one looks
onto the verdant gardens and pool; the other one, across the street, is in
a charming, historic building with a narrow courtyard. **Pros:** Mexican-
hacienda feeling; excellent location; pet friendly. **Cons:** staffing is minimal; noisy a/c units; some rooms get street noise. Ⓢ *Rooms from: $99*
✉ *Calle Morelos 133, Centro* ☎ 624/142–0388 ⊕ *www.elencantoinn.
com* ⌁ *12 rooms, 14 suites* ❘○❘ *No meals* ✛ *1:C1.*

$$ 🎬 **Holiday Inn Resort Los Cabos.** The former home of the Presidente
ALL-INCLUSIVE   InterContinental Los Cabos, the familiar Holiday Inn brand has taken
FAMILY   over this sprawling property featuring cactus gardens that surround
low-lying terracotta-colored buildings. **Pros:** Chiqui Kids' Club (ages
5–12); adults-only pool; generally mellow atmosphere is good for fami-
lies and those looking for a getaway; free Wi-Fi. **Cons:** rooms tend
to be basic; food is run-of-the-mill buffet-style restaurants, except at
Napa. Ⓢ *Rooms from: $200* ✉ *Blvd. Mijares and Paseo San José, cul-
de-sac at end of hotel zone, Zona Hotelera* ☎ 624/142–9229 ⊕ *www.
holidayinnresorts.com/loscabos* ⌁ *390 rooms, 7 suites* ❘○❘ *All-inclusive*
✛ *1:D4.*

$$$ 🎬 **Hotel El Ganzo.** The newest addition to San José del Cabo has an
HOTEL   uber-chic vibe where guests can interact with artists, musicians, and
Fodor's Choice   filmmakers in a creative and luxurious setting. **Pros:** an outlet for art-
★   ists; free beach cruisers to explore the marina and cactus gardens. ⚠ **As
of this writing, Hotel El Ganzo is scheduled to be closed for repairs and
remodeling until mid-2015 due to damages from Hurricane Odile.** **Cons:**
must spend a minimum of 500 pesos to use the beach club; service does
not match the price. Ⓢ *Rooms from: $300* ✉ *Tiburón s/n, La Playita,
Marina* ☎ 624/104–9000 ⊕ *www.elganzo.com* ⌁ *72 rooms, 6 suites*
❘○❘ *No meals* ✛ *1:D2.*

$$$ 🎬 **Hyatt Ziva.** This resort is great for both families and couples looking
ALL-INCLUSIVE   for a complete getaway, featuring 619 suites, eight restaurants rang-
ing from French to Italian and Spanish to Japanese, seven bars, four
pools (including an adults-only option), and a Kids' Club. **Pros:** great
à la carte restaurant selection; spacious suites; Kids' Club and adjacent
water park offer diversion for little ones. **Cons:** resort's size is a bit over-
whelming; slow elevator; 30% of rooms lack ocean views. Ⓢ *Rooms
from: $390* ✉ *Paseo Malecon, Lote 5, Zona Hotelera* ☎ 624/163–7730
⊕ *www.loscabos.ziva.hyatt.com* ⌁ *619 suites* ❘○❘ *All-inclusive* ✛ *1:B6.*

$ 🎬 **La Fonda del Mar.** If you're looking for a peaceful back-to-nature
B&B/INN   retreat, check out this hotel on a long, secluded beach that straddles
the line between desert and ocean. **Pros:** beautiful beachfront prop-
erty; excellent full breakfast included in room rate. **Cons:** located past
La Playita which is far from town; difficult to find; credit cards not
accepted; shared shower facilities. Ⓢ *Rooms from: $95* ✉ *Old East
Cape Rd., La Playita* ✛ *Follow the signs to El Encanto de La Laguna or
ask for directions to Buzzard's since many locals refer to the hotel by the
bar's name.* ☎ 624/145–2139 *cell,* 624/113–6368 *restaurant* ⊕ *www.
buzzardsbar.com* ⌁ *3 cabañas, 1 suite* ▬ *No credit cards* ❘○❘ *Breakfast*
✛ *1:D2.*

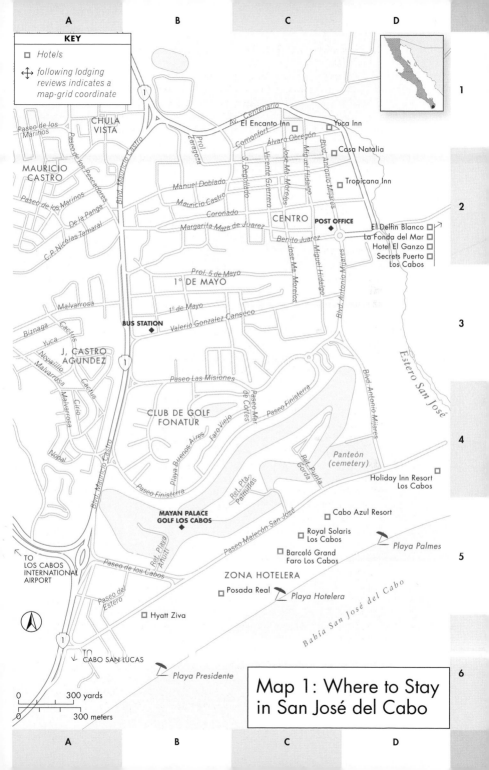

Map 1: Where to Stay in San José del Cabo

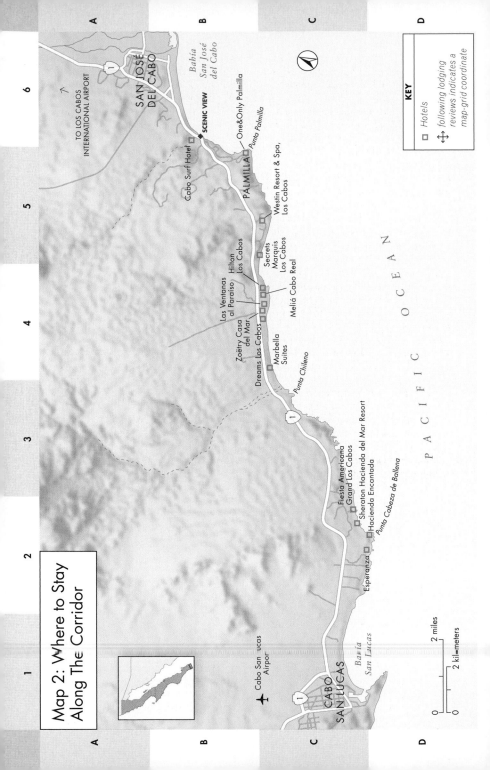

Map 2: Where to Stay Along The Corridor

TO LOS CABOS
INTERNATIONAL AIRPORT

SAN JOSÉ
DEL CABO

Bahía
San José
del Cabo

SCENIC VIEW

Cabo Surf Hotel

One&Only Palmilla

Punta Palmilla

PALMILLA

Westin Resort & Spa,
Los Cabos

Hilton
Los Cabos

Secrets
Marquis
Los Cabos

Meliá Cabo Real

Las Ventanas
al Paraíso

Zoëtry Casa
del Mar

Marbella
Suites

Dreams Los Cabos

Punta Chileno

Fiesta Americana
Grand Los Cabos

Sheraton Hacienda del Mar Resort

Hacienda Encantada

Punta Cabeza de Ballena

Esperanza

PACIFIC OCEAN

Cabo San Lucas Airport

CABO
SAN LUCAS

Bahía
San Lucas

KEY

☐ Hotels

↥ following lodging
reviews indicates a
map-grid coordinate

0   2 miles

0   2 kilometers

$ **Posada Real.** One of the better values in Hotel Zone, this tranquil
HOTEL   beachside property consists of two tri-level, Santa Fe–style buildings, and nice cactus gardens with fountains. **Pros:** hotel maintains an intimate feeling with a friendly staff; price is very reasonable compared to all of its neighbors; several meal plans available. **Cons:** slightly outdated rooms; no elevator; only one restaurant with all inclusive plan means limited dining options. $ *Rooms from: $133* ✉ *Malecón, Zona Hotelera* ☎ *624/142–0155, 800/448–8355 in U.S.* ⊕ *www.posadareal. com.mx* ⇲ *140 rooms, 8 suites* ❧ *Multiple meal plans* ⊹ *1:B5.*

$ **Royal Solaris Los Cabos.** Royal Solaris was the first all-inclusive in Los
ALL-INCLUSIVE   Cabos, and it runs smoothly, with plenty of entertainment options and
FAMILY   sports activities offered. **Pros:** Kids' Club entertains kids 4–12 year olds from 9 to 5; cooking classes and dancing lessons; best value of the all-inclusives. **Cons:** the accommodations and food veer toward only adequate here; this is not the place to go for romance-seeking couples; time-share salespeople are pushy. $ *Rooms from: $190* ✉ *Paseo Malecon, Lote 10, Colonia Campo de Golf, Zona Hotelera* ☎ *624/145–6800, 877/270–0440 in U.S.* ⊕ *www.hotelessolaris.com* ⇲ *387 rooms, 2 suites* ❧ *All-inclusive* ⊹ *1:C5.*

$$$$ **Secrets Puerto Los Cabos.** The first of the all-inclusive chains to reach
ALL-INCLUSIVE   La Playita, this adults-only resort has swim-up rooms, ocean views, seven restaurants, and a 13,000 square-foot Spa by Pevonia. **Pros:** isolated location (for now); plenty of activities; caters to adults. **Cons:** beach not swimmable; neighboring construction; annoying time-share pitches. $ *Rooms from: $550* ✉ *Avenida Paseo de los Pescadores s/n, La Playita* ☎ *624/144–2600* ⊕ *www.secretsresorts.com* ⇲ *500 rooms* ❧ *All-inclusive* ⊹ *1:D2.*

$ **Tropicana Inn.** It's not on the beach, but this hotel in a quiet enclave
HOTEL   along one of San José's main boulevards is a delightful, reasonable find. **Pros:** bustling on-site restaurant and bar with live entertainment; rooms are immaculate; small on-site spa; staff is attentive and courteous. **Cons:** kids are allowed even though the hotel is clearly oriented to adults seeking peace and relaxation; ice machine near several rooms can be loud; rooms at end of hotel have poor views and lighting. $ *Rooms from: $130* ✉ *Blvd. Mijares 30, Centro* ☎ *624/142–1580* ⊕ *www. tropicanainn.com.mx* ⇲ *36 rooms, 4 suites* ❧ *Breakfast* ⊹ *1:D2.*

THE CORRIDOR

Even before the Corridor had an official name or even a paved road, the few hotels here were ritzy and elite; one even had its own private airstrip. As the saying goes, the more things change, the more they stay the same—developers have deliberately kept this area high-end and private. The Corridor is the most valuable strip of real estate in the region, with guard-gated exclusivity, golf courses, luxury developments, and unsurpassed views of the Sea of Cortez.

$$ **Cabo Surf Hotel.** Professional and amateur surfers alike claim the
HOTEL   prime ocean-view rooms in this small hotel on the cliffs above Playa
Fodor's Choice   Costa Azul that has successfully blended surfing and pampering into
★   one property. **Pros:** blends surfing and pampering; hotel guests receive

15% discount on surf lessons and rental. **Cons:** traffic from the highway can be noisy; usually full as wedding parties tend to book the entire hotel. ⑤ *Rooms from: $265* ✉ *Hwy. 1, Km 28* ☎ *624/142-2676, 858/964–5117 in U.S.* ⊕ *www.cabosurfhotel.com* ↵ *36 rooms* ⦿ *No meals* ✛ *2:B6.*

$$$$
ALL-INCLUSIVE
FAMILY

⚏ **Dreams Los Cabos.** This casual, unfussy resort is touted as a romantic getaway, but it's more a destination for families and wedding parties with all ages of guests in attendance. **Pros:** Explorer's Club for kids ages 3–12; golf concierge; plenty to entertain. **Cons:** resort can sometimes feel overrun with children; food is abundant but cuisine is only average; $15 daily charge for Internet access. ⑤ *Rooms from: $400* ✉ *Hwy. 1, Km 18.5* ☎ *866/237–3267, 624/145–7600* ⊕ *www. dreamsresorts.com* ↵ *308 suites* ⦿ *All-inclusive* ✛ *2:C4.*

> ## AN ADVENTURE-A-DAY
>
> The Secrets Marquis has implemented a program that might just lure even its least active patrons off their beach chairs. The year-round Adventure-A-Day program offers trips and activities around the area that range from an easy visit to San José's Art District and barhopping in Cabo San Lucas to snorkeling the crystal clear bays of the Corridor and camel back rides through the desert. The adventures range in price from $15 to $220 and can be booked when reserving your room or through the concierge in the lobby.

$$$$
RESORT
Fodor's Choice
★

⚏ **Esperanza.** One of the most exquisite resorts in Los Cabos, focused on privacy and impeccable service, and home to one of the best spas in the region, Esperanza is true luxury. **Pros:** extra amenities included in the room rate; setting is exquisite; every casita has an ocean view. **Cons:** the high cost of incidentals can get exhausting; wind can be fierce on the rocky cliffs. ⑤ *Rooms from: $800* ✉ *Hwy. 1, Km 7, Punta Ballena* ☎ *624/145–6400, 866/311–2226 in U.S.* ⊕ *www.esperanzaresort. com* ↵ *57 suites, 60 villas* ⦿ *Breakfast* ✛ *2:C2.*

$$$$
ALL-INCLUSIVE

⚏ **Fiesta Americana Grand Los Cabos.** The dramatic lobby of this all-inclusive resort is eight stories above the beach, and every room looks out onto the Sea of Cortez. **Pros:** a good choice for couples wanting a relaxing getaway and golfers; every room has an ocean view; free kids' club ages 4–12. **Cons:** rocky beach; service is notoriously spotty. ⑤ *Rooms from: $450* ✉ *Cabo del Sol, Hwy. 1, Km 10.3* ☎ *624/145–6200, 866/927–7666* ⊕ *www.fiestamericanagrand.com* ↵ *235 rooms, 14 suites* ⅄ *Jack Nicklaus Ocean Golf Course at Cabo del Sol* ⦿ *All-inclusive* ✛ *2:C3.*

$$$$
RESORT

⚏ **Hacienda Encantada.** Despite the enormous size of this time-share resort hybrid, there are only 150 rooms, meaning guests are treated to 1,400 square-foot hacienda-styled suites. **Pros:** outstanding views; excellent taco bar; all-inclusive package includes dining at marina restaurants. **Cons:** beach not swimmable; stiff sheets; extra charge for premium alcohol and certain menu items; noisy golf carts putt around the property; room service not included in all-inclusive plan. ⑤ *Rooms from: $400* ✉ *Carretera Transpeninsular, Km 7.3* ☎ *624/163–5555, 877/797–0519 in U.S.* ⊕ *www.haciendaencantada.com* ↵ *150 rooms* ⦿ *Multiple meal plans* ✛ *2:C2.*

The intimate, 40-suite Marbella Suites is known for its laid-back atmosphere.

$$ **Hilton Los Cabos.** Rooms are spacious at this hacienda-style Hilton
RESORT built on one of the Corridor's few swim-friendly beaches. **Pros:** 24-hour
FAMILY gym; golf concierge service; great cocktail bar; no time-shares in main
building. **Cons:** spa services aren't up to par with the rest of the resort;
$10 charge for Wi-Fi per day; no activities; nothing extra included in
room rate; staff lacks attention to detail. *⑤ Rooms from: $279 ⊠ Hwy.
1, Km 19.5 ☎ 624/145–6500, 800/HILTONS ⊕ www.hiltonloscabos.
com ✍ 322 rooms, 53 suites ⑩ No meals ✛ 2:C4.*

$$$$ **Las Ventanas al Paraíso.** From the moment your private butler greets
RESORT you with a margarita and escorts you to the spa for a welcome mas-
Fodor'sChoice sage, you know you're in for some serious pampering and a special
★ experience. **Pros:** exceptional service; stellar dining and wine/tequila
selection; best spa in Los Cabos. **Cons:** there can be a 4- to 8-night
minimum depending on the season and holiday; 35% tax and gratuity
added to every bill; super-pricey. *⑤ Rooms from: $968 ⊠ Hwy. 1, Km
19.5 ☎ 624/144–2800, 888/ROSEWOOD in U.S. ⊕ www.lasventanas.
com ✍ 71 suites, 12 villas ⑩ Multiple meal plans ✛ 2:C4.*

$ **Marbella Suites en la Playa.** With all the sophisticated properties in Los
HOTEL Cabos, it's a treat to discover little Marbella Suites, one of the oldest
Fodor'sChoice hotels in Cabo, and one which still retains the flavor of the peaceful
★ and romantic East Cape properties. **Pros:** large rooms with kitchen-
ettes; gracious, friendly staff; homey, relaxed atmosphere; free Wi-Fi
Cons: not accessible for guests with wheelchairs; most rooms with only
minimal ocean views; no TVs (except in penthouse); bathrooms lack
tubs. *⑤ Rooms from: $112 ⊠ Trans. Hwy. 17 ☎ 624/144–1060 ⊕ www.
marbellasuites.com ✍ 41 suites ⑩ No meals ✛ 2:C4.*

One&Only Palmilla is a stunning seaside resort.

$$$$
ALL-INCLUSIVE

Meliá Cabo Real. Whether you're traveling for a business meeting or a family get-together, this all-inclusive property is one of the liveliest places in the Corridor and has the only swimmable beach thanks to a man-made cove. ⚠ As of this writing Meliá Cabo Real is scheduled to be closed for repairs and remodeling until July 1, 2015, due to damages from Hurricane Odile. **Pros:** near golf courses; decent rates; swimmable beach. **Cons:** no elevator; slippery pool area; loud music at pool carries into closed rooms; charge for Wi-Fi and room service. $ *Rooms from: $400 ✉ Hwy 1, Km 19.5 ☎ 624/144–2218, 866/43–MELIA ⊕ www. meliacaboreal.com ↪ 307 rooms* ◯ *All-inclusive ✛ 2:C4.*

$$$$
RESORT
Fodor's Choice
★

One&Only Palmilla. Built in 1956 by the son of the then-president of Mexico, the One&Only was the first resort introduced to the Los Cabos area, and it retains an old-world ambience and elegance that is without match in the region. **Pros:** lush landscape stands out from the rest; "Air to Go" meals for flight home; complimentary tequila and cocktail snacks delivered daily; morning yoga and boot camp classes. **Cons:** prices are high; increasing numbers of boisterous groups mar the otherwise genteel atmosphere. $ *Rooms from: $695 ✉ Hwy. 1, Km 27.5 ☎ 624/146–7000, 866/829–2977 in U.S. ⊕ www.oneandonlyresorts. com ↪ 172 rooms, 1 villa ⅂ Jack Nicklaus–designed 18-hole course* ◯ *No meals ✛ 2:B5.*

$$$$
ALL-INCLUSIVE

Secrets Marquis Los Cabos. Stunning architecture, a property-wide art collection of unique pieces, noticeable attention to detail, and loads of luxurious touches make the Marquis a standout. **Pros:** tranquility prevails for complete escape; exceptional full-service spa. **Cons:** weddings are frequently taking place on the premises; surf is unswimmable; extra charge for Wi-Fi. $ *Rooms from: $525 ✉ Carretera 1, Km.*

21.5 ☎ 624/144–2000, 877/238–9399 ⊕ *www.secretsresorts.com/marquis-los-cabos* ⤳ 206 suites, 26 casitas ⦿ All-inclusive ✢ 2:C5.

$$
RESORT
FAMILY
☒ **Sheraton Hacienda del Mar Resort.** Small domes and barrel tile roofs top eight buildings at this lovely, hacienda-style resort in the Cabo Del Sol development. **Pros:** rooms are serene and quiet; access to amazing golf courses; design reflects destination; children under 17 stay free. **Cons:** beach is not usually good for swimming; the mostly mediocre restaurants are expensive; daily Internet fee; time-share sales people can get pushy. ⑤ *Rooms from: $220* ✉ *Cabo del Sol, Hwy. 1, Km 10* ☎ *624/145–8000, 800/325–3535 in U.S.* ⊕ *www.sheratonloscabos.com* ⤳ *239 rooms, 31 suites* ⦿. *All Cabo del Sol's courses are available to guests* ⦿ *No meals* ✢ *2:C2.*

$
RESORT
FAMILY
☒ **Westin Resort & Spa, Los Cabos.** Built by prominent Mexican artist Javier Sordo Madaleno, the colorful design and architecture reflecting the famous Arco (arch) makes this Westin more memorable than some of the others in the Corridor. **Pros:** good children's center; great gym with yoga and Pilates classes; multiple pools including an adults-only option; every room has an ocean view. **Cons:** it's a trek from the parking lot and lobby to the rooms and pools; lots of groups; daily Internet surcharge. ⑤ *Rooms from: $189* ✉ *Hwy. 1, Km 22.5* ☎ *624/142–9000, 888/625–5144 in U.S.* ⊕ *www.starwood.com/westin* ⤳ *243 rooms, 12 suites* ⦿ *No meals* ✢ *2:C5.*

$$$$
ALL-INCLUSIVE
Fodor's Choice
★
☒ **Zoëtry Casa del Mar.** It's all about comfort and privacy at this award-winning, hacienda-style hotel that caters to couples and travelers with a healthy lifestyle. **Pros:** flexible check-in and checkout times; adults-only property; intimate and peaceful atmosphere; generous all-inclusive perks. **Cons:** the hotel is technically 53 rooms but it's surrounded by 220 time-share condos; undertow at beach; food can be hit-or-miss. ⑤ *Rooms from: $585* ✉ *Hwy. 1, Km 19.5* ☎ *624/145–7700, 888/4-ZOETRY in U.S.* ⊕ *www.zoetryresorts.com* ⤳ *63 suites* ⦿ *All-inclusive* ✢ *2:C4.*

CABO SAN LUCAS

In Cabo San Lucas, there's a massive hotel on every available plot of waterfront turf. A pedestrian walkway known as the Marina Golden Zone is lined with restaurants, bars, and shops. It's anchored by the sleek Puerto Paraíso mall that curves around the entire perimeter of Cabo San Lucas harbor, itself packed with wall-to-wall sportfishing and pleasure yachts. Unfortunately, a five-story hotel complex at one edge of the harbor blocks a small portion of the water view and sea breezes from the town's side streets, but it can't be denied that Cabo is a carnival and a parade, all at once. The short Pacific coast beach just over the rocky hills at the west end of the marina has a more peaceful ambience, though monstrous hotel projects have gobbled up much of

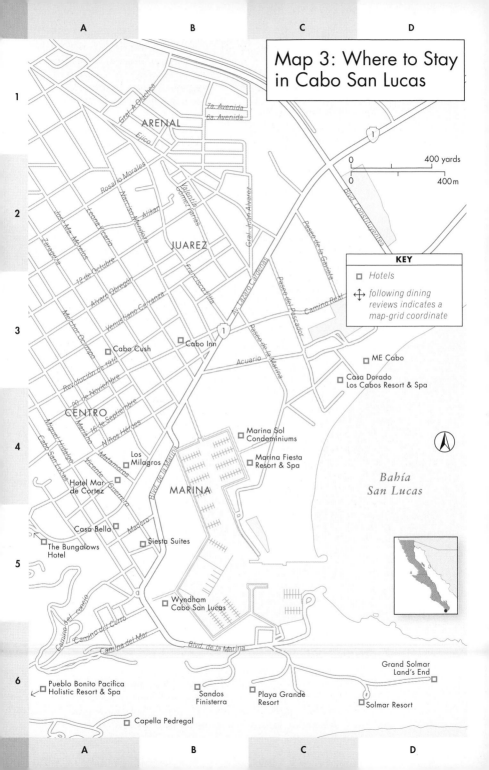

Map 3: Where to Stay in Cabo San Lucas

ARENAL

JUAREZ

CENTRO

MARINA

Bahía San Lucas

400 yards

400 m

KEY

□ Hotels

↔ following dining reviews indicates a map-grid coordinate

Cabo Cush

Cabo Inn

ME Cabo

Casa Dorado Los Cabos Resort & Spa

Marina Sol Condominiums

Marina Fiesta Resort & Spa

Los Milagros

Hotel Mar de Cortez

Casa Bella

The Bungalows Hotel

Siesta Suites

Wyndham Cabo San Lucas

Grand Solmar Land's End

Pueblo Bonito Pacifica Holistic Resort & Spa

Sandos Finisterra

Playa Grande Resort

Solmar Resort

Capella Pedregal

the sand here, too. If being right on the water isn't a primary concern, it is well worth checking out some of the smaller, independently owned hotels sprinkled around the downtown area. Several offer gracious, hacienda-style accommodations with a personal touch that huge hotels cannot match. For a tranquil setting close enough to all the action, opt for one of the resorts near Land's End.

$
B&B/INN
The Bungalows Hotel. If solitude and a reasonable room rate are more important than being in the center of the action, Bungalows is your place. **Pros:** oasis-like property; excellent value; personalized service; outstanding breakfasts. **Cons:** noise from traffic and surrounding neighborhood; a bit off the beaten path. ⓢ *Rooms from: $135* ✉ *Blvd. Miguel Angel Herrera* ☎ *624/143–5035, 624/143–0585* ⊕ *www.thebungalowshotel. com* ⤳ *16 suites, 6 bungalows* ⦿*Breakfast* ✛ *3:A5.*

$
HOTEL
Cabo Cush. By far one of the most affordable hotels in Cabo, this little gem is reminiscent of courtyard hotels in mainland Mexico, with a central breezeway running between the low-slung two-story buildings in the heart of town. **Pros:** fantastic price for a comfortable room; friendly staff will offer all sorts of recommendations; free Wi-Fi and long distance calls to the U.S. **Cons:** no swimming pool or gardens; no view; some street noise. ⓢ *Rooms from: $60* ✉ *Calle Zaragoza between Revolucion and Carranza* ☎ *624/143–9300* ⊕ *www.cabocush.com* ⤳ *22 rooms* ⦿*No meals* ✛ *3:A3.*

$
B&B/INN
Cabo Inn. The small, comfortable rooms at this affordable palapa-roofed, cactus lined, and jungle like hotel have brightly painted walls with murals and stained-glass windows above the headboards. **Pros:** very affordable hotel close to the beach; communal kitchen; free Wi-Fi and coffee. **Cons:** some rooms are dark and cramped; upper rooms can get very noisy. ⓢ *Rooms from: $39* ✉ *Calle 20 de Noviembre and Vicario, Centro* ☎ *624/143–0819, 619/819–2727 in U.S.* ⊕ *www. caboinnhotel.com* ⤳ *18 rooms, 2 suites* ⦿*No meals* ✛ *3:B3.*

$$$$
RESORT
Fodor'sChoice
★
Capella Pedregal. The sand-colored, 5-star resort near the tip of the Baja Peninsula where the Sea of Cortez meets the Pacific is one of Los Cabos' best places to vacation. **Pros:** every room has a plunge pool; stellar restaurant El Farallon is on-site; exceptional service and a staff that calls you by name. **Cons:** Pacific-side beach is not swimmable; not ideal for children. ⓢ *Rooms from: $595* ✉ *Camino del Mar 1, Marina* ☎ *877/247–6688* ⊕ *www.capellapedregal.com* ⤳ *52 rooms, 14 suites* ⦿*No meals* ✛ *3:A6.*

$$$$
RESORT
FAMILY
Fodor'sChoice
★
Casa Dorada Los Cabos Resort & Spa. Through the dramatic entry on the stone facade you'll find this seven-floor, all-suites combination hotel–time-share has it all. **Pros:** beautifully appointed rooms; ocean views from every room; located at the heart of Playa Médano; great online deals for up to 50 percent off advertised rates. **Cons:** the beach in front of the hotel is host to noisy bars and clubs; time-share salespeople are aggressive. ⓢ *Rooms from: $685* ✉ *Av. del Pescador, Medano Beach* ☎ *624/163–5757, 866/448–0151 toll-free from U.S.* ⊕ *www. casadorada.com* ⤳ *186 suites* ⦿*No meals* ✛ *3:C3.*

$$$$
RESORT
FAMILY
Grand Solmar Land's End Resort & Spa. With luxury villas situated between cliff and sea, this property is the closest to the famed landmark, El Arco, that you will sleep. **Pros:** ocean views; as close to El

5

Arco as you can get; villas give a sense of home and isolation; taxes and gratuities included in every bill. **Cons:** beach not safe for swimming; hefty charge for in-room coffee, water, and Wi-Fi. $ *Rooms from: $650* ✉ *Av Solmar No 1A, next to Solmar Resort, Centro* ☎ *624/144–2500* ⊕ *www.grandsolmarresort.com* ⮑ *246 rooms* ❚⊙❚ *Multiple meal plans* ✣ *3:D6.*

> ### WHALE-WATCHING FROM UP ON HIGH
>
> The tower at **Sandos Finisterra** is about as high you can get, geographically, and it's the best spot in Cabo San Lucas to watch the gray whales in their winter home.

$

HOTEL

⊞ **Hotel Mar de Cortez.** Another one of Cabo's original hotels, Hotel Mar is only a few blocks from the marina, a block from the main square, near *muchos* restaurants, bars, clubs, and shopping. **Pros:** clean rooms and pleasant surroundings; refreshing pool; free Internet; complimentary breakfast for guests that stay three plus nights. **Cons:** noisy air-conditioning units; surrounding streets are busy and loud; beds and pillows are too hard. $ *Rooms from: $67* ✉ *Av Lazaro Cardenas, between Vincente Guerrero and Matamoros* ☎ *624/143–0032, 800/347–8821 in U.S.* ⊕ *www.mardecortez.com* ⮑ *88 rooms, 16 suites* ⊙ *Closed Sept.* ❚⊙❚ *Breakfast* ✣ *3:A4.*

$

HOTEL

⊞ **Los Milagros.** A mosaic sign (crafted by co-owner Ricardo Rode) near the entrance hints at the beauty inside this small stylish inn offering a relaxed atmosphere and boutique feel without the heavy cost. **Pros:** quiet inn located close to everything in Cabo; one room is accessible to travelers with disabilities; free Wi-Fi and TVs in every room. **Cons:** air-conditioning units in rooms can be loud; pool is small and not heated; daily fee for parking in private lot. $ *Rooms from: $85* ✉ *Matamoros 116* ☎ *718/928–6647 in U.S., 624/143–4566* ⊕ *www.losmilagros.com.mx* ⮑ *12 rooms* ❚⊙❚ *No meals* ✣ *3:A4.*

$$

RESORT

⊞ **Marina Fiesta Resort & Spa.** Though this colonial-style building is not ocean-side, most rooms have a pleasant view of the cloverleaf-shape pool and the yacht-filled marina. **Pros:** close to popular bars and shops, walking distance to Playa Médano; side rooms remodeled in 2014; all-inclusive plan gives access to seven restaurants. **Cons:** staff not well trained; there is no buffer between guests and aggressive time-share salespeople; no ocean views; center rooms are dated. $ *Rooms from: $216* ✉ *Marina, Lots 36 and 37, Marina* ☎ *624/145–6020, 877/243–4880 in U.S.* ⊕ *www.marinafiestaresort.com* ⮑ *155 rooms* ❚⊙❚ *Multiple meal plans* ✣ *3:B4.*

$$$

RESORT

⊞ **ME Cabo.** In the middle of Médano's most popular beach is the ME, the Meliá brand's posh offering in Cabos San Lucas. **Pros:** great for adults and singles; ME's Passion Night Club (open Thursday–Saturday) is a popular Cabo destination; iPod docking stations and plasma TVs in every room. **Cons:** affordable rooms are limited; noise carries from Passion club; not child friendly; meals not included. $ *Rooms from: $350* ✉ *Playa Médano* ☎ *624/145–7800, 877/954–8363 in U.S.* ⊕ *www.me-cabo.com* ⮑ *92 rooms, 58 suites* ❚⊙❚ *No meals* ✣ *3:D3.*

$$

RESORT

FAMILY

⊞ **Playa Grande Resort.** This large, multicolor all suite hotel complex on the beach next to the original Solmar property (which is now an all-inclusive) looks a bit Las Vegas, even by Cabo standards, but it's got

TIME-SHARE BEWARE

For some families who frequently like to get away to resorts, the time-share concept can be a good, and economical, way to vacation. Time-shares are a big business in Los Cabos, and the offers are incessant, especially as you walk through the town of Cabo San Lucas. Indeed, pushy, in-your-face time-share representatives at the airport and in many hotel lobbies will try to entice you to attend a presentation by offering free transportation, breakfast, and activities, or even attractive amounts of cash. These aggressive salespeople are a major downside to many expensive lodgings where you might assume that you won't be harassed. Don't feel obligated to accept—presentations often last two hours or more, and can be physically and emotionally draining. If you're staying in a hotel that has time-share units, aggressive salespeople may call your room every morning asking you to attend a free breakfast. If you're not interested, nicely demand to be taken off their call list.

■**TIP**➜ If you want those time-share "sharks" off your back pronto, simply say "I live here"—and they'll leave you alone.

5

all kinds of activities and facilities, making it a great family vacation option. **Pros:** the Thalasso Spa is huge; putt-putt golf course and play structures; fabulous pools. **Cons:** fitness center and Internet charges apply; getting to and from rooms is time-consuming and confusing; ongoing neighboring construction. ⑤ *Rooms from: $200* ⊠ *Av. Playa Grande #1* ☎ *624/145–7524, 800/344–3349 in U.S.* ⊕ *www.solmar. com* ⇱ *358 rooms* ❍❘ *No meals* ✛ *3:C6.*

$$$$
ALL-INCLUSIVE

🏩 **Pueblo Bonito Pacifica Resort & Spa.** Soothing waterfalls, glass-domed ceilings, and pebbled floors bring nature indoors to complement this holistic approach to vacationing. **Pros:** adults only; truly tranquil lodgings; free gym and Wi-Fi. **Cons:** $40 charge for use of beach beds; beach is not swimmable; you must have a car or take a cab to get to town. ⑤ *Rooms from: $600* ⊠ *Predio Paraiso Escondido* ☎ *624/142–9696, 800/990–8250 in U.S.* ⇱ *140 rooms, 14 suites* ❍❘ *All-inclusive* ✛ *3:A6.*

$$$$
ALL-INCLUSIVE

🏩 **Sandos Finisterra Los Cabos.** One of the first hotels built in Cabo, the Sandos Finisterra is an all-inclusive perched on a hill overlooking the marina and the Pacific. **Pros:** full remodel in 2013; fantastic location; rooms have either bay or ocean view. **Cons:** beach is not swimmable because of rough waves and undertow; time-share sales pitch can be annoying. ⑤ *Rooms from: $500* ⊠ *Blvd. Marina* ☎ *624/145–6700* ⊕ *www.sandos.com* ⇱ *250 rooms* ❍❘ *All-inclusive* ✛ *3:B6.*

$
HOTEL

🏩 **Siesta Suites.** The owners keep a close eye on this four-story hotel—a calm refuge two blocks from the marina—and dispense great insider advice to visitors. **Pros:** great rates; friendly staff; barbecue area great for cooking up the catch of the day; free Wi-Fi. **Cons:** town noise can sometimes be intrusive; limited off-street parking; ongoing construction in this area; pool is small and is surrounded by tables from Salvatore's restaurant at night. ⑤ *Rooms from: $69* ⊠ *Calle Zapata at Guerrero, Centro* ☎ *624/143–2773, 866/271–0952 toll-free in U.S.* ⊕ *www. cabosiestasuites.com* ⇱ *5 rooms, 15 suites* ❍❘ *No meals* ✛ *3:A5.*

$$ ▦ **Solmar Resort.** The sandy colored Solmar sits against the rocks at
ALL-INCLUSIVE Land's End facing the surging Pacific. **Pros:** wide beach great for sunset
strolls; 10-minute walk to town; great spa. **Cons:** ongoing construction
at all Solmar properties through 2015; everything closes at 10 pm;
limited dining options. ⑤ *Rooms from: $250* ⊠ *Av. Solmar at Blvd.
Marina, Apdo. 8* ☎ *624/145–7575, 800/344–3349 in U.S.* ⊕ *www.
solmar.com* ⥲ *100 suites* ⎮◎⎮ *All-inclusive* ✛ *3:D6.*

SHOPS AND SPAS

Updated by
Marlise Kast

Los Cabos may not have a whole lot of homegrown wares, but the stores are filled with beautiful and unusual items from all over mainland Mexico. You can find hand-painted blue Talavera tiles from Puebla; blue-and-yellow pottery from Guanajuato; black pottery from San Bartolo Coyotepec (near Oaxaca); hammocks from the Yucatán; embroidered clothing from Oaxaca, Chiapas, and the Yucatán; silver jewelry from Taxco; fire opals from Queretaro; and the fine beaded crafts of the Huichol tribe from Nayarit and Jalisco.

Los Cabos manufactures good times under plenty of sunshine but very few actual products. One exception is glassware from Fábrica de Vidrio Soplado (Blown-Glass Factory). In addition, a burgeoning arts scene has national and international artists opening galleries and, in fact, a large number of galleries now abound throughout Los Cabos, with many in San José del Cabo's rapidly evolving city center and more dotted throughout Todos Santos's historic downtown. Dozens of shops will custom-design gold and silver jewelry for you, fashioning pieces in one to two days. Liquor shops sell a locally produced liqueur called *damiana*, which is touted as an aphrodisiac. A few shops will even create custom-designed bathing suits for you in a day or so.

No longer hawking only the requisite T-shirts, belt buckles, and trinkets, Cabo's improved shopping scene has reached the high standards of other Mexican resorts. Its once-vacant streets are today lined with dozens of new shops, from open-air bazaars and souvenir shops to luxury malls and designer boutiques.

PLANNING

HOURS OF OPERATION

Many stores are open as early as 9 am, and often stay open until 9 or 10 pm. A few close for siesta at 1 pm or 2 pm, then reopen at 4 pm. About half of Los Cabos' shops close on Sunday; those that do open usually close up by 2 or 3 in the afternoon.

It's not uncommon to find some shops and galleries closed in San José del Cabo or Todos Santos during the hot season (roughly June to September), though very few shops close in Cabo San Lucas. We've noted this whenever possible; however, some shops simply close up for several weeks if things get excruciatingly slow or hot. In any case, low-season hours are usually reduced, so call ahead during that time of year.

BUYER BEWARE

One of the benefits of traveling in Los Cabos is the low crime rate, thanks in part to the large population of expats and year-round tourists, and the *tranquilo* nature of locals. That being said, it's always wise to pay attention to what's going on when money is changing hands. Some tips: Watch that your credit card goes through the machine only once, so that no duplicates of your slip are made. If there's an error and a new slip needs to be drawn up, make sure the original is destroyed. Don't let your card leave a store without you. One scam is to ask you to wait while the clerk runs next door ostensibly to use another business's phone or to verify your number—but really to make extra copies. Again, this area is refreshingly safe and incident-free compared to many areas on the mainland, but it's always wise to be aware.

BEST BRING-BACKS

If you travel Los Cabos with a few extra pesos in your pocket it's likely you'll want to return home with a memento that reminds you of the spirit and vibrancy of this region.

Works of art by local artists make great treasures to take back home—and galleries will usually ship the items for you. For more packable take-home goodies, the clothing options are nearly endless: T-shirts, resort wear, and clothing from hip Mexican designers will all compete for space in your suitcase. Cabo San Lucas is a great shopping town; if you've got time and some money, there's no need to worry about purchasing your beach vacation clothing before leaving home.

If you're looking for something truly authentic and *hecho en Cabo* (made in Cabo), then check out the blown glass at the intriguing **Fábrica de Vidrio Soplado.** Other fun souvenirs include the new labels of tequila offered from such outlets as Cabo Wabo, Hotel California in Todos Santos, the Cabo Surf Hotel, and Las Veritas, a popular Cabo dance club and bar.

SENDING STUFF HOME

Better stores and galleries offer shipping services for large or unwieldy items.

If you are an avid shopper, it won't hurt to pack a duffel bag for all your new treasures to check as luggage on your way home.

For more shipping info, ⇨ see Travel Smart Los Cabos.

WHAT YOU CAN'T BRING HOME

Don't buy items made from tortoiseshell or any sea turtle products: it's illegal (Mexico's turtle species are endangered or threatened, and these items aren't allowed into the United States, Canada, or the United Kingdom). Cowboy boots, hats, and sandals made from the leather of endangered species such as crocodiles may also be taken from you at customs, as will birds, or stuffed iguanas or parrots. It isn't uncommon for U.S. Customs agents to seize seashells, so those and all sea creatures are best left where you find them.

Both the U.S. and Mexican governments also have strict laws and guidelines about the import–export of antiquities. Check with customs beforehand if you plan to buy anything unusual or particularly valuable.

Although Cuban cigars are readily available, American visitors aren't allowed to bring them into the United States and will have to enjoy them while in Mexico. However, Mexico produces some fine cigars from tobacco grown in Veracruz. Mexican cigars without the correct Mexican seals on the individual cigars and on the box may be confiscated. For those 21 and older, U.S. customs allows one liter of alcohol per person to be entered into the U.S. duty-free, which is something to keep in mind if you plan on gifting bottles of tequila.

TIPS AND TRICKS

Better deals are often given to cash customers—even though credit cards are nearly always accepted—because stores must pay a commission to the credit-card companies. If you are paying in cash, it is perfectly reasonable to ask for a 5%–10% discount—though you shouldn't assume you'll be given one.

U.S. dollars are widely accepted in Los Cabos, although most shops pay a lower exchange rate than a bank (or ATM) or *casa de cambio* (money exchange).

Bargaining is common in markets and by beach vendors, who may ask as much as two or three times their bottom line. Occasionally an itinerant vendor will ask for the real value of the item, putting the energetic haggler into the awkward position of offering far too little. One vendor says he asks *norteamericanos* "for twice the asking price, since they always want to haggle." The trick is to know an item's true worth by comparison shopping. It's not necessary to bargain for already inexpensive trinkets like key chains or quartz-and-bead necklaces or bracelets.

SHOPPING GLOSSARY

bakery: *panadería*	market: *mercado*
bookseller: *librería*	notions store: *mercería*
candy store: *dulcería*	perfume store: *perfumeria*
florist: *florería*	shoe store: *zapateria*
grocery store: *abarrotes*	stationery store: *papelería*
health-food store: *tienda naturista*	tobacconist: *tabaquería*
jewelry store: *joyería*	toy store: *juguetería*
laundromat: *lavanderia*	

HUICHOL SHOPPING TIPS

See also Art of the Huichol special feature in this chapter.

Beaded items: The smaller the beads, the more delicate and expensive the piece. Beads with larger holes are fine for stringed work, but if used in bowls and statuettes cheapen the piece.

Items made with iridescent beads from Japan are the priciest. Look for good-quality glass beads, definition, symmetry, and artful use of color. Beads should fit together tightly in straight lines, with no gaps.

Yarn paintings: Symmetry is not necessary, although there should be an overall sense of unity. Thinner thread results in finer, more costly work. Look for tightness, with no visible gaps or broken threads. Paintings should have a stamp of authenticity on the back, including artist's name and tribal affiliation.

Prayer arrows: Collectors and purists should look for the traditionally made arrows of brazilwood inserted into a bamboo shaft. The most interesting ones contain embroidery work, or tiny carved icons, or are painted with copal symbols indicative of their original, intended purpose, for example protecting a child or ensuring a successful corn crop.

SAN JOSÉ DEL CABO

Cabo San Lucas's sister city has a refined air, with many shops in old colonial buildings just a short walk from the town's *zócalo* (central plaza). Jewelry and art are great buys—this is where you'll find the best shopping for high-quality Mexican folk art. Many of the most worthwhile shops are clustered within a few of blocks around Plaza Mijares, where Boulevard Mijares and Avenida Zaragoza both end at the zócalo at the center of San José. Thursday nights from November to June are designated Art Nights, when galleries stay open until 9 serving drinks and snacks, with various performances, demonstrations, and dancing—it's a fun night out!

Use the coordinate (⊕ 1:B2) at the end of each listing to locate a site on the corresponding maps.

ART GALLERIES

Amber Gallery & Fine Art Annex. This is the store to visit if you're a fan of amber jewelry, sculptures, abstract art, and collector perfume bottles. The owner recently added photography, paintings, and fossils to his gallery collection. ⊠ *Obregón 18 B* ☎ *624/105–2332* ⊕ *www. amberart.net* ✠ *1:A3.*

Casa Dahlia Fine Art Gallery. Casa Dahlia Fine Art Gallery features contemporary artists from Mexico and abroad, and invites visitors to linger in its beautifully renovated historic building to enjoy organic teas and coffee. Movies are shown every Thursday and Friday night in the gallery's gardens. ⊠ *Morelos and Zaragoza* ☎ *624/166–0262 cell, 503/922–3434 in U.S.* ⊕ *www.casadahlia.com* ✠ *1:B3.*

ART WALKS

Thursday art walks happen in downtown San José from November to June. Participating galleries and shops stay open until 9 pm and serve drinks and snacks, and many arrange for special events or openings. There is usually music on Plaza Mijares, and it's not uncommon for the streets to be full of people, locals and tourists alike. "Historic Art District" brochures are in most galleries and shops.

Frank Arnold Gallery. Frank Arnold Gallery has two big draws: arguably the best gallery space in town, in a modern building by local architect Alfredo Gomez, and Frank Arnold's dramatic, widely acclaimed contemporary paintings that have been compared to de Kooning, Gorky, and Hans Hofmann. The gallery also features bronze sculptures and fine art prints. ⊠ *1137 Calle Comonfort* ☎ *624/142–4422, 559/301–1148 in U.S.* ⊕ *www.frankarnoldart.com* ✠ *1:B2.*

Galería de Ida Victoria. Galería de Ida Victoria has been designed with skylights and domes to show off the international art contained within its three floors, which includes paintings, sculpture, photography, and prints. ⊠ *Guerrero 1128, between Zaragoza and Obregon* ☎ *624/142–5772* ⊕ *www.idavictoriagallery.com* ♡ *Closed Sun.* ✠ *1:A3.*

La Dolce Art Gallery. Near San José's classic cathedral on the zócalo, La Dolce Art Gallery specializes in modern painting styles. ⊠ *Hidalgo between Zaragoza and Obregón* ☎ *624/142–6621* ⊕ *www.alecalderoni. com* ♡ *Closed Mon.* ✠ *1:C2.*

Fodor'sChoice ★ **Patricia Mendoza Gallery.** Explore works of art by Mexico's top contemporary artists such as Lucille Wong, Javier Guadarrama, Jorge Marín, Luis Filcer, and Joao Rodriguez, among others. All of the artists represented here are known nationally and internationally in important collections and museums. ⊠ *Obregón at Hidalgo* ☎ *624/158-6497, 624/105–2270* ⊕ *www.patriciamendozagallery.com* ✠ *1:C2.*

silvermoon gallery. Silvermoon gallery is remarkable in the Los Cabos region both for the assortment and the quality of art contained within its walls. Mexican folk art makes up most of the inventory here. Treasures include Carlos Albert's whimsical papier-mâché sculptures, Mata Ortiz pottery from the Quezada family, Huichol yarn "paintings," Alebrijes (colorful wooden animal sculptures) from Oaxaca, and fine jewelry.

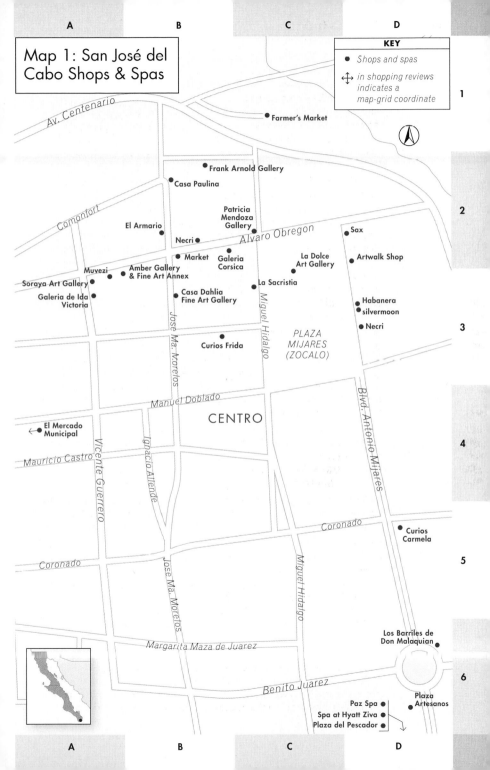

Map 1: San José del Cabo Shops & Spas

KEY

- Shops and spas
- in shopping reviews indicates a map-grid coordinate

Av. Centenario

Comonfort

Farmer's Market

Frank Arnold Gallery

Casa Paulina

Patricia Mendoza Gallery

El Armario

Necri

Alvaro Obregon

Sax

Market   Galeria Corsica

La Dolce Art Gallery

Artwalk Shop

Muvezi

Amber Gallery & Fine Art Annex

Soraya Art Gallery

La Sacristia

Galeria de Ida Victoria

Casa Dahlia Fine Art Gallery

Habanera

silvermoon

Necri

Jose Ma. Morelos

Curios Frida

PLAZA MIJARES (ZOCALO)

Miguel Hidalgo

Manuel Doblado

CENTRO

Blvd. Antonio Mijares

El Mercado Municipal

Mauricio Castro

Vicente Guerrero

Ignacio Allende

Coronado

Curios Carmela

Coronado

Jose Ma. Morelos

Miguel Hidalgo

Los Barriles de Don Malaquian

Margarita Maza de Juarez

Benito Juarez

Plaza Artesanos

Paz Spa

Spa at Hyatt Ziva

Plaza del Pescador

SELF-GUIDED GALLERY WALK IN SAN JOSÉ

A good number of galleries are closed, or have greatly reduced operating hours, during the hottest months of the year, usually late June through September. If there is one gallery you are particularly interested in, it's worth calling ahead to check on hours.

The Thursday art walks start at 5 pm, with galleries open until 9 pm. Start your walk on Hidalgo and Obregón, and wander down Obregón through the six or so galleries scattered on the next two blocks. Turning left on to Guerrero, you'll want to stop in to see **Galería de Ida Victoria** and

Casa Don Pablo. Turn right out of the galleries and walk a block over to Comonfort, where you'll connect to Morelos in another block to find the galleries in **Casa Paulina** awaiting, and the **Frank Arnold Gallery** a half block farther up on Comonfort. If you're hungry at this point, **Voilà Bistro** in Plaza Paulina and **Baan Thai**, across the street from each other on Morelos at Comonfort, are both excellent. Finish up by heading back to the zócalo and wandering among the shops on Plaza Mijares—making sure not to miss **Sax** and **silvermoon**.

Owner Armando Sanchez Icaza is gracious and knowledgeable; he knows volumes about the artists whose work he carries. His silversmiths can also make custom jewelry for you within a day or two. ⊠ *Plaza Mijares No. 10* ☎ *624/142–6077* ⊕ *www.silvermoongallerycabo. wordpress.com* ⊗ *Closed Sun.* ✛ *1:D3.*

Soraya Art Gallery. Soraya Art Gallery sells murals, faux finish, furniture, and trompe l'oeil art by local artists. ⊠ *Calle Guerrero #4* ☎ *044– 624/355–2819 cell* ⊗ *Closed weekends* ✛ *1:A3.*

FOLK ART AND CERAMICS

Curios Carmela. Curios Carmela displays an almost overwhelming array of Mexican textiles, pottery, glassware, hammocks, and souvenirs, but with a bit of searching you'll find some great bargains. ⊠ *Blvd. Mijares 43* ☎ *624/142–1617* ✛ *1:D5.*

La Sacristia. La Sacristia has a fine selection of Talavera pottery, traditional and contemporary Mexican jewelry, blown glass, and contemporary paintings. The glassware is incredible. ⊠ *Hidalgo #9, at Alvaro Obregón* ☎ *624/142–4007* ✛ *1:C3.*

Muvezi. Presenting the unexpected here in Baja Sur, Muvezi features fine Shona sculptures from Zimbabwe in a variety of breathtaking stones. It is the public face of an economic development project working to keep the ancient tradition of stone carving alive in Zimbabwe, and to provide desperately needed funds for health care at the grassroots level there. Don't worry about the weight of the stone. sculptures come in a variety of sizes and Muvezi will ship pieces to your home. Muvezi donates 20% of the revenues to help fight malaria throughout Africa. Buy a piece of art and affect a positive change. ⊠ *Alvaro Obregón 20* ☎ *624/157–2428* ⊕ *www.muvezi.com* ⊗ *Closed Sun.* ✛ *1:A3.*

A shop in San José del Cabo displays its colorful handmade wares.

Necri. Known for their hand-painted Talavera pottery from Puebla, this store also sells ceramics, handicrafts, black pottery, Majolica dinnerware, and pewter pieces. ⊠ *Calle Alvaro Obregón #17* ☎ *624/130–7500* ⊕ *www.necri.com.mx* ⊗ *Closed Sun.* ✢ *1:D3.*

HOME FURNISHINGS

Casa Paulina. More than just an art gallery, Casa Paulina inspires decorating ideas with items for the home. Candles, lamps, chairs, throws, and enormous clay pots are a few of the treasures you might find. ⊠ *Plaza Paulina, Morelos and Comonfort* ☎ *624/142–5555* ⊕ *www.casapaulina.com* ✢ *1:B2.*

JEWELRY

Artwalk Shop. This small boutique at Casa Natalia has jewelry, handbags, and art made from recycled metals. The organic soaps and oils are made from grapes in Baja's wine country. The owner, Natalia, helps support local women in need by selling their handmade products. Artwalk also has a good selection of brass jewelry from Mexico City. ⊠ *Blvd. Mijares, 4, at Casa Natalia* ☎ *624/146–7100* ⊕ *www.casanatalia.com* ⊗ *Closed Tues.* ✢ *1:D2.*

Sax. Owned by two talented sisters, Sax is a great place to find exceptional, eclectic silver jewelry designs. The artists will create a design of your choice in 72 hours. Although bargaining is not practiced, prices are very good here. There is another location in the Shoppes at Palmilla, or you can purchase directly from their online store. ⊠ *Plaza Mijares 1* ☎ *624/142–6053* ⊕ *www.saxstyle.com* ✛ *1:D2.*

MALLS

Plaza Artesanos. With a block of 30 stalls, Plaza Artesanos has a wide selection of handmade crafts and souvenirs, including pottery, jewelry, blankets, clothing, hammocks, leather bags, and even pure Mexican vanilla extract. Don't be afraid to barter by starting at half the asking price and then meeting somewhere in the middle. Drop by on Wednesday for live music, regional dance performances, and free margaritas from 6:30 to 8:30 pm. ⊠ *Blvd. Mijares, between Valerio Gonzalez and Paseo Finisterra* ☎ *624/143–7353, 762/105–5384* ✛ *1:D6.*

Plaza del Pescador. An outdoor mall conveniently located across the street from San José del Cabo's string of resorts, Plaza del Pescador offers guests an alternative to hotel dining. You'll find everything from sushi and gelato to tapas and a wine bar. Among the 25 shops and restaurants are a bookstore, jewelry store, fitness gym, and coffee shop. ⊠ *Paseo Malecon; Local 21–A, across from Cabo Azul Resort* ☎ *624/142–3436* ⊕ *www.plazadelpescador.com* ✛ *1:D6.*

MARKETS

El Mercado Municipal. San José's traditional market area is where you can stock up on fresh meats and produce, or visit the market's **Viva Mexico** stand for clothes, belts, spices, jewelry, and other curios—all at excellent prices. ⊠ *Castro and Coronado, off Calle Doblado* ✛ *1:A4.*

FAMILY **Farmer's Market** (*San José del Cabo Mercado Organico*). Get your organic fix at the *Mercado Organico* every Saturday from 9 to 3. Jewelry, artwork, soaps, fruit, and vegetables are a few of the goodies you'll find here. Food stalls serve everything from tacos to pizza and entertainment is offered for the kiddlets, making this an ideal outing for the whole family. ⊠ *Margarita Maza de Juarez, between Benito Juarez and Vincente Guerrero Col 8 de Octubre* ☎ *624/108–4235* ⊕ *www. sanjomo.com* ✛ *1:C1.*

SPAS

Paz Spa. Surrounded by natural stone walls, all of the treatment rooms at Cabo Azul's Paz Spa are named after semiprecious stones such as onyx, pearl, opal, lapis, jade, sapphire, and amber. Specialties include 50-minute massages to 210-minute complete experiences, as well as exfoliations, wraps, facials, manicures, and pedicures. A terrace suite can accommodate up to four treatments at one time for those looking for group relaxation. Seven other rooms round out the spa itself, and two double cabanas on the beach are available for those seeking the sound of the waves as backdrop to their treatment. Popular therapies include a Papaya Sugar Polish and Shea Butter Massage, as well as an Aloe Cooling Massage. An on-site salon is open Monday to Saturday from 9 to 5. ⊠ *Cabo Azul Resort, Paseo Malecón s/n Lote 11 Fonatur*

☏ 624/163–5100 ⊕ *www.caboazulresort.com* ✉ *Body treatments: $170–$250. Facials: $120–$190* ✛ *1:D6.*

The Spa at Hyatt Ziva. The concept at Hyatt Ziva's spa is to explore water, earth and air. Lounge by the communal pool, or duck into one of 19 treatment rooms for revitalizing massages, romantic packages, anti-aging facials, detoxifying body wraps, and deep-cleansing scrubs using local, natural ingredients. For those interested in a quick fix, manicures and pedicures are popular, and the on-site salon can help turn a bad-hair day into something grand. ⊠ *Hyatt Ziva Los Cabos, Paseo Malecon s/n Lote 5* ☏ *624/163–7730* ⊕ *www.loscabos.ziva.hyatt.com* ✉ *Body Treatments: $110–$280. Facials: $75–$240* ✛ *1:D6.*

SUNDRIES AND LIQUOR

Los Barriles de Don Malaquias. Go beyond Cuervo and Patrón at Los Barriles de Don Malaquias, which specializes in rare tequilas. The tequila selection is complemented by a good collection of Cuban cigars. Owner Rigoberto Cuervo Rosales is often on site to offer tequila tastings. ⊠ *Blvd. Mijares and Juárez* ☏ *624/130–7800, 624/142–5322* ✛ *1:B2.*

The Market. From the maker of Flora Farms, this corner store sells all things organic including fresh fruit, pickled vegetables, soaps, jams, honey, coffee, and body oils. It's a great place to grab a healthy snack or stock up on produce delivered daily from Flora's local farm. ⊠ *Morelos at corner of Alvaro Obregon* ☏ *624/142–1665* ⊕ *www.flora-farms.com* ⊘ *Closed Sun.* ✛ *1:B2.*

THE CORRIDOR

There are shopping options along the Corridor—the stretch of land between San José del Cabo to the east and Cabo San Lucas to the west—but the shops cater more to resort guests and American expats than to travelers looking to experience Los Cabos. The closest thing you'll find to a shopping mall here is Las Tiendas de Palmilla, across from Palmilla Resort, with fewer than a dozen shops, galleries, and restaurants. Unless you are intent on something specific at one of the shops on the Corridor, you'll have much more fun shopping in San José del Cabo, Cabo San Lucas, or Todos Santos.

HOME FURNISHINGS

Artesanos. Local homeowners and restaurateurs come to Artesanos for Mexican furnishings, dishes, and glassware, along with colorful handicrafts and ornaments. ⊠ *Hwy. 1, Km 2.5* ☏ *624/143–3850* ⊕ *www. artesanos.com* ⊘ *Mon.–Sat. 9–2.* ⊘ *Closed Sun.*

MALL

Las Tiendas de Palmilla. Las Tiendas de Palmilla is across from the posh Palmilla Resort. There is a smattering of shops and galleries, a couple of restaurants, a coffee shop, a nice terrace with a peaceful fountain, and a view of the Palmilla development with the Sea of Cortez beyond. **Antigua de México** is a branch of the famous Tlaquepaque store, and shoppers will discover distinctive furniture and bedding supplies, and many Mexican-flavor interior-decorating items. **Pez Gordo Art Gallery** is artist Dana Leib's second location, and offers her pieces, as well as those by other artists. You'll find beautifully designed furnishings, accessories, fabrics, and antique doors at **Casa Paulina.** Stop in **Casa Vieja** for beautiful women's apparel by Mexican designers, including Pineda-Covalin—you'll find a wide range of styles in fibers such as cotton, silk, linen, and even cactus. If you need to fuel up during your time here, there's an outpost of popular **Nick-San,** and **Cream Cafe.** ⊠ *Hwy. 1, Km 27.5* ☎ *624/144–6999* ⊕ *www.lastiendasdepalmilla.com.*

SPAS

Fodor's Choice
★ **One&Only Palmilla Spa.** Treatment villas are tucked behind white stucco walls, ensuring privacy. Therapists lead you through a locked gate into peaceful palm-filled gardens with a bubbling hot tub and a daybed covered with plump pillows. There are 13 private treatment villas, for either one or two people; six are equipped with an outdoor shower, bathtub, and thatched-roof daybed, for relaxing between or after treatments. There's a blend of Mexican and Asian, and other global accents; treatments use cactus, lime, and a variety of Mexican spices. Each treatment begins with a Floral Footbath—a symbolic Balinese ritual, which represents a cleansing of life's tensions to prepare you for total relaxation. One signature treatment is the Secret Garden Remedy, which starts with an exfoliation followed by an Indian influenced massage using oil infused with jasmine, lime, sweet orange, rosemary, and basil. For the ultimate in relaxation, try the Chocolate Synergy Treatment—two hours and two therapists that combine four massage techniques using a Mexican herbal compress and chocolate oil. ⊠ *Hwy. 1, Km. 27.5* ☎ *624/146–7000* ⊕ *www.palmilla.oneandonlyresorts.com* ✉ *Body treatments: $250–$450. Facials: $175–$250. Mani/Pedi: $55–$150.* ☞ *Parking: Valet (free).*

Secrets Spa by Pevonia. You'll enjoy the open-air hot tubs that face the Cape's blue sky and overlook the Sea of Cortez. Lounge chairs draped with thick towels tempt you to linger by the hot tubs, but floors inlaid with stones will lead you to the spa's treatment rooms and the amazing experiences within. Noteworthy are the seaweed wrap, the hot stone massage, and the myoxy caviar facial. The spa is only open to hotel guests or outside visitors willing to purchase a Day Pass for $150 per person. This gives access to the spa and other all-inclusive services at the resort from 9 am to 11 pm. Secrets Spa by Pevonia now has a second location past the marina in San José del Cabo. ⊠ *Secrets Marquis Los Cabos Resort, Hwy. 1, Km 21.5* ☎ *624/144–0906* ⊕ *www. secretsresorts.com/marquis-los-cabos* ✉ *Body treatments: $109–$235. Facials: $105–$275. Mani/Pedi: $45–$85. Waxing: $39–$85.* ☞ *Parking: Valet (free).*

SOMMA Wine Spa. SOMMA is the only spa of its kind in Mexico, with only six others throughout the world. The concept spa uses grapes from the up-and-coming Valle de Guadalupe wine region just outside of Ensenada. It's an unusual experience blended with classical treatments, focusing on the calming, cosmetic, and antioxidant properties of grapes and wine, or vinotherapy. It towers high above the Sea of Cortez with 15 treatment rooms, both indoor and open-air, and offers a geothermal hot spring and more than 33 facial and body treatments from a Champagne Mud Wrap to a Le Vine Massage. ⊠ *Fiesta Americana Grand Resort, Hwy. 1, Km. 10.3, Cabo del Sol* 🕾 *624/145–6287* ⊕ *www.fiestamericanagrand.com/mx-los-cabos/hotel-grand-los-cabos* ☕ *Body treatments: $80–$250. Facials: $170–$234. Mani/Pedi: $40–$60.* ᴄᵃ *Parking: Valet and self-parking.*

The Spa at Esperanza. At the exclusive, 17-acre Esperanza Resort between Cabo San Lucas and San José del Cabo the beautiful spa is reached by way of a stone path over a koi pond. At check-in you're presented with an *agua fresca*, a healthy drink made with papaya or mango, or other fruits and herbs. Before your treatment, linger in the grotto, enjoying the *Pasaje de Agua* (water passage) therapy, which includes steam caves and a waterfall. Treatments incorporate local ingredients, tropical fruits, and ocean-based products. Look for such pampering as the papaya-mango body polish, the grated-coconut-and-lime exfoliation, the four-hands massage, and the Mexican beer facial. Yoga classes are held at 7:45 and 9 each morning for $35. ⊠ *Esperanza Resort, Hwy. 1, Km 7* 🕾 *624/145–6406* ⊕ *www.esperanzaresort.com* ☕ *Body treatments: $160–$335. Facials: $160–$295. Mani/Pedi: $45–$200.* ᴄᵃ *Parking: Valet (free).*

Fodor's Choice **The Spa at Las Ventanas al Paraíso.** Known for its innovative treatments—
★ nopal (cactus) anticellulite and detox wrap, crystal healing massages, and raindrop therapy, the Spa at Las Ventanas has both indoor and outdoor facilities. Some of the eight treatment rooms have private patios, and the two couples' suites come with a private butler. Healing rituals like the Holistic Twilight Ceremony are performed daily. Salt glows and massages are available in a pavilion by the sea. Guests staying in beachfront villas are treated to a 30-minute complimentary water massage in a private plunge pool. There are also pampering treatments for kids (Mommy and Me) and couples (Sea and Stars). ⊠ *Las Ventanas al Paraíso Resort, Hwy. 1, Km. 19.5* 🕾 *624/144–0300* ⊕ *www.lasventanas.com* ☕ *Body Treatments: $185–$900. Facials: $220–$410. Mani/Pedi: $45–$145.* ᴄᵃ *Parking: Valet (free).*

The Spa at Westin Los Cabos. Massages and wraps are the specialties provided in seven treatment rooms at the Westin's Spa. Most popular is the four-hand massage, which takes guests to the peak of relaxation. Those craving body treatments can opt for the Cocolucious, which features coconut, or the Cucumber and Mint scrub. The hot stone Swedish massage is also a top seller. An on-site salon, barbershop, and fitness center round out the amenities. ⊠ *Westin Los Cabos, Hwy. 1, Km. 22.5* 🕾 *624/142–9000* ⊕ *www.westinloscabos.com* ☕ *Body Treatments: $128–$269. Facials: $75–$155.*

6

SUNDRIES

La Europea. La Europea carries a wide selection of imported wines and deli products. ⊠ *Hwy. 1, Km 5* ☎ *624/145–8755* ⊕ *www.laeuropea. com.mx.*

Trader Dick's. Located along the Costa Azul surf coast near the popular Zipper's Restaurant, Trader Dick's is a country store that's a favorite with Americans seeking newspapers from home, along with familiar deli meats and cheeses. ⊠ *Hwy. 1, Km 28* ☎ *624/142–2828.*

CABO SAN LUCAS

Cabo San Lucas has the widest variety of shopping options in Los Cabos area, with everything from intriguing Mexican folk art and designer clothing to beer holsters and touristy T-shirts. Bargains on typical Mexican tourist items can be found in the dozens of shops between Boulevard Paseo de la Marina and Avenida Lazaro Cárdenas.

If you get hungry when you're shopping, it's worth trying the inexpensive taco and juice stands tucked into the mini–flea markets that stretch between streets.

Many of the shops in malls like Puerto Paraíso are typical of those you'd find in any mall in the United States—with prices to match. All over the downtown and marina areas, however, are great shops and galleries with unique and compelling items.

Use the coordinate (✛ 2:B2) at the end of each listing to locate a site on the corresponding maps.

ART GALLERIES

Fodor'sChoice **Arte de Origen.** Everything at Arte de Origen is 100% made in Cabo.
★ Pan-American cultural traditions inform the original decorative art in this richly colored open space. Painting, ceramics, and inventive, painting-like collages are applied to a wide variety of objects like boxes, tables, and mirror frames. Small sculptures, jewelry, and some textiles are also part of a collection of art that is clearly meant to be part of your living space. Other locations can be found at the Puerto Paraíso Mall in Cabo, in Cancun Mexico, and in La Jolla California. ⊠ *Madero between Guererro and Blvd. Marina* ☎ *624/105–1965* ⊕ *www.artedeorigen.com* ۞ *Closed Sun.* ✛ *2:B4.*

Sergio Bustamante. The talented artist from Guadalajara now has a shop in the Puerto Paraíso Mall. Bustamante's works initially focused on painting and papier-mâché. His recent sculptures in wood and bronze, many reflecting animal themes, can be purchased at this wonderful gallery and store. Ceramic sculptures and an extensive line of exquisite jewelry in bronze, gold, and silver, many set with precious and semiprecious stones, are found here as well. Bustamante has recently expanded to handbags and shoes, both of which are also on sale here. Don't balk at the price tags: each piece belongs to a limited edition and is created by hand. ⊠ *Puerto Paraíso Mall* ☎ *866/300–8030 in U.S., 624/144–4895* ⊕ *www.sergiobustamante.com.mx* ✛ *2:C3.*

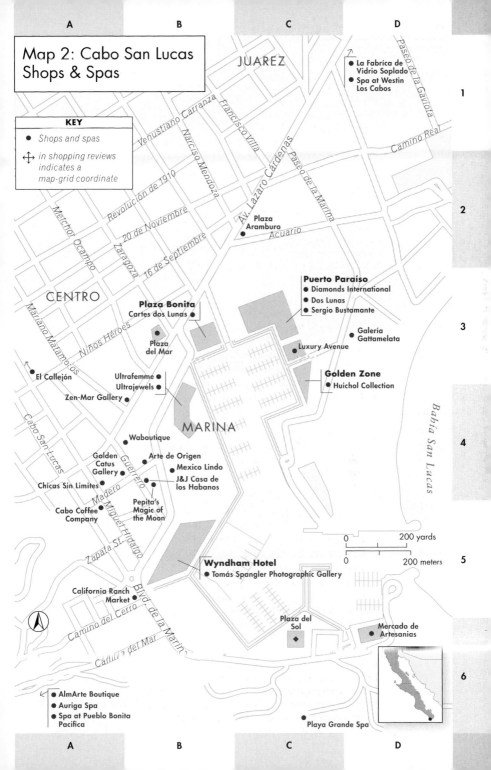

Map 2: Cabo San Lucas Shops & Spas

KEY

● Shops and spas

⇔ in shopping reviews indicates a map-grid coordinate

JUAREZ

● La Fábrica de Vidrio Soplado
● Spa at Westin Los Cabos

Paseo de la Gaviota

Camino Real

Venustiano Carranza

Francisco Villa

Naciso Mendoza

Av. Lázaro Cárdenas

Paseo de la Marina

Revolución de 1910

20 de Noviembre

Zaragoza

16 de Septiembre

Melchor Ocampo

Plaza Aramburo

Acuario

CENTRO

Mariano Matamoros

Niños Héroes

Plaza Bonita
Cartes dos Lunas ●

● Plaza del Mar

Puerto Paraíso
● Diamonds International
● Dos Lunas
● Sergio Bustamante

● Galería Gattamelata

● Luxury Avenue

● El Callejón

Ultrafemme ●
Ultrajewels ●

Zen-Mar Gallery ●

Golden Zone
● Huichol Collection

Cabo San Lucas

MARINA

Bahía San Lucas

● Waboutique

Golden Catus Gallery ●

● Arte de Origen
● Mexico Lindo

Chicas Sin Limites ●

Guerrero

Madero

Miguel Hidalgo

● J&J Casa de los Habanos

● Pepita's Magic of the Moon

Cabo Coffee Company ●

Zapata St.

200 yards

0   200 meters

Wyndham Hotel
● Tomás Spangler Photographic Gallery

California Ranch Market ●

Blvd. de la Marina

Camino del Cerro

Camino del Mar

Plaza del Sol ◆

Mercado de Artesanias ●

● AlmArte Boutique
● Auriga Spa
● Spa at Pueblo Bonita Pacifica

Playa Grande Spa ●

The inviting Plaza Bonita Shopping Mall in Cabo San Lucas

Tomás Spangler Photographic Gallery. Owner Tomás Spangler is an accomplished art photographer who has accumulated a number of stunning images from his travels throughout Mexico and the world; dozens are matted and mounted and on display at the Wyndham Hotel, and information about upcoming exhibitions can be obtained here, as well. This is the largest photo gallery in Baja. Orders can be shipped directly from his California studio. ⊠ *Wyndham Hotel Lobby, Calle Marina San Lucas* ☎ *831/480–4411 from U.S., 624/143–2001* ⊕ *www.fotomas. com* ⊕ *2:B5.*

CLOTHING

AlmArte Boutique. This lovely boutique sells designer clothing, silver jewelry, candles, art, books, and even items featured throughout the Capella Pedregal Resort such as headboards, doors, and tableware. If you've been admiring the glass-blown hearts dangling from leaf-barren Torote Trees throughout Cabo, this is the place to buy them. The women's line of beach-elegant clothing includes linens, silks, hats and loose-knitted flowing wraps. The store is open to the public; simply notify security at the main gate. ⊠ *Capella Pedregal Resort, Camino del Mar 1, El Pedregal, Marina* ☎ *624/163–4300* ⊕ *www.capellahotels. com* ☾ *Closed Tues.* ⊕ *2:A6.*

Chicas Sin Limites. Chicas Sin Limites translates to "girls without limits," which describes the apparel services here. Need your own custom-designed bathing suit—and fast? Select the fabric and cut, and your suit will be ready in 24 hours. ⊠ *Miguel Hidalgo s/n Col Centro, in front of Plaza Amelia* ☎ *624/143–1500* ⊕ *2:A4.*

Dos Lunas. Dos Lunas is full of trendy, colorful sportswear and straw hats, as well as a large selection of handcrafted accessories and gifts. ⊠ *Plaza Bonita, Blvd. Marina* ☎ *624/143–1969* ◎ *Closed Sun.* ✛ *2:C3*.

Pepita's Magic of the Moon. A favorite among locals and Cabo regulars, Magic of the Moon features clothing designed by Pepita Nelson, the owner. If you can't find anything that fits you or your style, she will design an outfit for you and finish it in three days. Also check out the handmade ceramic jewelry, beaded bustiers, and colorful bathing suits. ⊠ *Madero between Guererro and Blvd. Marina, next to Arte de Origen* ☎ *624/144–6133* ◎ *Closed Sun.* ✛ *2:B5*.

FOLK ART

Huichol Collection. Huichol Collection carries the Huichol Indian tribe's beautiful beaded crafts, as well as posters, postcards, and T-shirts in the vibrant colors and patterns typical of this ancient culture. ⊠ *Blvd. Marina and Ocampo* ☎ *624/143–4055* ✛ *2:C4*.

Mercado de Artesanías. This crafts market sells pottery, blankets, jewelry, and Mexican sombreros. It's a great place to find souvenirs for the folks at home. ⊠ *Blvd. Marina, south end* ✛ *2:D6*.

Zen-Mar Gallery. This friendly place carries hundreds of masks, Day of the Dead figures, rugs, glassware, bark-paper wall hangings from Puebla, and all sorts of other fun and captivating items. This is one of Cabo's more comprehensive folk-art shops. ⊠ *Cárdenas between Matamoros and Ocampo* ☎ *624/143–0661* ✛ *2:B4*.

FOOD

Cabo Coffee Company. The aroma of roasting coffee lures locals and visitors alike into Cabo Coffee company, where you can also find refreshing smoothies, cookies, and muffins. The organic green coffee beans are flown fresh from Oaxaca, and then roasted and bagged for sale. The store sells a number of Starbucks-like flavored coffee drinks, chai tea, and ice cream. There is also a book exchange with a few good beach reads. ⊠ *Madero and Hidalgo* ☎ *624/105–1130, 624/105–1754* ⊕ *www.cabocoffee.com* ✛ *2:A5*.

California Ranch Market (*Organic & Natural Groceries*). The area's best organic grocery store, California Ranch Market (formerly Tutto Bene), offers a good selection of imported wines, cheeses, and other gourmet delicacies, as well as American food brands. Freshly squeezed juices and handmade panini are also available. ⊠ *at Camino del Cerro, at the corner of Blvd Marina* ☎ *624/143–1947* ◎ *Closed Sun* ✛ *2:B5*.

GIFTS

Waboutique. Associated with the funky Cabo Wabo bar, waboutique sells memorabilia, excellent tequila, and souvenirs such as baseball hats, shot glasses, and mugs with the Cabo Wabo logo. Small bottles of tequila start at $24. ⊠ *Calle Guerrero between Madero and Lazaro Cárdenas* ☎ *624/163–7400* ⊕ *www.cabowabo.com* ✛ *2:B4*.

Continued on page 147

6

THE ART OF THE HUICHOL

The intricately woven and beaded designs of the Huichols' art are as vibrant and fascinating as the traditions of its people, best known as the "Peyote People" for their traditional and ceremonial use of the hallucinogenic drug. Peyote-inspired visions are thought to be messages from God and are reflected in the art.

Like the Lacandon Maya, the Huichol resisted assimilation by Spanish invaders, fleeing to inhospitable mountains and remote valleys. There they retained their pantheistic religion in which shamans lead the community in spiritual matters and the use of peyote facilitates communication directly with God.

Roads didn't reach larger Huichol communities until the mid-20th century, bringing electricity and other modern distractions. The collision with the outside world has had pros and cons, but art lovers have only benefited from their increased access to intricately patterned woven and beaded goods. Today the traditional souls that remain on the land—a significant population of perhaps 6,000 to 8,000—still create votive bowls, prayer arrows, jewelry, and bags, and sell them to finance elaborate religious ceremonies. The pieces go for as little as $5 or as much as $5,000, depending on the skill and fame of the artist and quality of materials.

(left) Huichol yarn painting, National Museum of Anthropology; (top) Huichol art, Puerto Vallarta

UNDERSTANDING THE HUICHOL

When Spanish conquistadors arrived in the early 16th century, the Huichol, unwilling to work as slaves on the haciendas of the Spanish or to adopt their religion, fled to the Sierra Madre. They lived there, disconnected from society, for nearly 500 years. Beginning in the 1970s, roads and electricity made their way to tiny Huichol towns. Today, about half of the population of perhaps 8,000 continues to live in ancestral villages and *rancherias* (tiny individual farms).

THE POWER OF PRAYER

They believe that without their prayers and offerings the sun wouldn't rise, the earth would cease spinning. It is hard, then, for them to reconcile their poverty with the relative easy living of "free-riders" (Huichol term for nonspiritual freeloaders) who enjoy fine cars and expensive houses thanks to the Huichols' efforts to sustain the planet. But rather than hold our reckless materialism against us, the Huichol add us to their prayers.

THE PEYOTE PEOPLE

Visions inspired by the hallucinogenic peyote plant are considered by the Huichol to be messages from God and to help in solving personal and

Huichol artisans and beadwork

communal problems. Indirectly, they provide inspiration for their almost psychedelic art. Just a generation or two ago, annual peyote-gathering pilgrimages were done on foot. Today the journey is still a man's chief obligation, but they now drive to the holy site at Wiricuta, in San Luis Potosi State. Peyote collected is used by the entire community—men, women, and children—throughout the year.

SHAMANISM

A Huichol man has a lifelong calling as a shaman. There are two shamanic paths: the path of the wolf, which is more aggressive, demanding, and powerful (wolf shamans profess the ability to morph into wolves); and the path of the deer, which is playful—even clownish—and less inclined to prove his power. A shaman chooses his own path.

Huichol bird, Jalisco

HOW TO READ THE SYMBOLS

Spiders that come out at dawn are thought to welcome the rising sun.

The deer is the animal manifestation of the god Kahumari, who intercedes in heaven on earthlings' behalf.

Anything with horns or antlers symbolizes communion and oneness with God.

Yarn painting

■ The trilogy of corn, peyote, and deer represents three aspects of God. According to Huichol mythology, peyote sprang up in the footprints of the deer. Depicted like stylized flowers, peyote represents communication with God. Corn, the Huichols' staple

Corn symbol

food, symbolizes health and prosperity. An image drawn inside the root ball depicts the essence of God within it.

■ The double-headed eagle is the emblem of the omnipresent sky god.

Peyote

■ A nierika is a portal between the spirit world and our own. Often in the form of a yarn painting, a nierika can be round or square.

■ Salamanders and turtles are associated with rain; the former provoke the clouds. Turtles maintain underground springs and purify water.

■ A scorpion is the soldier of the sun.

Scorpion

■ The Huichol depict raindrops as tiny snakes; in yarn paintings they descend to enrich the fields.

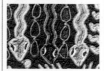
Snakes

Jose Beníctez Sánchez, (1938—) may be the elder statesman of yarn painters and has shown in Japan, Spain, the U.S., and at the Museum of Modern Art in Mexico City. His paintings sell for upward of $3,000 a piece.

TRADITION TRANSFORMED

The art of the Huichol was, for centuries, made from undyed wool, shells, stones, and other natural materials. It was not until the 1970s that the Huichol began incorporating bright, zingy colors, without sacrificing the intricate patterns and symbols used for centuries. The result is strenuously colorful, yet dignified.

YARN PAINTINGS
Dramatic and vivid yarn paintings are highly symbolic, stylized visions of life.

MASKS AND ANIMAL STATUETTES
Bead-covered wooden or ceramic masks and animal statuettes are other adaptations made for outsiders.

PRAYER ARROWS
Made for every ceremony, prayer arrows send petitions winging to God.

VOTIVE BOWLS
Ceremonious votive bowls, made from gourds, are decorated with bright, stylized beadwork.

WOVEN SHOULDER BAGS
Carried by men, the bags are decorated with traditional Huichol icons.

For years, Huichol men as well as women wore **BEADED BRACELETS**; today earrings and necklaces are also made.

Diamond-shape **GOD'S EYES** of sticks and yarn protect children from harm.

People in Glass Houses

Fábrica de Vidrio Soplado. A beautiful glass mosaic over the entrance to Fábrica de Vidrio Soplado (Blown-Glass Factory) welcomes Los Cabos' most famous artisans every day. Founded in 1988 by engineer Sebastian Romo, the factory uses a glassmaking process close to the one first developed in western Asia 4,000 years ago, later refined into glass-blowing during the Roman empire. At the factory, 35 artisans produce more than 450 pieces a day from hundreds of pounds of locally recycled glass. Visitors watch while crushed recycled glass is liquefied in gas-fired ovens and, seconds later, transformed into exquisite figures. Secrets for making

the thick glassware's deep blues, greens, and reds—the result of special mixtures of metals and gold—are passed from generation to generation. You are sometimes invited to make your own glassware by blowing through a hollow rod to shape a glob of molten glass at the end. The results are usually not impressive, but it's good fun nonetheless. ⊠ *Lazaro Cardenas s/n Edificio Posada ✛ Drive toward San José on Av. Cárdenas, which turns into Hwy. 1; the fábrica is 2 blocks northwest of Hwy. 1, near the bypass road to Todos Santos* ☎ *624/143–0255* ⊕ *www.glassfactory. com.mx.*

6

HOME FURNISHINGS

Cartes dos Lunas. This tiny shop at Plaza Bonita has hand-painted pottery and tableware, pewter frames, handblown glass, and carved furniture. ⊠ *Plaza Bonita, Blvd. Marina* ☎ *624/143–1770* ◷ *Closed Sun.* ✛ *2:B3.*

El Callejón. El Callejón is known for its stock of gorgeous Mexican furniture, lamps, dishes, home decor, tableware, lamps, accessories, and pottery. ⊠ *Miguel Hidalgo 2518, at 12 de Octubre* ☎ *624/143–3188, 624/144–4008* ⊕ *www.elcallejoncabo.wordpress.com* ✛ *2:A4.*

JEWELRY

Diamonds International. Certified master jewelers are on staff at Diamonds International. This store sells impressive diamonds, designer jewelry, and luxury timepieces. A second branch is in the Puerto Paraíso Mall. ⊠ *Corner of Vicente Guerrero* ☎ *624/143–3954 Vincente Guerrero location, 624/105–0810 Puerto Paraíso Mall* ⊕ *www. diamondsinternational.com* ✛ *2:C3.*

Mexico Lindo. Mexico Lindo has more than a dozen years of experience custom-designing sterling and 14k- and 18k-gold jewelry. Watch their craftsmen work at the store in the Puerto Paraíso Mall, which also sells a fair amount of Mexican artwork from around the country. ⊠ *Puerto Paraíso Mall, Av. Cárdenas* ☎ *624/144–3868* ◷ *Closed Sun.* ✛ *2:B4.*

Ultrajewels. Rolex, Cartier, Tiffany & Co., Mikimoto, TAG Heuer, Omega, Montblanc, and many other top names are offered at Ultrajewels, often at discounted prices. ⊠ *Blvd. Marina, Luxury Avenue* ☎ *624/163–4280* ⊕ *www.ultrajewels.com* ✛ *2:B4.*

MALLS

Golden Zone Shopping Center. There's a number of good shops and attractions at The Golden Zone Shopping Center, including the Tequila Museum, a Huichol Souvenir Shop, the Baja Lobster Company, and Los Deseos, known for their great margaritas. Recently added is Luxury Avenue, a collection of famous designer boutiques selling Coach, Fendi, Chopard, and Montblanc, all under one roof. ⊠ *Marina San Lucas* ⊕ *www.goldenzonecabo. com* ✛ *2:C3.*

Luxury Avenue. An indoor mall housing luxury boutiques like Coach, Fendi, Montblanc, and Cartier, Luxury Avenue is your one-stop shopping for upscale items in Cabo. It's open daily from 11 am to 10 pm. There is a second branch in Cancun, Mexico. ⊠ *Av. Lazaro Cardenas, adjacent to Puerto Paraíso Mall, Marina San Lucas* ☎ *624/163–4280* ⊕ *www.luxuryavenue.com* ✛ *2:C3.*

Plaza Aramburo. Plaza Aramburo is a primarily service-oriented shopping area with a pharmacy, bank, dry cleaner, and grocery store. But it also has clothing and swimwear shops and a nice but small Internet café and inexpensive "phone home" service. ⊠ *Av. Cárdenas and Zaragoza* ✛ *2:B3.*

Plaza Bonita. Plaza Bonita is a pleasant place to stroll; it's located at the western edge of the marina and has restaurants and bars catering to the cruise-ship crowd, with shops ranging from leather and clothing to local artwork and souvenirs. You'll also find an ATM, pharmacy, and Starbucks. ⊠ *Blvd. Marina and Av. Cárdenas* ✛ *2:B3.*

Plaza del Mar. Plaza del Mar, across from the Plaza Bonita Mall, sells T-shirts, tank tops, sweatshirts, and more, at its souvenir boutiques. ⊠ *Av. Cárdenas* ✛ *2:B3.*

Plaza del Sol. This open-air market has vendors selling local souvenirs like sarongs, sombreros, bathing suit cover-ups, and beaded necklaces. ⊠ *Blvd. Marina* ✛ *2:C6.*

Puerto Paraíso Mall. As Los Cabos continues on its upscale trajectory, it's safe to declare that this region has arrived and the shopping here has gone palatial. There is no better, or more apt, way to describe Puerto Paraíso, the city's thriving, air-conditioned, three-story marble- and glass-enclosed mall. With well more than 100 stores, boutiques, restaurants, galleries, and services, it's quickly becoming the social center of San Lucas. Paraíso offers a dizzying selection, from "A" as in **Arte de Origen,** an upscale shop selling art and local handicrafts, to "Z" as in the **Zingara Swimwear** shop. You can have a steak at **Ruth's Chris Steak House;** custom-design your own bikini; check your email at an Internet café; shop for beautiful art glass; or rent (or even buy) a Harley-Davidson motorcycle—almost anything is possible in this shopper's paradise. **Sergio Bustamante,** an acclaimed silversmith and sculptor, has recently opened a store here, and clothing shops include **Tommy Bahama, Hugo Boss,** and **Nike.** Beachwear boutiques such as **Allegra, Azul, Blu Lagoon, Pacific Blue, Tropica Calipso, Squalo Surf Shop,** and **Nautica** fulfill your beach-going needs. A 10-screen movie-theater complex provides cinematic respite, and the third floor is home to a play area for children and a small casino. Puerto Paraíso is connected to the newly opened Luxury Avenue, a string of designer boutiques offering top brands like Cartier, Coach, Fendi and Montblanc. ⊠ *Av. Cárdenas, Marina San Lucas* ⊕ *www.puertoparaiso.mx* ✛ *2:C3.*

SPAS

Auriga Spa. Named for a constellation in the northern hemisphere, Auriga Spa has a distinctive approach to wellness and beauty based on the cycles of the moon, each of which is said to impact the body in specific ways. Auriga's four signature treatments represent the varying energies of the lunar phases to align you with the rhythms of nature for enhanced well-being. The 10 treatment rooms in this body-melting spa, easily one of the best in the region, offer guests passage to the ultimate in relaxation. Cascading pools create a soothing sound track to the kneading of top technicians. Opt for the popular Full Body Massage or Full Moon Signature Treatment, or duck into the Julien Farel salon for full salon services. The Ancient Traditional Massage is a combination of detoxing, stretching, massage, and relaxation. ⊠ *Capella Pedregal Resort, Camino Del Mar, Marina* ☎ *624/163–4300* ⊕ *www. capellahotels.com* 🛏 *Body treatments: $145–$360. Facials: $175–$240* ✛ *2:A6.*

Playa Grande Spa. Playa Grande's spa is known for its thalassotherapy treatments, which come from the practice of using seawater baths and seaweed-based treatments for prevention and curative purposes. Treatments may include combinations of seaweed and seawater, and the minerals in both will rejuvenate and renew your skin like you've never experienced. ⊠ *Playa Grande Resort, Av. Playa Grande No. 1, Playa Solmar* ☎ *624/145–7575* ⊕ *www.playagranderesort.com* 🛏 *Body treatments: $175–$250. Facials: $130–$175. Hair: $30–$190. Mani/Pedi: $30–$60. Waxing: $20–$60* ✛ *2:C6.*

Spa at Pueblo Bonito Pacifica. This small, tranquil hotel on the Pacific side of Cabo is an adults-only property, filled with feng shui design, immaculately kept cactus gardens, and water, everywhere. Treatments at the Aromian Spa run the gamut from crystal Reiki healing to a yogurt-and-violets exfoliation, and even an intriguing temazcal (Maya sweat lodge) experience. ⊠ *Pueblo Bonita Pacifica Resort, Predio Paraíso Escondido* ☎ *624/143–9696* ⊕ *www.pueblobonitopacifica. com* 🛏 *Body treatments: $130–$330. Facials: $90–$275. Hair: $25–$110. Mani/Pedi: $35–$62.* ☞ *Parking: Valet (free)* ✛ *2:A6.*

TOBACCO AND LIQUOR

J&J Casa de los Habanos. This is the best place to find quality Cuban and international cigars, lighters, and ashtrays as well as tequila, and Cuban coffee. You can schedule a tequila tasting while you shop for cigars. ⊠ *Madero and Blvd. Marina* ☎ *624/143–6160* ⊕ *www.jnjcabo. com* ✛ *2:B4.*

NIGHTLIFE

Updated by
Marlise Kast

Party-minded crowds roam the main strip of Cabo San Lucas every night from happy hour through last call, often staggering home or to hotel rooms just before dawn. It's not hard to see why this is *the* nightlife capital of southern Baja.

Indeed, Cabo is internationally famous (or infamous, depending on your view) for being a raucous party town, especially during spring break. On the other hand, nightlife in San José del Cabo is much more low-key: it's more about a good drink and conversation as opposed to the table-dancing chaos you'll find in some Cabo hot spots.

Between the two towns, the self-contained resorts along the Corridor have some nightlife, mainly in ever-improving restaurants and bars, which can mix up some fabulous cocktails themselves.

The lines between "bar," "nightclub," and "restaurant" are blurry here. Never forget that enjoying a fine dinner is a time-honored way to spend a Los Cabos evening. Also, don't forget that things shift into lower gear during the lowest of the low season—those slow, sweltering months of August and September when some places curtail their offerings, or may close for a few weeks altogether. Never fear though: you'll find nighttime fun here no matter what season you visit.

PLANNING

WHAT'S WHERE

San José del Cabo: Proprietors here say that you "graduate" to San José del Cabo after you sow the wild oats of your youth in Cabo San Lucas. It's quieter and more intimate here, and for a cozy, romantic evening, nothing beats San José's nightlife.

The Corridor: This sprawling strip between the two cities is the province of big resorts and their in-house bars. Expect upscale venues (and patrons). A few nightspots not affiliated with any hotel do exist here and are quite popular.

Cabo San Lucas: Had the phrase "What happens in Vegas, stays in Vegas" not already been taken, Cabo San Lucas might have snapped it up. You can experience spring break here, even if you went to college 30 years ago. Quiet Cabo nightlife does exist; you just need to look a bit harder.

WHAT TO WEAR

"Informal" is the word, although there's some wiggle room in that label. The more authentic a place is, the more likely patrons dress to impress. (Think casual-classy when taking in dance clubs such as El Squid Roe.) For the upscale bars and clubs such as Privé, you'll feel out of place wearing flip-flops. "Gringo" means less formal. (Shorts and T-shirts are acceptable at the Giggling Marlin.) But do keep those signs you see back home in mind: "No shoes, no shirt, no service" is always followed here.

WHAT IT COSTS

Want to drink inexpensively? Think beer, especially Baja's very own Tecate. Many places compete for the best happy-hour prices, often about $2 for a cerveza. Margaritas, the other keep-'em-coming drink, cost around $5. A glass of wine in an upscale venue should run $7 and up. The rowdy beach bars in Cabo San Lucas have waitresses blowing whistles while handing out test tubes of vodka. Don't be fooled—there's a charge and tip behind each offer, so expect to pay around $5 each. Many places add a 10%–15% tip to your tab; others do not. (Look for the word "*servicio*" on your bill.) A big musical event means a nominal cover charge of a few dollars; those are rare.

WHAT'S GOING ON

You'll find copies of Los Cabos publications in hotels, restaurants, and bars all over the city. The most helpful are *Los Cabos Visitors Guide* and *Los Cabos Magazine.* Both provide a wealth of information on everything Los Cabos, from the restaurant, hotel, bar, and shopping scenes, to the many activities. The free English-language newspapers *Gringo Gazette* (⊕ *www.gringogazette.com*) and *Destino: Los Cabos* (⊕ *www.destinomagazine.com*) offer timely and cultural articles on the ever-changing scene. (We especially like the *Gringo Gazette* for its fun-loving, humorous look at expatriate life in Los Cabos.) The English-Spanish *Los Cabos News* (⊕ *www.loscabosnews.com.mx*) is also a good source for local event listings. These publications are available free at many hotels and stores or at racks on the sidewalk.

SAFETY

Nighttime is reasonably safe and secure here. Ask the bar or restaurant to call a taxi for you if you have far to go. Taxis aren't cheap, but you shouldn't put a price on getting home safely. All the standard precautions apply: Stick to well-lighted areas where people congregate. Wandering dark, deserted streets or lonely stretches of beaches is never wise, nor is staggering home in a state of inebriation.

DRINKING AGE/SMOKING RULES

Mexico's nationwide drinking age is 18. Bars here check IDs at the door if they have any doubts about your age. Consumption of alcohol or the possession of an open beverage container is not permitted on public sidewalks, streets, or beaches (outside of licensed establishments), or in motor vehicles, whether moving or stationary.

Smoking is prohibited in all enclosed businesses, including bars and restaurants. Lighting up is allowed at outdoor-seating areas provided by such venues, but not indoors.

SAN JOSÉ DEL CABO

After-dark action in San José del Cabo caters mostly to locals and tourists seeking tranquillity and seclusion. There are no big dance clubs or discos in San José. What little nightlife there is revolves around restaurants, casual bars, and large hotels. A pre- or post-dinner stroll makes a wonderful addition to any San José evening. When night falls, people begin to fill the streets, many of them hurrying off to evening Mass when they hear the church bells peal from the central plaza.

A number of galleries hold court in central San José del Cabo, creating the **San José del Cabo Art District**. It's just north and east of the town's cathedral, primarily along Obregón, Morelos, and Guerrero streets. On Thursday nights (5–9 pm) from November to June, visit the **Art Walk**, where you can meander around about 15 galleries, sampling wine and cheese as you go.

Use the coordinate (⊕ 1:B2) at the end of each listing to locate a site on the corresponding maps.

BARS

Baja Brewing Co. The Baja Brewing Co. serves cold, on-site–microbrewed cerveza and international pub fare. You'll find entrées ranging from ahi tuna quesadillas to shepherd's pie, plus more basic pub food such as basil-and-blue-cheese burgers and pizzas. As for the eight beers, we recommend the Baja Blond Ale; the BBC also brews Oatmeal Stout, Raspberry Lager, homemade root beer, and a dark, smooth Black Scorpion. If you can't make up your mind, order the sampler. ⊠ *Morelos 1277 and Obregón* ☎ *624/146–9995* ⊕ *www.bajabrewingcompany.com* ⊕ *1:C1.*

Jazz Tapas Bar. Paying tribute to jazz legends, this bar in Plaza del Pescador combines wine, tapas, and musically inspired artwork in a stylish setting. Try their Tapas Sampler and Big Jazz Mojito while listening to the smooth sounds of the live band, which plays most weekends. ⊠ *Plaza del Pescador, Paseo Malecon San Jose, Local 8, Across from Cabo Azul Resort* ☎ *624/130–7267* ⊕ *www.jazztapasbar.com* ⊗ *Sun.–Wed. 1 pm–12 am.; Thurs.–Sat. 1 pm–1 am* ⊕ *1:C5.*

La Osteria. Live music on Thursday and Friday coupled with the refreshing cocktails make this one of the best spots to grab a drink in San José del Cabo. Acoustic guitars add to the quaint atmosphere you'll find in the lantern-lit, stone courtyard. Tapas make a tasty accompaniment

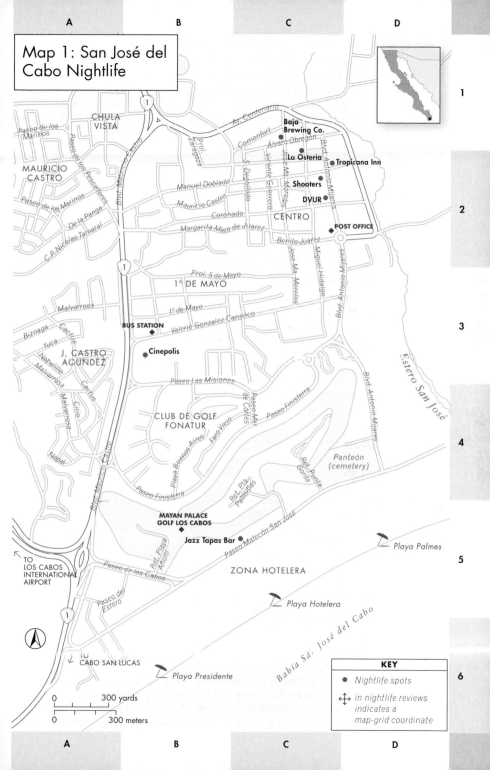

Waking the Dead

Celebrated throughout Mexico, the most important religious and indigenous festival in Los Cabos takes place November 1 and 2: All Saints' and All Souls' Day, more commonly referred to as **Día de los Muertos** (Day of the Dead). Long before Spain conquered Mexico, the festival was part of Indian culture and held during the winter equinox. In true colonial spirit, Spain changed the timing to coincide with its religious All Saints' and All Souls' Day.

Not as macabre as it sounds, the festival is a joyous celebration to welcome a visit from the souls of deceased loved ones. Family and friends prepare favorite foods and drink of the dearly departed, burn candles and incense, and place flowers in cemeteries and at memorials along the road. Shops carry candy shaped like skulls and coffins, and bread is baked to look like ghosts. No tears are to be shed, as it is said that the path back to the living world must not be made slippery by tears.

to the house sangrias. ⊠ *Alvaro Obregon #1207, Across from Salsitas* ☎ *624/146–9696* ⊗ *Closed Sun.* ✛ *1:C2.*

Restaurante Dvur. Come here for the ambience and cocktails (the food has mixed reviews) like the blackberry mojito or house margarita. Once the home of the owner's grandparents, the building dates back to 1927, and you can still see the original brick walls, adorned with historic family photographs. The courtyard, strung with lanterns and fairy lights, is a pleasant place to enjoy the live mariachi, offered Thursday to Saturday from 8 to 10. ⊠ *Blvd Antonio Mijares* ☎ *624/166–9439, 624/142–0418* ✛ *1:C2.*

Shooters. For a gringo-friendly atmosphere where you can order your Bud in English and watch sports on big-screen TVs, head to Shooters, located on the rooftop of the Tulip Tree restaurant. Open daily from 9 to 11 pm, days are busy, with breakfast and lunch served as well as Shooters's heavily promoted 15-peso (just more than $1) beers. ⊠ *Manuel Doblado at Blvd. Mijares* ☎ *624/146–9900* ⊕ *www.shootersbar.com.mx* ✛ *1:C2.*

Tropicana Inn. The Tropicana Inn's bar is a great place to mingle and enjoy live music. Conversation is usually possible on the terrace overlooking the bar and stage, though when a really hot band gets going, you'll be too busy dancing to talk. Mariachi bands play Thursday through Monday from 7:30 to 10:30. ⊠ *Blvd. Mijares 30* ☎ *624/142–1580* ⊕ *www.tropicanainn.com.mx* ✛ *1:C2.*

THE CORRIDOR

Nightlife along Highway 1 between San José del Cabo and Cabos San Lucas historically consists of hotel bars in big resorts, most of which are frequented only by their guests. A few stand-alone places have sprung up in recent years, including the chic Privé nightclub. A taxi or car is the

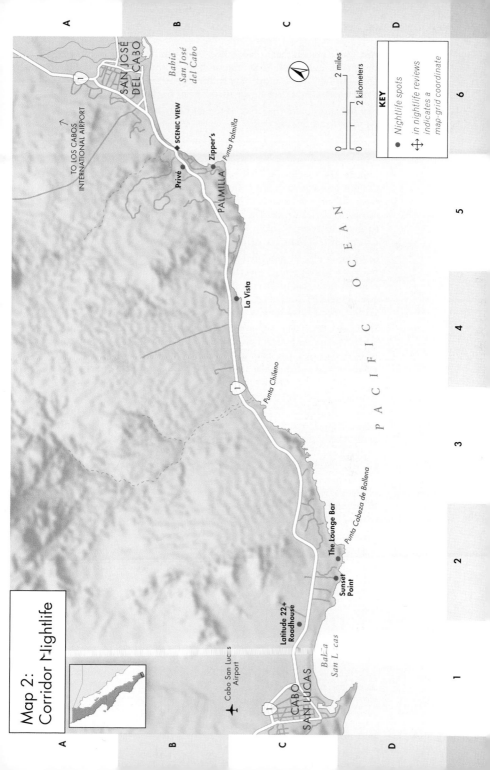

Map 2:
Corridor Nightlife

TO LOS CABOS
INTERNATIONAL AIRPORT

SAN JOSÉ
DEL CABO

*Bahía
San José
del Cabo*

SCENIC VIEW

Privé

Zipper's

Punta Palmilla

PALMILLA

La Vista

Punta Chileno

P A C I F I C   O C E A N

The Lounge Bar

Sunset
Point

Punta Cabeza de Ballena

Latitude 22+
Roadhouse

*Bahía
San Lucas*

Cabo San Lucas
Airport

CABO
SAN LUCAS

KEY

● *Nightlife spots*

⊕ *in nightlife reviews
indicates a
map-grid coordinate*

0   2 kilometers
0   2 miles

A   B   C   D

1   2   3   4   5   6

best way to reach these places. Because walking home is generally not an option, unless you're staying in-house or next door, nightlife ends early out here, with most bars turning off the lights around 10 or 11 pm. Head to Cabo San Lucas if you want to party later.

Use the coordinate (✛ 2:B2) at the end of each listing to locate a site on the corresponding maps.

BARS

Latitude 22+ Roadhouse. This noisy, friendly roadhouse always attracts gringos looking to down a shot of tequila, sip cold beer, and mingle with old or new friends. The menu features good, dependable, and mostly American fare. There is live music, ranging in style from pop to blues to country, from October to June. ⊠ *Hwy. 1, Km 4.5, near Costco* ☎ *624/143–1516* ⊕ *latno2baddays.com* ☉ *Closed Sun.* ✛ *2:C1.*

La Vista. For posh hotel bars, it's hard to top the Hilton Los Cabos' La Vista whose terrace overlooks the Sea of Cortez. There's nothing raucous here; just intimate conversation over wine and cocktails, with complimentary hors d'oeuvres from 5 to 6 pm. ⊠ *Hilton Los Cabos, Hwy. 1, Km 19.5* ☎ *624/145–6500* ⊕ *www.hiltonloscabos.com* ✛ *2:C4.*

The Lounge Bar. The name sounds rather utilitarian, but the dim lighting and intimate ambience here are anything but. Enjoy stunning views of El Arco—you are, after all, on the Cabo San Lucas end of the Corridor—at Esperanza's elegant bar and lounge on lush couches. Linger over quiet drinks or smoke a cigar as you listen to the sounds of the ocean. ⊠ *Esperanza Resort, Hwy. 1, Km 7, Manzana 10, Punta Ballena* ☎ *624/145–6400* ⊕ *www.esperanzaresort.com* ✛ *2:D2.*

Sunset Point. This casual wine-and-pizza lounge is a colorful rooftop hot spot that shares the same stunning view of the famous Los Cabos Arch as its downstairs counterpart, Sunset de Mona Lisa. With a selection of over 140 wines and champagnes, complimented by free tapas daily from 5 to 6 pm, this is the place to watch the sun set over light bites and cocktails. ⊠ *At Mona Lisa Sunset Restaurant, near Misiones Condos and Hotel, Carretera Transpeninsular Km 6.5, Bello Plaza del Rey 7 y 8* ☎ *624/581–6066, 624/145–8077* ⊕ *www.sunsetmonalisa.com* ✛ *2:D2.*

Zipper's. Named for the nearby surf break, beachfront Zipper's attracts a mixed crowd of surfers and nonsurfers alike. A good selection of beer, as well as ribs and burgers, is always on hand, with live music every night. ⊠ *Hwy. 1, Km 28.5* ☎ *624/172–6162* ⊕ *www.loscabosguide.com/zippers* ✛ *2:B5.*

CABO SAN LUCAS

The epicenter of Cabo San Lucas nightlife is along the Marina San Lucas and the two streets that run parallel beyond it. You'll walk a gauntlet of servers waving menus in your face, but the many fun sidewalk bars along the marina between Plaza Bonita and Puerto Paraíso are great during Happy Hour and late into the night. Many nightlife places do a brisk daytime business, too, especially when cruise ships are in port, which is several days a week.

Watch out for the tequila shooters and Jell-O shots forced upon revelers by merry waiters—they usually cost at least $5 each. Topless bars and "gentlemen's" clubs are abundant, too. (Their "showgirls" signs give away what—and where—they are.) Single men are often accosted outside San Lucas bars with offers for drugs and sex. Be careful in this area, and be aware that the police may be behind some of these solicitations.

Use the coordinate (✛ 3:B2) at the end of each listing to locate a site on the corresponding maps.

BARS

Baja Brewing Co. The Cabo San Lucas branch of the microbrewery in San José del Cabo shares the same menu and selection of beers on tap. Yet, the partially open space atop a seaside hotel lends a decidedly different, relaxed vibe. Perfect after a day at the beach, enjoy live music, ranging from Cuban to rock to funk, on Monday, Thursday, Friday, and Saturday. There is a third, additional BBC location on the ground floor of the nearby Cabo Marina's Puerto Paraíso Mall. ⊠ *Rooftop of Cabo Villas, Médano Beach* ☎ *624/143–9199* ⊕ *www.bajabrewingcompany. com* ✛ *3:C4.*

Billygan's Island. Celebrate Spring Break year-round at the boisterous Billygan's Island on Médano Beach. The crowd, largely bikini-clad twentysomethings, drink margaritas and beer while reveling in bikini dance contests. ⊠ *Médano Beach* ☎ *624/143–3435, 624/144–3908* ✛ *3:C4.*

Dos Mares. Sophisticated, tranquil, and comfortable, Dos Mares offers a peaceful, panoramic view of the fishing yachts in the Marina San Lucas. Inside, a flat screen shows sports, and outside, tables on the boardwalk overlook the pier. Snack on tacos, pizza, and pasta while sipping 2-for-1 Coronas during Happy Hour from 11–5 pm. Tuesday through Sunday, a live band plays Latin and American Pop. ⊠ *De la Darsena Lote 18 Col. Centro, on Marina boardwalk, near Puerto Paraíso Mall, Marina* ☎ *624/143–0582* ⊕ *www.barometro.com.mx* ✛ *3:B4.*

Las Varitas. Las Varitas, one of Cabo's most popular clubs, is a branch of the La Paz rock club favored by young Mexicans. Local and internationally famous Latin rock bands perform here almost every night, and the establishment even boasts its own label of house tequila. ⊠ *Paseo de la Marina, near corner of Camino Viejo San Jose* ☎ *624/143–9999* ☾ *Closed Sun.* ✛ *3:C3.*

Mango Deck. Feel like getting a little bit rowdy and dancing in the sand? Overlooking the Arch, Mango Deck is a happening spot every night of the week, with DJs spinning late into the hours of the early morning, and revelers partying at all hours of the day. ⊠ *At the western end of El Medano Beach, near the Casa Dorada resort* ☎ *624/143–0901* ⊕ *www. mangodeckcabo.com* ✛ *3:C4.*

Nikki Beach. If you've ever wanted to feel like you're in a music video this is your chance. Miami meets Cabo at this restaurant, bar, and club with an over-the-top feeling of luxury. White gauze canopies shade plush sun

7

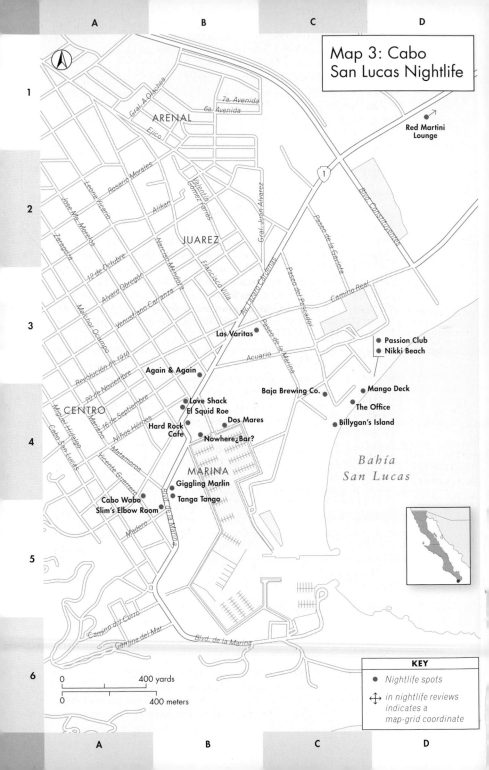

Map 3: Cabo San Lucas Nightlife

A   **B**   **C**   **D**

1

ARENAL

7a. Avenida
6a. Avenida

Gral. A Olachea

Ejica

Red Martini
Lounge

2

JUAREZ

Rosario Morales

Valentín Gómez Farías

Narciso Mendoza

Francisco Villa

Gral. Juan Alvarez

Leona Vicario

Jose Ma. Morelos

Zaragoza

Atikan

Av. Lazaro Cardenas

Paseo de la Gaviota

Blvd. Constituyentes

3

12 de Octubre

Alvaro Obregón

Venustiano Carranza

Melchor Ocampo

Revolución de 1910

90 de Noviembre

Paseo del Pescador

Camino Real

Las Varitas

Acuario

Paseo de la Marina

Passion Club
Nikki Beach

4

CENTRO

16 de Septiembre

Niños Héroes

Matamoros

Vicente Guerrero

Miguel Hidalgo

Cabo San Lucas

Again & Again

Love Shack
El Squid Roe
Dos Mares
Hard Rock
Cafe
Nowhere¿Bar?

Baja Brewing Co.

Mango Deck
The Office
Billygan's Island

*Bahía
San Lucas*

5

MARINA

Giggling Marlin
Tanga Tanga

Cabo Wabo
Slim's Elbow Room

Madera

Blvd. de la Marina

Camino del Cerro

Camino del Mar

Blvd. de la Marina

6

0   400 yards

0   400 meters

KEY

●   *Nightlife spots*

⬦   *in nightlife reviews
indicates a
map-grid coordinate*

A   **B**   **C**   **D**

beds and lounge chairs around multiple swimming pools, while DJs spin at all hours of the day. Try the Sexy Salad with lobster, shrimp, avocado, and mango or their satay chicken; both pair well with a fruity cocktail and will help keep the buzz under control. ✉ *ME Cabo Hotel, Playa Médano* ☎ *624/145–7800* ⊕ *www.nikkibeach.com* ✛ *3:D3.*

Nowhere ¿Bar?. Local professionals loosen up over beers while exuberant tourists have too much fun at the Nowhere ¿Bar?. Two-for-one drinks and a lively dance floor are a big draw here. Reckless gyrating isn't strictly limited to the dance floor, though—don't be at all surprised to see people busting a move on the tables from early evening on. On weekend nights, especially over holidays and spring break, it's a madhouse scene. Sushi and tacos are served from adjacent restaurants. ✉ *Plaza Bonita, Blvd. Marina 17* ☎ *624/143–4493* ⊕ *www.nowherebar. com* ✛ *3:B4.*

The Office. The Office began as a place to rent windsurfing equipment but expanded into a bar/eatery now famous for its seafood and goblet-size margaritas. Despite the fact that the floor here is the sand, this place is a tad more upscale than the other venues on Médano Beach. On Thursdays from 7 to 9 is a musical show with Mexican folk dancer—a little touristy, but always a crowd pleaser. ✉ *Médano Beach, between Mango Deck and Billygan's Island* ☎ *624/143–3464* ⊕ *www. theofficeonthebeach.com* ✛ *3:C4.*

Fodor's Choice ★ **Slim's Elbow Room.** Slim's calls itself "the world's smallest bar," and you'll be lucky to get a seat at this kitschy four-seat space that plays honkytonk music and serves $3 beers and tequila shots. Signed dollar bills line the walls and ceiling, and a buzzing, standing crowd loiters out the door and onto the Boulevard Marina sidewalk each evening, vibing off its energy. ✉ *Blvd. Marina, Plaza de los Mariachis* ⊕ *www.slimscabo. com* ✛ *3:B5.*

Tanga Tanga. A hot and popular spot for listening to live music, playing pool or darts, and watching sports on big-screen TVs, the sidewalk bar Tanga Tanga has a bar outdoors and another one inside. Local reggae and rock groups play here most afternoons and nights. Margaritas are plentiful and the wings are extra spicy! ✉ *Plaza de la Danza, Blvd. Marina, outside Wyndham Hotel* ☎ *624/144–4501* ✛ *3:B4.*

DANCE CLUBS

El Squid Roe. If you are easily offended, have a hard time letting loose, or have a heart condition, you may want to think twice before entering this four-story party spot where anything goes. Waiters dance and gyrate with female patrons, roaming waitresses pour Jell-O shots down your throat, frat-boy wannabes attempt beer-chugging contests, and scantily clad dancers undulate in a makeshift penitentiary. During spring break or high season, more than 3,500 revelers come here on any given night—and many stay until sunrise. Feeling out of place? Head for one of the balconies on the third and fourth floors (which can be reached by elevator) where the scene is a bit less lurid. Around the corner stands the bar's souvenir shop with humorous T-shirts. If you need to soak up some of that alcohol before heading home, grab

A Shot of Tequila

What once was the drink of the poor Mexican farmer is now produced en masse and enjoyed internationally, with countless varieties crowding shelves across the world. Unfortunately, lower-quality brands make up the bulk of exports, so if the thought of sipping this heady liquor turns your stomach, take some time to seek out some of a higher quality while you're in Los Cabos.

Tequila must contain at least 51% blue agave, a plant related to the lily. The best tequilas are 100% blue agave. Liquid is distilled from the sap of seven- to 10-year-old plants and fermented. If you buy tequila with a worm, it was probably bottled in the United States, and is likely not a good-quality tequila.

Most of the good stuff is made in the town of Tequila, near Guadalajara. Labels bearing *reposado* indicate up to a year of aging; *añejo,* from one to three years. The longer tequila ages, the smoother it tastes.

Getting your fill of taste-testing is an easy thing to do in Los Cabos, because every bar will have at least a couple of bottles on the shelves, but you should visit at least one establishment that specializes in the good stuff. There are a number of locations in Los Cabos to do so: **Pancho's Restaurant & Tequila Bar** comes to mind, as does the **Tequila & Ceviche Bar** at the posh Las Ventanas al Paraíso Resort. **Habanero's** located in San José del Cabo has a tequila pairing course, instructed by certified Tequilier (Tequila Sommelier) Tadd Chapman.

Pancho's might as well be a tequila museum. Hundreds of tequilas are available for tasting, and many of the colorfully named brands up on the shelves are no longer manufactured. Schedule a private tasting, at $50 per person, with Bernard Corriveau, the official "Tequila Ambassador" of Mexico, who will teach you a bit about the history, production process, and art of this complex liquor. Corriveau, appointed a "Maestro Tequilero" by the Consejo Regalador de Tequila (loosely, the industry's Tequila Board), just might be the most knowledgeable person on tequila in Los Cabos. Pancho's holds group tequila tastings in English each Tuesday night at 7 pm.

Only guests at Las Ventanas al Paraíso Resort can enjoy the small, intimate Sushi, Tequila & Ceviche Bar set off from its lobby. The resort's "Tequileros" conduct the lessons for a maximum of 10 guests where you'll learn the history, classifications, distillation process, and different types of tequila along with the appropriate way to drink it. Of the 95 different varieties available for sampling, some are affordable, while others—the Clase Azul Ultra, aged five years, produced in numbered batches of 100 bottles and $254 per shot—are literally liquid gold. Other favorites include the Don Julio Real, $74 per shot; the Chinaco Negro, extra añejo, $79 per shot; the Casa Dragones Joven, $65 per shot; the Gran Centanario Reserva, $44 per shot; and the Reserva de la Familia, $32 per shot. Classes are held on Tuesday and Friday at 5 pm, at a cost of $86 per person. Tequilas are served with ceviche sampler, guacamole, and homemade tortillas chips.

At the **Antigua Los Cabos Museum and Store**, located on the *zócalo* (town square). You can sample various tequilas and other interesting liquors free of charge.

DID YOU KNOW?

One of the best places to see Mexican folk dancing is actually a Cabo San Lucas beach bar known as The Office on the Beach. Thursday nights see not only colorful dance performances but also a mean music show.

a taco from Billy Kitchen just at the front of the club. El Squid Roe also has a full menu, serving pastas, steaks, and salads. ⊠ *Av. Lazaro Cárdenas, between Zaragoza and Morelos* ☎ *624/143–0655* ⊕ *www. elsquidroe.com* ⊹ *3:B4.*

Giggling Marlin. Giggling Marlin has been around forever and predates Cabo's tourism explosion, though its gimmicks remain popular. Watch brave (and inebriated) souls be hoisted upside down at the mock fish-weighing scale, or join in an impromptu moonwalk between tables. Many fun (albeit risqué) floor shows seem to relax people's inhibitions. The age of the clientele varies, as does the music, but the dance floor is usually jammed. A nightly two-for-one drinks special packs 'em in from 11 pm until 1 am. The bartender may place a shot of tequila in front of you the minute you sit down—but you'll pay at least $5 if you drink it. Look for Giggling Marlin's drink coupon inside Cabo's free city map. ⊠ *Blvd. Marina and Matamoros* ☎ *624/143–0606* ⊕ *www. gigglingmarlin.com* ⊹ *3:B4.*

Fodor'sChoice ★ **Passion Club.** There is no doubt that the swankiest (and priciest) spot in Los Cabos is the Passion Club. Top DJs from around the world come to play their sets and fuel the cozy, neon club. The Passion Club alway has a full dane floor and hosts various VIP events throughout the year. ⊠ *At ME Cabo, on El Médano Beach* ☎ *624/145–7800* ⊕ *www. me-cabo.com* ⊹ *3:D3.*

ROCK CLUBS

Cabo Wabo. American rock plays over an excellent sound system at Cabo Wabo, though the jam sessions with owner Sammy Hagar and his many music-business friends are the real highlight. Plan way in advance to attend Hagar's Birthday Bash Week—usually the second week in October—as tickets sell out. It's a large venue, with a raised stage, a tall ceiling resembling an auditorium, the longest bar in town, and, for VIPs, a lounge upstairs. Strong air-conditioning scores lots of points in the heat of summer. ■TIP➔ Make dinner reservations to avoid the long lines to get into the club. Lunch and dinner are served with extensive menus, and a taco grill cooks up tasty munchies outside if you wish to cool off after dancing. Shops on-site or at the international airport sell Cabo Wabo souvenir clothing. ⊠ *Calle Guerrero* ☎ *624/143–1901, 624/163-7400* ⊕ *www.cabowabo.com* ⊹ *3:A4.*

Hard Rock Cafe. With a '59 white Cadillac jutting through the window and dozens of rock-and-roll albums and memorabilia on the walls, this Hard Rock Cafe might be in Mexico, but it is a typical member of the chain. Live rock music starts at 8 pm every Tuesday, Friday, and Saturday and 2-for-1 Corona drink specials are offered daily from 6 to 10 pm. Ladies drink free from 9 pm to 11 pm on Thursday. On the first floor is the requisite shop where you can purchase your "Hard Rock Cafe Cabo San Lucas" caps and T-shirts. ⊠ *Blvd. Marina across from El Squid Roe* ☎ *624/143–3779* ⊕ *www.hardrock.com* ⊹ *3:B4.*

Hagar's Hangout: Cabo Wabo

According to local lore, in the mid-1980s former Van Halen lead singer Sammy Hagar and a friend were walking along the beach in Cabo San Lucas when they passed a drunk man stumbling. Hagar remarked, "Hey, he's doing the Cabo Wabo." A few years later, in 1990, Hagar and the rest of Van Halen opened the bar called Cabo Wabo—establishing one of the premier stops on the Cabo party circuit. When the group broke up in 1996, all but Hagar sold their shares in the bar.

Mexican and American rock bands perform every night. Almost always packed, the place erupts when Hagar comes to play. When he's on tour, he may only make it to the club four or five times a year. Three of those visits fall on April 22 (the bar's anniversary), October 3–4 for the bar's MELT DOWN celebration, and the week around

October 13 (for Hagar's birthday celebration). When not on tour, Hagar hits Cabo Wabo up to 12 times a year. The dates are usually announced on the club's website, ⊕ *www.cabowabo. com.*

Often accompanying Hagar are some of his rock-and-roll friends. These have included Chris Isaak, Kirk Hammett of Metallica, David Crosby, Slash, Rob Zombie, the Cult, and the Sex Pistols.

Easily seen from afar due to a light-house replica at the main entrance, the bar was designed by architect Marco Monroy. He built high, cavern-ous ceilings and painted the walls with zebra stripes and psychedelic neon patterns. Hagar liked Monroy's work so much that the design of the bar was replicated for his set on the "Red Voodoo" tour.

7

SUNSET CRUISES

Several companies run nightly cruises for dinner or drinks that capture stunning sunsets as their vessels rounds the cape. Stands around the marina act as agents and can book excursions for you, but some manage to rope you into a time-share visit in the process. Better to book through your hotel's front desk or directly through the company.

Caborey. Caborey offers a nightly 2½-hour sunset-dinner cruise on a three-deck catamaran. Cost is $97 and includes a full prix-fixe dinner with your choice of one of six main courses, an open bar for domestic beverages, and a Las Vegas–style show of Mexican music. Departure time is 6 pm September–April, and 5 pm the rest of the year. Check online for ticket discounts. ⊠ *Caborey Office located inside Hotel Wyndham* ☎ *624/143–8060, 866/460–4105 in North America* ⊕ *www. caborey.com.*

Tropicat. Jazz plays every evening as the passengers aboard the Tropicat watch the sun set over the 65-foot catamaran, which departs at 6 pm September–April and at 5 pm the rest of the year. The two-hour excursion is $59 per person and includes premium wines and hors d'oeuvres. Check online for ticket discounts. The catamaran departs from Dock #4, next to the main cruise ship terminal. ⊠ *Camino Del Cerro 215 El*

A CAVALCADE OF STARS

It can only be Los Cabos' proximity to Southern (upper) California: at 2½ hours by air from L.A., the southern tip of Baja has become a fabled getaway for all manner of Hollywood celebs. Stars like John Wayne and Bing Crosby vacationed here a half century ago and put Los Cabos on the map, and the area never looked back. Not all today's stars opt for the flash and glitz of Cabo San Lucas. Many prefer quieter San José del Cabo with its selection of small inns and intimate restaurants.

Sammy Hagar, formerly of the rock group Van Halen, is the celebrity most associated with Los Cabos; he's part owner of Cabo Wabo. But the list (in no particular order) of those who have vacationed here is impressive: Leonardo DiCaprio, Jennifer Lopez, George Clooney, Oprah Winfrey, Brad Pitt, Beyoncé Knowles, Michael Douglas, Catherine Zeta-Jones, Michael Jordan, Brooke Shields, Madonna, Demi Moore, Ashton Kutcher, Meg Ryan, Adam Sandler, Celine Dion, Gwyneth Paltrow, Spike Lee, Jennifer Aniston, Bono, Charlize Theron, Halle Berry, Jessica Simpson, Sarah Jessica Parker, Salma Hayek, Goldie Hawn, Kurt Russell, Sylvester Stallone— and that's just to name a few. Ryan Seacrest often pops over for an afternoon lunch at Las Ventanas.

Many fly into a small airstrip near Cabo San Lucas that handles private jets—as does one terminal at Los Cabos International Airport. Call it a hunch, but we mere mortals probably won't be sitting next to JLo or Oprah in coach. You never know who you might see after you arrive, though, so keep your eyes peeled. Do remember that "Be cool" is one of Los Cabos' cardinal rules: gawking, staring, and taking photos are frowned upon.

Pedregal, across from the Electric Company ☎ *624/143–3797* ⊕ *www. tropicatcabo.com.*

LOS CABOS SIDE TRIPS

Todos Santos and La Paz

WELCOME TO LOS CABOS SIDE TRIPS

TOP REASONS TO GO

★ **Shopping Todos Santos:** An influx of artisans and craftspeople has turned Todos Santos into the region's snazziest, high-quality shopping destination.

★ **Lodging Value:** Todos Santos offers a selection of charming inns at just a fraction of the cost—but all at full quality—of Los Cabos hostelries down the coast.

★ **The Aquarium of the World:** So Jacques Cousteau christened the Sea of Cortez; La Paz makes the perfect launching point for exploring this body of water's rich marine life.

★ **The Best of Urban Baja:** La Paz is your bet for the urban pleasures of a charming, low-key Mexican city that lines a grand seaside promenade to boot.

★ **A Whale of a Time:** The annual December-through-April migration of gray whales to and from Alaska is visible from various points on the Baja coast and a guaranteed stunner.

1 Todos Santos. Todos outgrew its surfing roots without abandoning them entirely, but you'll more likely come here for its growing number of galleries and craft shops. The arts scene has fueled a rise in gracious small inns, making this popular Los Cabos–area day trip an overnight destination in its own right.

2 La Paz. Don't let La Paz's workaday hustle and bustle fool you. This seaside state capital is one of Mexico's loveliest small cities—you'll be sold after an evening stroll on the oceanfront *malecón*, ice cream cone in hand—and the launching point for Baja's best diving, fishing, and whale-watching excursions.

GETTING ORIENTED

In Todos Santos climb the hill north of the bus terminal to reach the original colonial town center with its stupendous views, landmark mission church, and several small inns and galleries. Coming into Todos Santos from the south, Highway 19 parallels area beaches without necessarily hugging the coastline. Roads leading to the shore are in decent shape, but twist and turn at points. Follow the signs; things are well marked.

The focal point of La Paz is the dense grid of streets in the city center, with most sights, lodgings, and restaurants either on the *malecón*, (aka Paseo Alvaro Obregón), or a few blocks inland at most. (Remember: The odd curvature of the coast means that you are looking *west* out over the Sea of Cortez here.) The alternative to staying in the city is the 18-km (11-mile) highway leading north from La Paz to its port of Pichilingue, lined with a few small seaside hotels.

8

Updated by
Chris Sands

At the risk of sounding glib, we might suggest that you skip Los Cabos altogether. The highlights of your visit to the far southern tip of the Baja peninsula may include two very un-Cabo-like destinations. One is objectively a small community; the other is actually the region's largest city, but will always be an overgrown small town at heart.

Their tranquil, reverent names—Todos Santos ("all saints") and La Paz ("peace")—are the first hint that you have left the glitz of Los Cabos behind, and that it's time to shift gears and enjoy the enchantment of Mexico. As an added bonus, both are positioned in such a way on the peninsula that you can enjoy beautiful sunsets over the sea. (Los Cabos gives you only ocean sun*rises*.)

The appeal of Todos Santos is becoming more well known, as a growing number of expats—American and European alike—move to the area. There's a lot to love here: the surf on the Pacific, just a couple of miles west of town, is good; weather is always a bit cooler than in Los Cabos; and the lush, leisurely feel of this artsy colonial town—think a smaller version of central Mexico's San Miguel de Allende—is relatively undisturbed by the many tourists who venture up from Los Cabos for the day. Todos Santos has always been the quintessential Los Cabos day trip, especially for the myriad cruise passengers who call there. As the town's tourism offerings grow, it's becoming a destination in its own right. Break the typical pattern of day-tripping to Todos Santos and spend at least one night here amid the palms, at one of the pleasant, small inns.

La Paz plants itself firmly on the Sea of Cortez side of the Baja peninsula. A couple of hours north of Los Cabos, it remains slightly outside the Cabo orbit, and it has always attracted visitors (and an expanding expat population) who make La Paz their exclusive Baja destination. Of course, 200,000-plus Paceños view their city as being the center of the universe, thank you very much. (La Paz is the capital of the state of Baja California Sur and Los Cabos is in *their* orbit.) In addition to many urban trappings, La Paz offers a growing number of outdoor-travel options. This city *on* the water has become all about what's *in* the water. Sportfishing and scuba diving are big here, and La Paz is now a major launching point for whale-watching excursions.

WHAT IT COSTS IN DOLLARS			
$	**$$**	**$$$**	**$$$$**
Restaurants	Under $12	$12–$20	$21–$30	over $30
Hotels	Under $150	$150–$250	$251–$350	over $350

Restaurant prices are the average cost of a main course at dinner or, if dinner is not served, at lunch. Hotel prices are the lowest cost of a standard double room in high season.

Hotel reviews have been shortened. For full information, visit Fodors. com.

TODOS SANTOS

73 km (44 miles) north of Cabo San Lucas, 81 km (49 miles) south of La Paz.

From the hodgepodge of signs and local businesses you see on the drive into Todos Santos, south on Highway 19, it appears that you're heading to the outskirts of a typical Baja town. But climb the hill to its old colonial center with its mission church and blocks of restored buildings, and the Todos Santos that is gaining rave reviews in tourism circles is revealed.

Todos Santos was designated one of the country's Pueblos Mágicos (Magical Towns) in 2006, joining 82 other towns around Mexico chosen for their religious or cultural significance. Pueblos Mágicos receive important financial support from the federal government for development of tourism and historical preservation. Architects and entrepreneurs have restored early-19th-century adobe-and-brick buildings around the main plaza of this former sugar town and have turned them into charming inns, whose hallmark is attentive service at prices far more reasonable than a night in Los Cabos. A good number of restaurateurs provide sophisticated, globally inspired food at hip eateries.

Todos Santos has always meant shopping, at least since about three decades ago when the first U.S. and Mexican artists began to relocate their galleries here. Day-trippers head up here from Los Cabos, enjoying lunch and a morning of shopping. The growing number of visitors who buck that trend and spend a night or two here leave feeling very satisfied indeed.

Los Cabos visitors typically take day trips here, though several small inns provide a peaceful antidote to Cabo's noise and crowds. El Pescadero, the largest settlement before Todos Santos, is home to ranchers and farmers who grow herbs and vegetables. Business hours are erratic, especially in September and October.

8

GETTING HERE AND AROUND

Highway 19, now upgraded to four lanes, connects Todos Santos south with Cabo San Lucas and north with La Paz, making the drive easier than ever. Nonetheless, we recommend making the trip before dark; the occasional cow or rock blocks the road. Autotransportes Aguila provides comfortable coach service over a dozen times a day in both directions between Los Cabos (San José and San Lucas) and La Paz, with an intermediate stop in Todos Santos. Plan on an hour from La Paz or Cabo San Lucas and 90 minutes from San José del Cabo. Ecobaja Tours offers scheduled shuttle service ($22 one-way) three times daily between Todos Santos and Los Cabos Airport, 90 minutes away.

VISITOR INFORMATION

Baja California Sur State Tourist Office. The Baja California Sur State Tourist Office is in La Paz about a 10-minute drive north of the *malecón* (seaside promenade). It serves as both the state and city tourism office. There's also an information booth on the malecón (no phone) that can give you info on La Paz and surrounding areas. Both offices and the booth are open weekdays 9–5. ⊠ *Km. 5.5, Carretera al Norte, La Paz* ☎ *612/124–0100* ⊕ *www.explorebajasur.com.*

EXPLORING

WORTH NOTING

Nuestra Señora del Pilar. Todos Santos was the second-farthest south of Baja California's 30 mission churches, a system the Spanish instituted to convert (and subdue) the peninsula's indigenous peoples. Jesuit priests established an outpost here in 1723 as a *visita* (circuit branch) of the mission in La Paz, a day's journey away on horseback. The original church north of town was sacked and pillaged twice during its existence, before being relocated in 1825 to this site in the center of town. Additions in the past two centuries have resulted in a hodgepodge of architectural styles, but the overall effect is still pleasing, and the structure serves to this day as the community's bustling parish church. ⊠ *Calle Márquez de León, between Centenario and Legaspi* ☎ *612/145–0043* ⊙ *Daily 7 am–8:30 pm.*

Teatro Cine General Manuel Márquez de León. The mouthful of a name denotes Todos Santos's 1944 movie theater, which was quite a grand movie palace back in the day for remote, small-town Mexico. A few cultural events take place here, including the annual Todos Santos Film Festival each February. ⊠ *Calle Legaspi s/n* ☎ *612/145–1083* ⊙ *Weekdays 9–2, weekends 9–1* ⊙ *Closed June.*

WHERE TO EAT

Todos Santos's dining selection echoes the town—stylish expat with traditional Mexican—and makes a nice outing during any Los Cabos–area stay. Restaurants here do a brisk business at lunch, less so at dinner. It's a real treat to drive up from Los Cabos or down from La Paz for a special meal. At an hour each way, that's easier to do before dark.

$ ✗ **Baja Beans.** Although Los Cabos and Baja are not coffee-growing
CAFÉ regions, the folks in the town of El Pescadero roast the finest beans
from the Sierra Norte mountains in the Mexican state of Puebla. They
turn them into the area's best gourmet coffee drinks, which may be
enjoyed at tables in the adjoining garden. Baked goods and light fare
headline the daily menu offerings, with more filling options—such
as vegetarian frittatas—available for Sunday brunch. Other Sunday
specials include live music and a farmers' market. ⑤ *Average main:*
$5 ⊠ *Km 64, Hwy. 19, Pescadero* ☎ *612/130–3391* ⊕ *bajabeans.com*
⊙ *No dinner. Closed Mon.*

$$$ ✗ **Café Santa Fe.** The setting, with tables situated in an overgrown court-
ITALIAN yard, is as appealing as the food, which includes salads and soups
made with organic vegetables and herbs, homemade pastas, and fresh
fish with light sauces. Many Cabo-area residents lunch here regularly.
The marinated seafood salad is a sublime blend of shrimp, octopus,
and mussels with olive oil and garlic, with plenty for two to share
before dining on lobster ravioli. ⑤ *Average main: $22* ⊠ *Calle Cen-*
tenario, between Márquez de León and Hidalgo ☎ *612/145–0340*
⊕ *cafesantafetodossantos.com* ⊙ *Closed Tues.; closed Aug. 25–Nov. 1.*

$ ✗ **Caffé Todos Santos.** Omelets, bagels, granola, and whole-grain breads
ECLECTIC delight the breakfast crowd at this casual small eatery; deli sandwiches,
fresh salads, and an array of burritos, tamales, and *flautas* (fried tortillas
rolled around savory fillings) are lunch and dinner highlights. Check
for fresh seafood on the daily specials board. Gourmet pizzas and pasta
dishes are also available. ⑤ *Average main: $10* ⊠ *Calle Centenario 33*
☎ *612/145–0300* ▭ *No credit cards* ⊙ *No dinner Mon. Closed last*
two weeks of Sept.

$$ ✗ **El Gusto! At Posada La Poza.** Even if you don't stay at the sumptuous
ECLECTIC Posada La Poza just outside town, lunch or dinner at its equally lovely
Fodor's Choice restaurant will be one of the highlights of your Los Cabos vacation.
★ Owners Jürg and Libusche Wiesendanger call their offerings "Swiss-
Mex"—Mexican food with European touches, and careful attention to
detail. Start with the vegetarian-based tortilla soup with three different types of dried chilies to give it just enough kick. Then sample the
smoked-tuna flautas with raspberry-chipotle sauce, quesadillas with
mushroom or shrimp, or marinated *arrachera* (flank steak) strips. You'll
find dishes such as lamb shoulder in winter. Believe it or not, there is
enough of an evening chill in the air that time of year that dining next
to the fireplace feels cozy. Top your meal off with a sorbet, flan, or
mousse, and possibly the best selection of wines in the region (all Mexican from northern Baja's Guadalupe Valley). Dinner is served from 6
to 8, which gives you time to catch the sunset. Reservations are recommended. ⑤ *Average main: $19* ⊠ *Camino a La Poza #282, follow signs*
on Hwy. 19 and Benito Juárez to beach, La Poza ☎ *612/145–0400,*
612/145–0461 ⊕ *www.lapoza.com* ⊙ *Closed Thurs.*

$$ ✗ **Los Adobes.** Locals swear by the fried, cilantro-studded local cheese
MEXICAN and the beef tenderloin with huitlacoche at this pleasant outdoor res-
taurant. The menu is ambitious and includes tapas and several organic,
vegetarian options—rare in these parts. At night the place sparkles
with star-shape lights. Take a stroll through the adjoining landscaped

8

desert garden while you wait for your food. If you're here during the July–October low season, make it an early dinner; the place closes at 7 on weeknights. $ *Average main: $17* ⊠ *Calle Hidalgo, between Juárez and Colégio Militar* 🕿 *612/145–0203* ⊕ *www.losadobesdetodossantos. com* ⊗ *Closed Sun. No dinner Sat.*

$$ ✕ **Michael's at the Gallery.** Everybody who dines here seems to know one
ASIAN   another, but visitors are always welcome. The attraction at Michael's—not to be confused with Miguel's, the equally recommended Mexican place as you come into town—is an Asian menu combining Chinese, Japanese, Thai, and Vietnamese cuisines. Share an order of Mu Shu chicken or Vietnamese crab cakes as an appetizer. You'll dine on the patio behind the Galería de Todos Santos; you can browse while you wait for your food. Michael's keeps *very* limited hours, open just two evenings per week. $ *Average main: $20* ⊠ *Calle Juárez and Calle Topete, Centro* 🕿 *612/145–0500* 🍽 *Reservations essential* ⊗ *Closed Sun.–Thurs. No lunch.*

$ ✕ **Miguel's.** Deliciously prepared chiles rellenos are the attraction at
MEXICAN   Miguel's. The sign out front says so, and so does a faded *New York*
Fodor's Choice   *Times* article, which proclaims them the best in all of Baja. If you're
★   skeptical, owner Miguel Torres will be happy to show you a framed copy of the story. The hearty peppers come in cheese, shrimp, vegetarian, and other options, but the signature version is made with shrimp and scallops. Breakfast is served during the high-season months—October through May—and features egg dishes and breakfast burritos. Don't confuse this semi-outdoor place on the edge of town with Michael's, the Asian restaurant several blocks away near the church. $ *Average main: $8* ⊠ *Degollado at Calle Rangel* 🕿 *612/145–0733, 612/145–0814* ⊕ *miguels-restaurant.com* ▭ *No credit cards* ⊗ *Closed 3 weeks in Sept.*

WHERE TO STAY

The quality of lodgings in Todos Santos is surprisingly high. It's a much better value to stay here than along the Corridor or in Los Cabos—and there isn't a megaresort to be found. In fact, some of the best lodging in the region is found right here, among the lush palm trees of this former sugarcane town.

$$ 🏨 **Hacienda Todos los Santos.** Within each of the three *casitas* (guest-
HOTEL   houses) here, you'll find canopied beds and antique art. **Pros:** three casitas have private terraces and fully equipped kitchens; wonderful views from upstairs rooms. **Cons:** little to do here for young children. $ *Rooms from: $190* ⊠ *End of Benito Juárez* 🕿 *612/145–0547* ⊕ *www. tshacienda.com* 🛏 *4 suites, 3 casitas* ▭ *No credit cards* ⦿ *No meals* ⊕ *B2.*

$ 🏨 **Hotel California.** This handsome structure with two stories of arched
HOTEL   terraces and rich, vibrant colors on the walls is a testament to the artistic bent of owner Debbie Stewart. **Pros:** inn feels exotic and lush; convenient location; good value. **Cons:** some street noise; service not as smooth as other hotels in town. $ *Rooms from: $135* ⊠ *Benito*

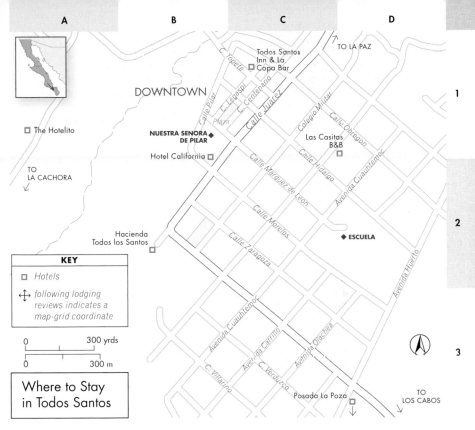

TO LA PAZ

Todos Santos
Inn & La
Copa Bar

DOWNTOWN

NUESTRA SENORA
DE PILAR

Hotel California

Las Casitas
B&B

TO
LA CACHORA

Hacienda
Todos los Santos

ESCUELA

KEY

☐ Hotels

✥ following lodging
reviews indicates a
map-grid coordinate

| 0 | | 300 yrds |
| 0 | | 300 m |

Where to Stay
in Todos Santos

Posada La Poza

TO
LOS CABOS

Juárez at Morelos ☎ *612/145–0525* ⊕ *www.hotelcaliforniabaja.com*
↩ *11 rooms* ⦿| *No meals* ✥ *B2.*

$ 🛏 **The Hotelito.** Original art is found throughout this modern lodging
HOTEL and has been mixed with contemporary and antique Mexican decora-
Fodor'sChoice tive pieces; the sculptural furniture is as comfortable as it is captivating.
★ **Pros:** saltwater swimming pool is fabulous; generous breakfasts are
delicious (mangoes right off the tree!); boogie boards, beach towels
and umbrellas available for beach use; five-minute walk to the beach.
Cons: 10-minute walk to downtown. ⑤ *Rooms from: $105* ⊠ *Rancho
de la Cachora* ☎ *612/145–0099* ⊕ *www.thehotelito.com* ↩ *4 rooms*
⊘ *Closed Sept.* ⦿| *Breakfast* ✥ *A1.*

$$ 🛏 **Posada La Poza.** West of town, overlooking a bird-filled lagoon that
HOTEL gives way to the Pacific, this is the only Todos Santos property right on
Fodor'sChoice the water. **Pros:** gracious owners; very generous, delicious breakfasts;
★ gorgeous saltwater pool and hot tubs; free Wi-Fi. **Cons:** no children
under 12; no TV or phones; need car to stay here. ⑤ *Rooms from:*
$200 ⊠ *Camino a La Poza #282, follow signs on Hwy. 19 and on*
Benito Juárez to beach, La Poza ☎ *612/145–0400, 855/552–7692 in*
U.S. ⊕ *www.lapoza.com* ↩ *8 suites* ⦿| *Breakfast* ✥ *C3.*

$$
B&B/INN
Fodor's Choice
★

⌂ **Todos Santos Inn.** This converted 19th-century house, with only eight guest rooms, is unparalleled in design and comfort, owing to the loving care and attention of the owners. **Pros:** traditional Mexican elegance and hospitality at its best; the interior courtyard of this property is a verdant oasis. **Cons:** street parking only; no kids under 12. $ *Rooms from: $180* ✉ *Calle Legaspi 33* ☏ *612/145–0040* ⊕ *www.todossantosinn.com* ⇌ *2 rooms, 6 suites* ❍ *Breakfast* ✛ *C1.*

NIGHTLIFE AND THE ARTS

As tourism grows in Todos Santos, so do its nightlife options. You'll never mistake this place for Los Cabos, however, and the town is quite fine with that state of affairs. Lingering over dinner remains a time-honored way to spend a Todos Santos evening.

FESTIVALS

Todos Santos holds three annual arts-related festivals during the high season in January and February. It's a good idea to make reservations weeks in advance if you plan to be here at those times.

Festival de Cine de Todos Santos (*Todos Santos Film Festival*). Todos Santos screens several new Latin American films during a 10-day festival in late February. The 1940s-era Teatro Cine General Manuel Márquez de León serves as the main venue, with some films shown at other sites in Todos Santos and La Paz. ⊕ *www.todossantoscine.org.*

Festival del Arte Todos Santos (*Todos Santos Art Festival*). The city goes all out to celebrate Mexican dance, music, folklore, and culture for a week in early February each year. Several of the downtown galleries hold special events in conjunction with the festival. ✉ *Centro.*

Todos Santos Music Festival. Former R.E.M. guitarist Peter Buck is the major force behind the Todos Santos Music Festival, which premiered in 2012, and is now held annually in January. The festival typically features seven nights of live music spread across two weekends, with an international lineup of performers appearing at Hotel California and the Todos Santos town square. Proceeds benefit local children's charities. ✉ *Centro* ⊕ *todossantosmusicfestival.com.*

BARS AND WINE BARS

La Bodega de Todos Santos. Twice-weekly wine tastings at this downtown wine shop make an interesting twist on a night out in Todos Santos. Stop by Monday or Wednesday evening during the October–June high season for a taste of Baja wines—a couple of vintages are featured each time—and an appetizer supplied by a rotating selection of local restaurants. La Bodega also organizes the town's largest food and wine festival, Gastrovino, which takes place each May. ✉ *Calle Hidalgo, between Juárez and Colegio Militar* ☏ *612/152–0181* ⊕ *www.gastrovino.mx* ☉ *Wine tastings Oct.–Jun., Mon. and Wed. 5–8 pm.*

La Santeña. You'll find this upscale rendition of a Mexican cantina (with a restaurant, too) in the Hotel Casa Tota. It's a great place to stop for a quiet drink. ✉ *Hotel Casa Tota, Calle Alvaro Obregón* ☏ *612/145–0590* ⊕ *www.hotelcasatota.com* ☉ *Daily 7 am–11 pm.*

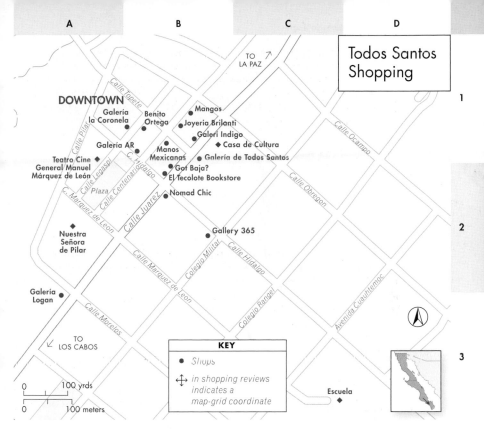

Shut Up Frank's. Take your pick from the sporting events shown on six big-screen TVs at the consummate sports bar in Todos Santos. Enjoy the scrumptious burgers here, too. ⊠ *Degollado and Rangel, across from Pemex station* ☎ *612/145–0707* ⊕ *www.shutupfranks.com* ⊗ *Daily 10–10.*

EN ROUTE

If you're headed to La Paz on Highway 1 from San José del Cabo, a large globe-shaped monument marks 23.27° latitude north, or the Tropic of Cancer. You cross the line between the earth's temperate zone and the tropics here. Of course, Baja is Baja, and you won't detect any difference in climate no matter which side of the line you are on. Many stop for a photo posing in front of the monument, which is 2 km (1 mile) south of the turnoff to Santiago. You can decide how obligatory that seems.

The Tropic of Cancer also crosses Highway 19 on the West Cape, just outside Todos Santos. There is no marker there.

SHOPPING

Although Todos Santos is gaining renown in all aspects of its tourism offerings, the name still means shopping to most Los Cabos–area visitors. Artists from the U.S. Southwest (and a few from Mexico) found a haven here some two decades ago. Their galleries and shops showcase traditional and contemporary work. There is a strong Baja emphasis in the art, and you'll find beautiful jewelry and fine crafts from all over Mexico.

Use the coordinate (✛ B2) at the end of each listing to locate a site on the corresponding map.

ART GALLERIES

Benito Ortega Vargas, Sculptor. Sculptor Benito Ortega Vargas's studio and gallery showcases evocative, often sea-inspired works in wood, bronze, stone, and other materials. ⊠ *24 Centenario at Obregon, Centro* ☎ *612/136–2760* ⊕ *www.sculpturemexico.com* ✛ *B1.*

Gallery 365. The colors of Todos Santos provide the inspiration for the abstract paintings of artist Steve Thurston. ⊠ *Colegio Militar and Hidalgo, Centro* ☎ *612/145–0001* ⊕ *www.gallerysteve.com* ✛ *B2.*

Galería AR. The colorful contemporary paintings of Arturo Mendoza Elfeo are the main attraction at Galería AR, although the artist's relation to the Brilanti family of jewelry makers—owners of several downtown galleries and boutiques, including Joyería Brilanti and Manos Mexicanas—ensures the gallery always has an excellent selection of hand-crafted jewelry. ⊠ *Centenario at Hidalgo* ☎ *612/145–0502* ⊗ *Mon.–Sat. 10–6* ✛ *B1.*

Galería de Todos Santos. Since opening in 1994, Michael and Pat Cope's *galeria* has represented a diverse group of Mexican and American painters and sculptors working in a variety of artistic mediums. The gallery's terrace opens as an Asian restaurant, Michael's at the Gallery, on Friday and Saturday evenings. (⇨ *Where to Eat.*) ⊠ *Calle Juárez at Calle Topete, Centro* ☎ *612/145–0500* ⊕ *galeriatodossantos-com.webs.com* ⊗ *Mon.–Sat. 10–4:30, Sun. 11–4* ✛ *B1.*

Galería Indigo. Local artists exhibit their works, primarily Baja-themed landscapes and abstracts, at this Belgian-owned gallery; gourmet panini, wraps, and salads are on hand to enhance the browsing experience. ⊠ *Calle Juárez at Calle Topete* ☎ *612/145–0808* ⊗ *Mon.–Sat. 10–5* ✛ *B1.*

Galería La Coronela. Galería La Coronela exhibits the work of prodigious painter Victor Vega, as well as paintings by his daughter, Sofía. ⊠ *Calle Legaspi between Hidalgo and Topete* ☎ *612/102–9851* ⊗ *Daily 10–5* ✛ *A1.*

Galería Logan. The namesake gallery features the work of Jill Logan, a Southern Californian who has been in Todos Santos since 1998. Jill does bold oil-on-canvas paintings and complexly layered multimedia pieces. ⊠ *Calle Juárez and Morelos* ☎ *612/145–0151* ⊕ *www.jilllogan.com* ⊗ *Mon.–Sat. 10–5* ✛ *A3.*

BOOKS

El Tecolote Bookstore. El Tecolote Bookstore is the best bookstore in the Los Cabos region. Stop here for Latin American literature, poetry, children's books, current fiction and nonfiction, and books on Baja. Take a break with a coffee or juice in the back. ⊠ *Calle Juárez at Calle Hidalgo* ☎ *612/145–0295* ⊗ *Mon.–Sat. 9–5, Sun. noon–3* ✛ *B2.*

Colorful blankets for sale in a Todos Santos market

CLOTHING AND FOLK ART

Mangos. Mangos is filled with gorgeous Guatemalan textiles, Mexican folk art, belts, purses, wood carvings, and Day of the Dead figurines, as well as paintings by esteemed Baja California Sur artists like Ezra Katz and Rafael Chávez. ⊠ *Calle Centenario, between Topete and Obregón* ☎ *612/145–0315* ⊗ *Mon.–Sat. 10:30–4:30* ⊗ *Closed Jun.–Nov.* ✛ *B1.*

Manos Mexicanas. Manos Mexicanas is a treasure trove of fine Mexican crafts, jewelry, decorative objects, and work by local potter Rubén Gutiérrez. Owner Alejandra Brilanti has amassed an incredible collection of affordable pieces. You are not likely to leave empty-handed. ⊠ *Topete at Centenario* ☎ *612/145–0538* ⊗ *Mon.–Sat. 10–5* ✛ *B1.*

Nomad Chic. Eastern simplicity and the romance of exotic travel influence Nomad Chic's eclectic collection of apparel, jewelry, and accessories. ⊠ *Juárez at Hidalgo, Centro* ☎ *612/105–2857* ⊕ *www.nomadchic. mx* ✛ *B2.*

JEWELRY

Joyería Brilanti. Joyería Brilanti is a showcase for the stunning jewelry and design works of famed Taxco silversmith Ana Brilanti, in addition to a number of other contemporary jewelry artists—including Ana's son and the store's proprietor, José—whose work shares the same dramatic aesthetic. Be sure to look at the silver tea services and other functional pieces. You'll also find selected stone carvings and bronzes from local artists. ⊠ *Centenario near Topete* ☎ *612/145–0799* ⊗ *Mon.–Sat. 10–5* ✛ *B1.*

ART WALKS IN TODOS SANTOS

The shops and galleries in the downtown area can be explored in an hour or two, or you can easily make a day of it. Start at **Nuestra Señora de Pilar** church in the morning, when it's cooler. Head up Legaspi a block to **Galería la Coronela**. Make a left out of the gallery and then make a right onto Topete to head over one block to Centenario—to the left is **Joyeria Brilanti**, and on the corner is **Manos Mexicanas**. Continue heading south on Topete and on Juarez you'll find **Galería de Todos Santos** at the intersection. Between the galleries mentioned you'll find dozens of additional shops to wander through, too.

MARKETS

The Pescadero-based café Baja Beans hosts a Sunday farmers' market, with arts and crafts offerings, stands featuring locally grown produce, live music, and healthy brunch options like vegetarian frittatas.

SOUVENIRS

Got Baja?. You'll find a nice selection of Baja-themed souvenirs at this small downtown shop, located next to Cafélix Coffee & Kitchen. ⊠ *Calle Juárez, between Márquez de León and Hidalgo* ☎ *612/178–0067* ⊕ *www.gotbaja.mx* ☉ *Daily 10–5* ✛ *B2.*

SPORTS AND THE OUTDOORS

ECOTOURISM

Todos Santos Eco Adventures. Todos Santos Eco Adventures offers a number of land- and water-based adventures. Choose from cliff walks, rock climbing, mountain treks, or fishing trips. Friendly guides pride themselves on thorough knowledge of the area, the environment, and the culture of the region. Their weeklong Todos Santos Cooking Adventure combines Mexican lessons with local sightseeing. Whichever of the offerings you choose, you'll feel like you're traveling with a savvy friend. The Jauregui family runs the operation with great care, and it's apparent. Ask about the casitas if you need overnight accommodations. ⊠ *Guaycura #88, La Poza* ✛ *West on Calle Olachea, follow signs toward La Poza. (Call for detailed directions)* ☎ *612/145–0189, 619/446–6827 in U.S.* ⊕ *www.tosea.net.*

SURFING

Todos Santos offers great surfing areas for beginners to experts. The advantage here is that the crowds, including the swarming masses from the cruise ships, don't head up to these waters, which makes for a much more relaxed scene in the water and on the beach.

Los Cerritos, south of Todos Santos on Mexico 19, offers gentle waves to beginners during the summer and more challenging breaks for advanced surfers during the northwest swell from December to March. San Pedrito, also south of town, offers great surfing for experienced surfers during the winter swells, with a number of popular, low-key, surf-oriented motels along the beach. In summer, the surf is generally pretty mellow along this stretch, so locals and surfers who demand greater challenge head to the Corridor or areas along the east side of the Cape for more satisfying breaks.

Costa Azul Surf Shop. Costa Azul Surf Shop is a small shop on the north end of the beach by the cliffs at Los Cerritos. The staff is friendly, and, for such a small space, there's a good selection of board rentals, as well as T-shirts, shorts, and accessories to buy. You'll see its stickers on cars all over the Cape, and the interactive map on its website is a great resource for information on surf spots all over Baja Sur. ⊠ *Playa Los Cerritos, Los Cerritos* ☎ *624/142–2771 San José del Cabo office* ⊕ *www.costa-azul.com.mx* ⊗ *Daily 8–6.*

Todos Santos Surf Shop. Swing by Todos Santos Surf Shop for board rentals, to arrange a lesson, buy gear, or get that ding in your board repaired. Other activities options are also available, including day trips to Magdalena Bay during whale-watching season, and to La Paz to swim with sea lions and whale sharks. ⊠ *Calle Hidalgo, between Colégio Militar and Rangel* ☎ *612/145–1114* ⊗ *Closed Sun.*

LA PAZ

81 km (49 miles) north of Todos Santos, 178 km (107 miles) north of San José del Cabo (via Hwy. 1), 154 km (92 miles) north of Cabo San Lucas (via Hwy. 19).

Tidy, prosperous La Paz may be the capital of the state of Baja California Sur and home to about 220,000 residents, but it still feels like a small town in a time warp. This east-coast development could easily be the most traditional Mexican city in Baja Sur, the antithesis of the "gringolandia" developments to the south. Granted, there are plenty of foreigners in La Paz, particularly during snowbird season. But in the slowest part of the off-season, during the oppressive late-summer heat, you can easily see how La Paz aptly translates to "peace," and how its residents can be called Paceños (peaceful ones).

Travelers use La Paz as both a destination in itself and a stopping-off point en route to Los Cabos. There's always excellent scuba diving and sportfishing in the Sea of Cortez. La Paz is the base for divers and fishermen headed for Cerralvo, La Partida, and the Espíritu Santo islands, where parrot fish, manta rays, neons, and angels blur the clear waters by the shore, and marlin, dorado, and yellowtail leap from the sea. Cruise ships are more and more often spotted sailing toward the bay as La Paz emerges as an attractive port. (Only small ships can berth at La Paz itself; most cruise liners dock at its port of Pichilingue, about 16 km [10 miles] north of town.)

La Paz officially became the state capital in 1974, and is its largest settlement (though the combined Los Cabos agglomeration is quickly catching up). All bureaucracy holds court here, and it's the site of the ferry port to Mazatlán and Topolobampo, the port of Los Mochis, on

LA PAZ LANGUAGE SCHOOLS

La Paz is a laid-back city with a picturesque waterfront and some fine beaches—a great spot to work on your Spanish skills at one of the good language schools in the area. Perhaps the only drawback to learning Spanish in this area is that its large tourism industry has made English widely spoken. (It still doesn't compare to the numbers of foreigners living in Los Cabos.) Resist the temptation to hang out with other English speakers. Plunge in and practice your Spanish outside class.

Centro de Idiomas, Cultura y Comunicación. This language school offers personalized classes and immersion programs at all levels. It arranges for students to live with local families to get the maximum possible exposure to the language and daily practice. ⊠ *Francisco Madero 2460* ☎ *612/125-7554* ⊕ *www.cicclapaz.com.*

Se Habla . . . La Paz. Se Habla is an American-owned language school with regular classes and cultural interactions. It also offers special programs for health-care and legal professionals. ⊠ *Francisco Madero 540* ☎ *612/122-7763* ⊕ *www. sehablalapaz.com.*

the mainland. There are few chain hotels or restaurants, but that's sure to change as resort developments come to fruition around the area.

La Paz region, including parts of the coastline south of the city, is slated as the future building site of several large-scale, high-end resort developments with golf courses, marinas, and vacation homes. Economic doldrums of recent years put brakes on those projects, but as Mexico's tourism finally, slowly, cautiously begins to rebound, plans have moved to the front burner again.

8

GETTING HERE AND AROUND

Aeropuerto General Manuel Márquez de León (LAP) is 11 km (7 miles) northwest of La Paz. Alaska Air partner Horizon Air flies daily from Los Angeles. Aereo Calafia connects La Paz with Los Cabos. Several airlines connect La Paz with Mexico City and various domestic airports in Mexico. Flying into the Aeropuerto Internacional de Los Cabos, two hours away near San José del Cabo, offers a far better selection of fares and itineraries. Ecobaja Tours operates shuttles five times daily between Los Cabos Airport and La Paz for $33 one-way. In La Paz, taxis are readily available and inexpensive. Taxis between La Paz airport and towns are inexpensive (about $15) and convenient. A ride within town costs under $5; a trip to Pichilingue costs around $15. In La Paz the main Terminal de Autobus is on the malecón at Independencia. Bus companies offer service to Todos Santos (one hour), Los Cabos (two hours).

Baja Ferries connects La Paz with Topolobampo, the port at Los Mochis, on the mainland, with daily high-speed ferries. The trip takes seven hours and costs $72 per person. Baja Ferries also connects La Paz and Mazatlán; it's a 16-hour trip and costs $88 per person. You can buy tickets for ferries at La Paz Pichilingue terminal. The ferries carry passengers with and without vehicles. If you're taking a car to

THE STEINBECK CONNECTION

For an account of the Baja of years past, few works beat John Steinbeck's *The Log from the Sea of Cortez*, published in 1951. It recounts a six-week voyage he took in 1940 with marine biologist Ed Ricketts for the purpose of cataloging new aquatic species on the gulf side of Baja California. (*Phialoba steinbecki*, a previously unknown species of sea anemone discovered during the excursion, was later named for the author.)

Steinbeck lamented what he was sure would one day be the inevitable tourism growth to arrive on the peninsula. The author was mistaken on one key point however: he was certain the megaboom would come to La Paz and not to then-sleepy Cabo San Lucas.

the mainland, you must obtain a vehicle permit before boarding. Ferry officials will ask to see your Mexican auto-insurance papers and tourist card, which are obtained when crossing the U.S. border into Baja.

ESSENTIALS

Airlines Aereo Calafia ☎ *612/123–2643* ⊕ *www.aereocalafia.com.mx.* **Horizon Air** ☎ *800/252–7522* ⊕ *www.alaskaair.com.* **Aeropuerto Manuel Márquez de León** ☎ *612/124-6307* ⊕ *www.aeropuertosgap.com.mx.*

Bus Contacts Autotransportes Aguila ✉ *Av. Álvaro Obregón #125, between Independencia and 5 de Mayo, Malecón* ☎ *800/824-8452* ⊕ *www. autotransportesaguila.net.* **Ecobaja Tours** ✉ *5 de Mayo, Malecón* ☎ *612/123–0000* ⊕ *www.ecobajatours.com.*

Currency Exchange Banamex ✉ *Esquerro 110, Zona Comercial* ☎ *612/122–1011* ⊕ *www.banamex.com.mx.*

Emergencies ☎ *Dial 065, 060, or 066.* **Highway Patrol** ☎ *612/122–0369.* **Police** ☎ *066.*

Ferry Lines Baja Ferries ✉ *La Paz Pichilingue Terminal* ☎ *612/123–0508, 612/125-6324* ⊕ *www.bajaferries.com.*

Hospitals Centro de Especialidades Médicas ✉ *Calle Delfines 110* ☎ *612/124–0400.*

EXPLORING

TOP ATTRACTIONS

Malecón. Offically the Malecón Alvaro Obregón, this seaside promenade is La Paz's seawall, tourist zone, and social center all rolled into one. It runs for 5 km (3 miles) along Paseo Álvaro Obregón and has a sidewalk as well as several park areas in the sand just off it. Paceños are fond of strolling the malecón at sunset when the heat of the day finally begins to subside. Teenagers slowly cruise the street in their spiffed-up cars, couples nuzzle on park benches, and grandmothers meander along while keeping an eye on the kids. (You will see people swimming here, and the water is cleaner than it used to be, but the

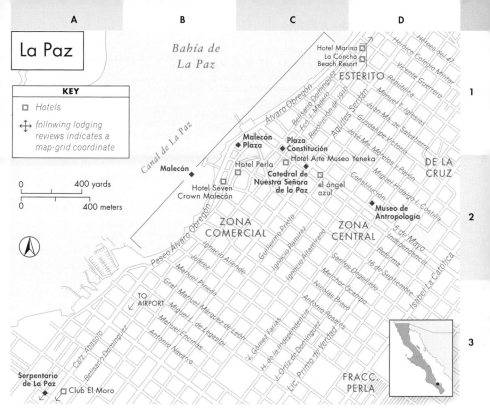

La Paz

KEY

☐ Hotels

✛ following lodging reviews indicates a map-grid coordinate

0 ——— 400 yards

0 ——— 400 meters

Bahía de La Paz

Hotel Marina La Concha Beach Resort

ESTERITO

DE LA CRUZ

Malecón Plaza

Plaza Constitución

Malecón

Hotel Perla

Hotel Arte Museo Yeneka

Catedral de Nuestra Señora de la Paz

el ángel azul

Museo de Antropología

Hotel Seven Crown Malecón

ZONA COMERCIAL

ZONA CENTRAL

TO AIRPORT

Serpentario de La Paz

Club El Moro

FRACC. PERLA

beaches outside town are a far surer bet in that regard.) ✉ *Paseo Alvaro Obregón* ✛ *B2.*

Malecón Plaza. A two-story white gazebo is the focus of Malecón Plaza, a small concrete square where musicians sometimes appear on weekend nights. An adjacent street, Calle 16 de Septiembre, leads inland to the city. ✉ *Paseo Alvaro Obregón and Calle 16 de Septiembre* ✛ *B2.*

Plaza Constitución. Plaza Constitución, the true center of La Paz, is a traditional zócalo that also goes by the name Jardín Velazco. Concerts are held in the park's gazebo and locals gather here for art shows and fairs. Day-to-day life here entails shoeshines and local bingo games. ✉ *Bordered by Av. Independencia, Calles 5 de Mayo, Revolución de 1910, and Madero, Centro* ✛ *C2.*

WORTH NOTING

Catedral de Nuestra Señora de la Paz. The downtown church, Catedral de Nuestra Señora de la Paz, is a simple, unassuming stone building with a modest gilded altar but beautiful stained glass windows. The church was built in 1861 near the site of La Paz's first mission, which no longer exists. The two towers of the present cathedral were added a half-century later. ✉ *Revolución de 1910, between 5 de Mayo and Independencia, Centro* ☎ *612/122–2596* ⊕ *www.diocesislapaz.org* ☾ *Daily 9–3* ✛ *C2.*

FAMILY **Museo de Antropología.** La Paz's culture and heritage are well represented at the Museo de Antropología, which has re-creations of indigenous Comondu and Las Palmas villages, photos of cave paintings found in Baja, and copies of Cortés's writings on first sighting La Paz. All exhibit descriptions are labeled in Spanish only, but the museum's staff will help you translate as best they can. If you're a true

SUNRISE, SUNSET

La Paz sits on the east coast of the Baja peninsula, but a convoluted curvature of the shoreline here positions the city to look out west over the Sea of Cortez. That means that you can enjoy beautiful sunsets over the water here at the end of the day.

Baja aficionado and want to delve into the region's history, this museum is a must; otherwise, a quick visit is all you need, if even that. ⊠ *Calle Altamirano at Calle 5 de Mayo, Centro* ☎ *612/122–0162* ⌸ *$3* ⊙ *Daily 9–6* ✥ *D2.*

Serpentario de La Paz. Better that you encounter all the creatures that slip and slither here in the safety of Mexico's largest serpentarium than out in the wilds of Baja. More than 100 species are on display in indoor and outdoor exhibits, including turtles, pythons, rattlesnakes, and a rather large iguana. For less than $3, visitors may take photos with their choice of two pythons or a baby crocodile. Labeling is entirely in Spanish, but the staff offers guided tours in English with advance notice. A gift shop sells reptile-themed souvenirs. ⊠ *Calle Brecha California, between Nueva Reforma and Guaycura, Centro* ☎ *612/122–5611* ⊕ *www.elserpentario.org* ⌸ *$6* ⊙ *Tues.–Sun. 10–4* ✥ *A3.*

BEACHES

Around the malecón, stick to ambling along the sand while watching local families enjoy the sunset. Just north of town the beach experience is much better; it gets even better north of Pichilingue. Save your swimming and snorkeling energies for this area. All facilities listed here exist on the weekends. Their existence on weekdays may be spottier.

Playa Balandra. A rocky point shelters a clear, warm bay at Playa Balandra, 21 km (13 miles) north of La Paz. Several small coves and pristine beaches appear and disappear with the tides, but there's always a calm area where you can wade and swim. Snorkeling is fair around Balandra's south end where there's a coral reef. You may spot clams, starfish, and anemones. Kayaking and snorkeling tours usually set out from around here. If not on a tour, bring your own gear, as rentals aren't normally available. Camping is permitted but there are no hookups. The smallish beach gets crowded on weekends, but on a weekday morning you may have the place to yourself. Sand flies can be a nuisance here between July and October. **Amenities.** toilets, food concession, parking lot, camping. **Best for:** swimming, walking, snorkeling.

Playa Caimancito. Situated just beyond La Concha Beach Club Resort, 5 km (3 miles) north of La Paz, Caimoncito is home to a scenic stretch of sand and some sun-shading palapas. Locals swim laps here, as the water is almost always calm and salty enough for easy buoyancy. There aren't any public facilities here, but if you wander over to the hotel for lunch or a drink you can use its restrooms and rent water toys. **Amenities:** parking lot. **Best for:** sunsets, swimming, walking.

Playa El Tecolote. Spend a Sunday at Playa El Tecolote, 25 km (15 miles) north of La Paz, and you'll feel like you've experienced the Mexico of old. Families set up house on the soft sand, kids race after seagulls and each other, and *abuelas* (grandmothers) daintily lift their skirts to wade in the water. Vendors rent out beach chairs, umbrellas, kayaks, and small, motorized boats; a couple of restaurants serve up simple fare such as ceviche and *almejas* (chocolate clams). These eateries are usually open throughout the week, though they sometimes close on chilly days. Facilities include public restrooms and trash cans. Camping is permitted, but there are no hookups. **Amenities:** toilets, food concession, playground, parking lot, camping. **Best for:** sunsets, swimming, walking.

FAMILY **Playa Pichilingue.** Starting in the time of Spanish invaders, Pichilingue, 16 km (10 miles) north of La Paz, was known for its preponderance of oysters bearing black pearls. In 1940 a disease killed them off, leaving the beach deserted. Today it's a pleasant place to sunbathe and watch sportfishing boats haul in their daily catches. Locals set up picnics here on weekend afternoons and linger until the blazing sun settles into the bay. Restaurants consisting of little more than a palapa over plastic tables and chairs serve oysters *diablo,* fresh clams, and plenty of cold beer. Pichilingue curves northeast along the bay to the terminals where the ferries from Mazatlán and Topolobampo arrive and many of the sportfishing boats depart. If La Paz is on your cruise itinerary, you'll likely dock at Pichilingue, too. One downside to this beach: traffic buzzes by on the nearby freeway. The water here, though not particularly clear, is calm enough for swimming. **Amenities:** toilets, food concession, parking lot. **Best for:** sunset, walking.

8

WHERE TO EAT

$ ✕ **Bandido's Grill.** Bandido's has come a long way since opening nearly
BURGER a decade ago with three plastic tables and a grill fixed under the hood of an old pickup truck. The unique truck-grill is still around, but the restaurant's latest alfresco setting suggests it may be transitioning from working-class pit stop into romantic burger joint. Red- and white-checkered tablecloths are scattered amidst dozens of palm trees festooned with lanterns, and tropical breezes blow in past the nearby marina. Bandido's is very popular with locals, who crowd the place nightly for enormous half-pound burgers and barbecue ribs, ice cold cervezas, and old-time rock and roll. $ *Average main: $10* ✉ *Calle Navarro at Topete, Centro* ☎ *612/128–8338.*

$ ✕ **Caffé Gourmet.** Not far from hotels, restaurants, and important down-
CAFÉ town sights, this small cafe is a great place to recharge with a morning espresso, chai, or smoothie, along with great pastries. Wi-Fi is available here, so you can catch up on your email. Credit cards are accepted.

$ *Average main: $3* ✉ *Esquerro at Calle 16 de Septiembre* ☎ *612/122–7710* ⊗ *Closed Sun.*

$$
MEXICAN
✕ **El Bismark.** The original Bismark is a bit out of the way, but it attracts families who settle down for hours at long wood tables, while waitresses divide their attention between patrons and telenovelas (Latin American soap operas) on the TV above the bar. Tuck into seafood cocktails, enormous grilled lobsters, or carne asada served with beans, guacamole, and homemade tortillas. Seafood tacos and *micheladas* are specialties at the malecón location, called Bismark-cito. $ *Average main:* *$15* ✉ *Av. Degollado at Calle Altamirano, Centro* ☎ *612/122–4854* $ *Average main: $15* ✉ *Alvaro Obregón, between Constitución and Hidalgo* ☎ *612/128–9900.*

$$$$
MEXICAN
Fodor's Choice
★
✕ **El Tupé.** Due to the talent and creativity of chefs Uziel Leaño and Luis González, El Tupé has become one of the darlings of the La Paz dining scene. They dish up exquisitely prepared and presented regional favorites in unexpected ways: Serving vessels often include abalone and chocolate clam shells, or cross-sections of indigenous trees. They conceived of El Tupé during backpacking trips. The two Sudcalifornianos were so impressed with some of the traditional dishes they found in their native state's less-traveled areas, they decided to open a restaurant to showcase the region's unique flavors and signature culinary style. Six- and twelve-course menus change daily to take advantage of the freshest local, organic ingredients. Seatings for both are at 6 pm daily and include excellent pairing options from Baja's wine country, Valle de Guadalupe. $ *Average main: $38* ✉ *Calle Mutualismo, between Nicolás Bravo and Ocampo, Centro* ☎ *612/158–9524, 612/159–0339* ⊗ *No lunch.*

$$
SEAFOOD
✕ **Los Laureles.** A small stand that looks as if it might have been rolled along the street by a vendor is just the entryway decoration for this well-established restaurant. Whether you eat at a bench at the stand outside or dine within in the air-conditioning, if you like seafood, you will enjoy Los Laureles. It offers all sorts of *fruits de mer* served in many different ways, but the seafood cocktails are notable for their freshness (you can even try the shrimp raw) and variety (abalone is an option). $ *Average main: $12* ✉ *Paseo Alvaro Obregón at Salvatierra, Centro* ☎ *612/128–8532.*

$$
SEAFOOD
✕ **Mar y Peña.** The freshest, tastiest seafood cocktails, ceviches, and clam tacos imaginable are served in this nautical restaurant crowded with locals. If you come with friends, go for the *mariscada,* a huge platter of shellfish and fish for four. The shrimp *albondigas* (meatballs) soup has a hearty fish stock seasoned with cilantro; and the crab *ranchero* is a savory mix of crabmeat, onions, tomatoes, and capers. Portions are huge. $ *Average main: $15* ✉ *Calle 16 de Septiembre, between Isabel la Católica and Albáñez, Centro* ☎ *612/122–9949.*

$
BAKERY
✕ **Pan d'Les.** Fortify yourself for a morning of sightseeing—the place is open only until 2:30 pm—at Pan d'Les in La Paz's central business district. Transplanted U.S. pastry chef Les Carmona hand-forms his European-style breads and pastries at his small bakery. It's all flour, water, yeast, and salt here, but no preservatives. You'll find a good selection each morning. Every day is the day for his slow-rising *rústico* sourdough

bread; the specialty on individual days of the week might be focaccia or a red wine-nut bread. An extra yummy treat in this warm climate is the homemade ice cream sandwiches. $ *Average main: $4* ✉ *Madero, between 5 de Mayo and Constitución, Centro* ☎ 612/122–5339 ⊟ *No credit cards* ☾ *No dinner. Closed Sun.*

$ ✕ **Rancho Viejo.** Everything is delicious, and prices are reasonable at this
MEXICAN cheerful little restaurant painted in bright yellow and orange. Meats are the specialty here, but just about everything on the menu is good and choices are abundant. The *tacos de arrachera,* a kind of beef taco, are particularly tasty. You can pop in any time, day or night, since this restaurant is open 24 hours. $ *Average main: $10* ✉ *Márquez de León at Dominguez, Centro* ☎ 612/128–4647, 612/125–6633 ⊕ *www.ranchoviejolapaz.com.*

$$ ✕ **Restaurant Zoe.** Following a makeover and name change from the
EUROPEAN cutesy portmanteau La Pazta, this popular eatery at the Hotel Mediterrane added colorful new accents and a bit of international flair to a menu best known for its homemade pasta and pizzas. Tasty additions like carrot, ginger, and honey cream soup, grilled scallops with ginger and lime butter, and green curry with tofu are now served with lasagna, ravioli, and other traditional Italian favorites. Restaurant Zoe opens only for dinner, but you can enjoy coffee, fresh pressed juices, and freshly baked bread in the hotel's adjacent café, open for breakfast and lunch. $ *Average main: $15* ✉ *Hotel Mediterrane, Allende 36, Centro* ☎ 612/125–1195 ⊕ *www.hotelmed.com* ☾ *No lunch.*

$ ✕ **Tacos Hermanos González.** La Paz has plenty of great taco shacks, but
MEXICAN none is better than the small stand of the González brothers who serve up hunks of fresh fish wrapped in corn tortillas and offer bowls of condiments with which to decorate your taco. The top quality draws sizable crowds of satisfied sidewalk munchers. $ *Average main: $3* ✉ *Madero at Degollado, Centro* ☎ 612/120–5074 ⊟ *No credit cards.*

8

WHERE TO STAY

$ ⊡ **Club El Moro.** Possibly the best bargain on the malecón, although
RESORT a bit away from the city center itself, this vacation-ownership resort has very reasonable suite rentals on a nightly and weekly basis. **Pros:** good value; shallow pool great if you don't care to swim. **Cons:** some dated decor; rooms facing pool area can be noisy. $ *Rooms from: $85* ✉ *Hwy. to Pichilingue, Km 2* ☎ 612/122–4084, 866/375–2840 ⊕ *www.clubelmoro.com.mx* ⌕ *18 rooms, 20 suites* ⊺⊘⎪ *Breakfast* ⊹ *A3.*

$ ⊡ **el ángel azul.** Owner Esther Ammann converted La Paz's historic
B&B/INN courthouse into a bed-and-breakfast that's a comfortable retreat in
Fodor's Choice the center of the city. **Pros:** lovely owner; attentive service; historic
★ building; terrific value. **Cons:** street parking only; no kids under 12. $ *Rooms from: $105* ✉ *Av. Independencia 518, at Guillermo Prieto, Centro* ☎ 612/125–5130 ⊕ *www.elangelazul.com* ⌕ *9 rooms, 1 suites* ⊺⊘⎪ *Breakfast* ⊹ *C2.*

$ ⊡ **Hotel Arte Museo Yeneka.** Thirteen budget-friendly rooms fringe a court-
HOTEL yard strewn with art and artifacts, each individually decorated to reflect this hotel's bohemian sensibility. **Pros:** affordable room rates; central

location; laundry service; motorcycle parking; pets are welcome. **Cons:** patchy Wi-Fi; noisy ceiling fans and air-conditioning units. $\boxed{\$}$ *Rooms from: $42* ⊠ *Calle Madero 1520, Centro* ☎ *612/125–4688* ⊕ *www. hotelyeneka.com* ⤳ *13 rooms* ▭ *No credit cards* ⦿ *Breakfast* ✚ *C2.*

$ ⊡ **Hotel Marina.** Here's a hotel with a full-service marina offering fish-
RESORT ing, scuba diving, and kayaking. **Pros:** good value; amenities for fishing vacations; tennis court. **Cons:** you may feel out of place if you're not here on a fishing vacation. $\boxed{\$}$ *Rooms from: $85* ⊠ *Hwy. to Pichilingue, Km 2.5* ☎ *612/121–6254, 866/262–7187 in U.S.* ⊕ *www.hotelmarina. com.mx* ⤳ *84 rooms, 5 suites* ⦿ *Breakfast* ✚ *D1.*

$ ⊡ **Hotel Perla.** The brown low-rise faces the malecón and has seen a flurry
HOTEL of activity since 1940, due largely to its nightclub, La Cabaña, which opens on Saturday night. **Pros:** central location; friendly staff; decent value for the price. **Cons:** room facing street can be noisy. $\boxed{\$}$ *Rooms from: $94* ⊠ *Paseo Alvaro Obregón 1570, Malecón* ☎ *612/122–0777* ⊕ *www.hotelperlabaja.com* ⤳ *110 rooms* ⦿ *No meals* ✚ *C2.*

$ ⊡ **Hotel Seven Crown Malecón.** This very reasonable, modern, minimal-
HOTEL ist hotel is perfectly situated to one side of the malecón's action. **Pros:** central location; affordable. **Cons:** very simple rooms; some rooms fac-ing street can be noisy. $\boxed{\$}$ *Rooms from: $102* ⊠ *Paseo Alvaro Obregón 1710, Centro* ☎ *612/128–7787* ⊕ *www.sevencrownhotels.com* ⤳ *55 rooms, 9 suites* ⦿ *No meals* ✚ *B2.*

$ ⊡ **La Concha Beach Club Resort and Condominiums.** On a long beach with
RESORT calm water, this older resort (built in 1984) has a water-sports center
FAMILY and a notable restaurant. **Pros:** renovated rooms in good shape; lower-priced rooms are good value; private beach; gym access or one hour of free kayaking per day. **Cons:** you'll need a car to stay here. $\boxed{\$}$ *Rooms from: $90* ⊠ *Hwy. to Pichilingue, Km 5* ☎ *612/121–6161* ⊕ *www. laconcha.com* ⤳ *99 rooms* ⦿ *Breakfast* ✚ *D1.*

NIGHTLIFE AND THE ARTS

BARS AND DANCE CLUBS

La Terraza. The best spot for both sunset- and people-watching along the malecón is La Terraza at the Hotel Perla. The place makes killer margaritas, too. ⊠ *Hotel Perla, Paseo Alvaro Obregón 1570, Malecón* ☎ *612/122–0777* ⊕ *www.hotelperlabaja.com.*

Las Varitas. This club heats up after midnight, with live music acts play-ing Banda, Norteño, and other Mexican musical styles. Ladies Night is Friday 9–11, with cheap drinks and performances by male exotic danc-ers. ⊠ *Av. Independencia 111, at Domínguez, Centro* ☎ *612/125–2025* ⊕ *lasvaritas.com.mx* ☻ *Thurs.–Sun. 8 pm–5 am.*

PERFORMING ARTS

El Teatro de la Ciudad. La Paz's cultural center seats over 1,100 and stages shows by visiting and local performers. ⊠ *Av. Navarro 700, at Héroes de Independencia, Centro* ☎ *612/125–0207, 612/122–3113.*

SHOPPING

ART AND SOUVENIRS

Antigua California. Antigua California has the nicest selection of Mexican folk art in La Paz, including wooden masks and lacquered boxes from the mainland state of Guerrero. ⊠ *Paseo Alvaro Obregón 220, Malecón* ☎ *612/125–5230* ☉ *Mon.–Sat. 9:30–8:30.*

Got Baja?. You'll find a nice selection of Baja-themed souvenirs, including quality T-shirts, at this downtown shop. There's also a branch in Todos Santos. ⊠ *Calle Madero 1240, Between 5 de Mayo and Constitución, Centro* ☎ *612/125–5991* ⊕ *www.gotbaja.mx.*

Ibarra's Pottery. The Ibarra family oversees the potters and painters at their namesake shop. Their geometric designs and glazing technique result in gorgeous mirrors, bowls, platters, and cups. ⊠ *Guillermo Prieto 625, between Torre Iglesias and República, Centro* ☎ *612/122–0404* ☉ *Weekdays 9–3, Sat. 9–2.*

BOOKS

Allende Books. This bookstore stocks La Paz's best selection of English-language works, mainly about Baja and Mexico, as well as laminated nature field guides. You'll also find a terrific selection of gifts here, including handcrafted jewelry, table runners, and wall hangings. ⊠ *Independencia 518, between Serdán and Guillermo Prieto, Centro* ☎ *612/125–9114* ⊕ *www.allendebooks.com* ☉ *Mon.–Sat. 10–6.*

SPORTS AND THE OUTDOORS

BOATING AND FISHING

The considerable fleet of private boats in La Paz now has room for docking at several marinas, including Marina Palmira north of the malecón, and Marina de La Paz and Marina Cortez to the south. Most hotels can arrange trips. Fishing tournaments are typically held in August, September, and October.

Fishermen's Fleet. The Fishermen's Fleet has daylong fishing on *pangas* (skiffs), as well as multiday excursions to Magdalena Bay. ☎ *612/122–1313, 408/884–3932 in U.S.* ⊕ *www.fishermensfleet.com.*

Mosquito Fleet. The Mosquito Fleet has 22 pangas starting at $300 for two people, and cabin cruisers from $550 for four people. ⊠ *Hwy. to Pichilingue, Km 5, between downtown and Pichilingue* ☎ *612/121–6120, 877/408–6769 in U.S.* ⊕ *www.bajamosquitofleet.com.*

KAYAKING

The calm waters off La Paz are perfect for kayaking, and you can take multiday trips along the coast to Loreto or out to the nearby islands.

Baja Expeditions. Baja Expeditions, one of the oldest outfitters working in Baja (since 1974), offers several kayak tours, including multinight trips between Loreto and La Paz. A support boat carries all the gear, including ingredients for great meals. The 10-day trip in the Sea of Cortez with camping on remote island beaches starts at $1,550 per person, based on double occupancy. ⊠ *Calle Sonora 585, between*

A diver gets up close and personal with a sea lion in the waters of the Sea of Cortez.

Topete and Abasolo, Manglito ☎ *612/125–3828, 800/843–6967 in U.S.* ⊕ *www.bajaex.com.*

Fun Baja. Fun Baja offers land tours, scuba and snorkel excursions with sea lions, seasonal whale-watching trips, and camping safaris to Isla Espíritu Santo. ⊠ *Carretera Federal La Paz-Pichilingue, Km 6.1, Marina Costa Baja, Local 61* ☎ *612/106–7148* ⊕ *www.funbaja.com* ✏ *Two-tank scuba trips from $135.*

SCUBA DIVING AND SNORKELING

Popular diving and snorkeling spots include the coral banks off Isla Espíritu Santo, the sea-lion colony off Isla Partida, and the seamount 14 km (9 miles) farther north (best for serious divers).

Cortez Club. The Cortez Club is a full-scale water-sports center with equipment rental and scuba, snorkeling, kayaking, and sportfishing tours, as well as the complete slate of PADI instructional courses. ⊠ *Hwy. to Pichilingue, Km 5, between downtown and Pichilingue* ☎ *612/121–6120, 877/408–6769 in U.S.* ⊕ *www.cortezclub.com* ✏ *Two-tank dives from $140.*

TOUR OPERATORS

KAYAKING

Nichols Expeditions. Nichols Expeditions arranges kayaking tours to Isla Espíritu Santo and between Loreto and La Paz, with camping along the way. It also offers a combination of sea kayaking in the Sea of Cortez with whale-watching in Magdalena Bay. ⊠ *497 N. Main, Moab, Utah* ☎ *800/648–8488 in U.S.* ⊕ *www.nicholexpeditions.com* ✏ *Four-day trip $725; nine-day trip $1,350.*

SCUBA DIVING

Baja Expeditions. Snorkel in sheltered coves off the coast of La Paz, or with sea lions at Los Islotes. Two- or three-tank dives at pristine sites near Isla Espíritu Santo are facilitated by a 28-foot custom dive boat. The 45-foot catamaran *El Mechudo* can carry up to eight people for week-long snorkel and dive charters. ⊠ *Calle Sonora 585, between Topete and Abasolo, Manglito* ☎ *612/125–3828, 800/843–6967 in U.S.* ⊕ *www.bajaex.com* ✉ *Snorkeling from $65 per person; scuba dives from $140.*

WHALE-WATCHING

La Paz is a good entry point for whale-watching expeditions to **Bahía Magdalena,** 266 km (165 miles) northwest of La Paz on the Pacific coast. Note, however, that such trips entail about six hours of travel from La Paz and back for two to three hours on the water. Only a few tour companies offer this as a daylong excursion, however, because of the time and distance constraints.

Many devoted whale-watchers opt to stay overnight in San Carlos, the small town by the bay. Most La Paz hotels can make arrangements for excursions, or you can head out on your own by renting a car or taking a public bus from La Paz to San Carlos, and then hire a boat captain to take you into the bay. The air and water are cold during whale season from December to April, so you'll need to bring a warm windbreaker and gloves. Captains are not allowed to "chase" whales, but that doesn't keep the whale mamas and their babies from approaching your panga so closely you can reach out and touch them.

An easier expedition is a whale-watching trip in the Sea of Cortez from La Paz, which involves boarding a boat in La Paz and motoring around until whales are spotted. They most likely won't come as close to the boats and you won't see the mothers and newborn calves at play, but it's still fabulous watching the whales breeching and spouting nearby.

Baja Expeditions. Seasonal five-day, four-night gray whale-watching excursions are offered for $2,675 per person, double occupancy. Tours are typically scheduled in February and March, and include flights, meals, an expert natural guide, and comfortable camping conditions at Laguna San Ignacio. ⊠ *Calle Sonora 585, between Topete and Abasolo, Manglito* ☎ *612/125–3828, 800/843–6967 in U.S.* ⊕ *www. bajaex.com.*

Cortez Club. The water-sports center Cortez Club runs extremely popular full-day whale-watching trips in winter. Transportation, guide, breakfast and seafood lunch are included. ⊠ *Hwy. to Pichilingue, Km 5, between downtown and Pichilingue* ☎ *612/121–6120, 877/408–6769 in U.S.* ⊕ *www.cortezclub.com* ✉ *$180 per person.*

8

BAJA CALIFORNIA BEACH TOWNS

With Ensenada and the Valle de Guadalupe Wine Region

WELCOME TO BAJA CALIFORNIA BEACH TOWNS

TOP REASONS TO GO

★ **Scenic Driving:** Along the Pacific Coast, south of Tijuana, the Carretera Transpeninsular (Highway 1) makes getting to Baja's historic missions and remote beaches half the fun.

★ **Sampling Mexico's Wine:** The Valle de Guadalupe, near Ensenada, is a gorgeous valley blanketed with sprawling vineyards and charming inns.

★ **Whale Watching:** Gray whales swim to Baja California every winter to mate and calve in three lagoons on the peninsula's west coast.

★ **Shopping for Handicrafts:** In Ensenada stores are filled not only with sunglasses and sombreros, but with interesting souvenirs that make for authentic bring backs.

1 Rosarito. Just 16 km (10 miles) south of the U.S. border are Rosarito's beautiful wide beaches, fronted by a less-than-beautiful town full of touristy bars targeting college students looking for a "what happens in Mexico, stays in Mexico" kind of weekend.

2 Puerto Nuevo. San Diegans cross the border for the fried lobster that made this sleepy fishing village famous.

3 Valle de Guadalupe. Explore the Ruta de Vino dotted with award-winning wineries, farm-to-table restaurants, and boutique hotels with unpretentious hosts.

4 Ensenada. A seaport town sandwiched by beaches, Ensenada is home to some of the best fish tacos and margaritas Mexico has to offer.

GETTING ORIENTED

Flanked by the Pacific Ocean to the west and the Sea of Cortez to the east, Baja California (also called Baja California Norte, or just Baja Norte) comprises the northern half of the Baja Peninsula. The majority of the narrow state is accessible by the Carretera Transpeninsular (Highway 1), but it's easy to feel as if you've gone far off the grid when a hundred miles of barren land stands between you and the nearest town or gas station. Embrace the feeling because Baja is really Mexico's wild, wild west, and still has the stark desert landscapes, secluded coves, and striking mountains to show for it.

9

Valle de Guadalupe **3**

3

San Antonio de las Minas

Cibola del Mar

0   5 miles

0   5 kilometers

1

3

4

Ensenada

Bahía Todos Santos

Ejido Chapultepec

1

Updated by
Marlise Kast

The beaches of the northern peninsula are like a dream: fine sand, water that's refreshing but not too cold, excellent sunshine and, for the surfer, some of the west coast's top waves. Part of that dream can evaporate, however, when you venture into the beach towns themselves.

More than a few of the stops along Highway 1 have been run down by years of American spring-breakers looking for a good time, and then leaving that good time's remnants behind. Ensenada is an exception: a charming fisherman's enclave, something-larger-than-a-village with a village's sleepy feel, complete with beachside trinket stores and fish taco stands (the town's beaches, conversely, are nothing special at all). Along this part of the peninsula, towns are close together, and the essentials (gas, food, lodging) are never far.

PLANNING

GETTING HERE AND AROUND

The main artery of the Baja Peninsula is a road of legend: Highway 1 winds down from Tijuana to Los Cabos through deserts and coastal bluffs, past fertile estuaries and through bleak towns which eke out a few crops from the dry soil.

If you're driving into Baja California from San Diego during peak hours, you might try heading 35 km (19 miles) east to the much less congested border crossing at Tecate. From there, Highway 3 takes you south through the Valle de Guadalupe to Ensenada.

Highway 3 continues southeast from Ensenada over the San Martír pass, where it meets Highway 5. From here, you can head north to Mexicali or south to San Felipe, where the road ends. In northern Baja, Highway 2 hugs the border from Mexicali to Tijuana. Although the hairpin turns make for beautiful overlooks during the day, the road east of Tecate is best avoided at night.

If you're driving in from the United States, purchase Mexican insurance (required) from any of the brokers near the border. It's also possible to rent a car in Tijuana or Mexicali from any of the major chains. Pack plenty of water and make sure your tires are in good shape: although the major highways are well maintained, a number of smaller roads—especially in Valle de Guadalupe—are unpaved.

There are few international flights into Tijuana, Baja California's only major airport; most travelers access the area from the border at San Diego. Aeroméxico flies to Los Cabos, to La Paz on the Baja Peninsula, and to several cities in mainland Mexico. Aeroméxico also connects Tijuana with Mexico City, and offers service between Tijuana and Oaxaca. Alaska Airlines, Spirit, US Airways, United, and American all fly into Los Cabos. Delta, Interjet, and Aeroméxico fly into La Paz.

ABOUT THE RESTAURANTS

With a modern history not much older than the Carretera Transpeninsular, most Baja California towns have appropriated their local cuisine from the cultures of mainland Mexico. In many regions, the best lunches and dinners are had at curbside taco stands, where fried fish is served atop tortillas—with shredded cabbage and salsa to add at your discretion. It's hard to find a good sit-down restaurant south of Ensenada, but the few that exist usually serve fantastic local seafood. There are a handful of exceptional restaurants popping up in Ensenada and Valle de Guadalupe where award-winning chefs are offering a farm-to-table experience. When restaurants are limited, opt for the local hot spot, which is always a better option than paying premium for a chef's half-baked take on "international cuisine."

ABOUT THE HOTELS

Expect your own bathroom, daily maid service, a secure parking lot, and clean quarters in all but the most basic of establishments. Many hotels offer breakfast for an extra fee, and swimming pools are prevalent. Luxury is never far in Baja Norte; almost every touristed locale has at least one "Resort & Spa" that tacks on Jacuzzis, massages, and dollar signs to the above basics (especially along the coast near Ensenada). Be aware that only camping (no hotels) is available in some of Baja Norte's smaller towns, including those on Highway 1 between Ensenada and San Quintín, and those on Highway 3 between Ensenada and San Felipe.

WHAT IT COSTS IN DOLLARS				
	$	$$	$$$	$$$$
Restaurants	Under $12	$12–$20	$21–$30	over $30
Hotels	Under $150	$150–$250	$251–$300	over $300

Restaurant prices are the average cost of a main course at dinner or, if dinner is not served, at lunch. Hotel prices are the lowest cost of a standard double room in high season.

Hotel reviews have been shortened. For full information, visit Fodors. com.

WHEN TO GO

Like the American southwest, Baja California's weather is conducive to year-round travel, though "peak season" will have a different meaning for beach bums and marine-life enthusiasts. The deserts can be sweltering between May and October, and parts of the Pacific coast are chilly between November and February. Whale-watching season on the Pacific runs roughly from December to late March, and although fishing is possible all year-round, local experts consider the summer months the best time to hook a big one.

ROSARITO

29 km (18 miles) south of Tijuana.

Southern Californians use Rosarito (population 150,000) as a weekend getaway, and during school vacations, especially spring break, the crowd becomes one big raucous party. Off-season, the place becomes a ghost town, which is arguably even less appealing than the frat scene. The beach, which stretches from the power plant at the north end of town about 8 km (5 miles) south, is long with beautiful sand and sunsets, but it's less romantic for the amateur explosives that boom every few minutes.

If you do wind up here for a night, head out to the wooden pier ($1 entrance fee) that stretches over the ocean in front of the Rosarito Beach Hotel, or hire a horse at the north or south end of Boulevard Benito Juárez for $30 per hour. ATVs are also available at the base of the pier for $25 per hour.

GETTING HERE AND AROUND

Rosarito is off of Highway 1 about 45 minutes south of the border. Follow the exit road directly into town.

Car Rental Alamo ⊠ *Blvd Sanchez Taboada, Zona Río, Tijuana* ☎ *664/686–4040* ⊕ *www.alamomexico.com.mx.*

EXPLORING

WORTH NOTING

Claudius. As Rosarito's only wine production facility, this winery brings grapes from neighboring valleys to create remarkable blends unlike anything on the market, such as their 2011 Merlot. All of the wines by owner Julio Benito Martin are organic, and are best appreciated with the winemaker himself, who has passion behind every pour. Be sure to try the Rosado de Grenache, a creamy buttery blend unique to his line. The tasting room is ideal for those who want to enjoy local wines near the border, without driving the distance to Valle de Guadalupe. To create your own blend, inquire about Julio's wine academy. ⊠ *Blvd. Sharp*

3722, col Amp Benito Juarez ☎ *661/100–0232* ⊕ *www.claudiusvino. com* ✉ *7 wine tastings cost $30* ☉ *Daily 8–5.*

WHERE TO EAT

$$$ ✕ **El Nido Steakhouse.** A dark, wood-paneled restaurant with leather
STEAKHOUSE booths and a large central fireplace, this is one of Rosarito's oldest eat-eries, and the best in town for atmosphere. Diners unimpressed with newer, fancier places come here for mesquite-grilled venison, lamb, rabbit, and quail from the owner's farm in the Baja wine country. They serve organic vegetables, have a delicious flan, and offer wine tastings in their small damp cellar. Ask for a table on the back patio where potted plants and a waterfall make a pleasant setting in the charming greenhouse. ⑤ *Average main: $30* ⊠ *Benito Juárez 67* ☎ *661/612–1430* ⊕ *www.elnidorosarito.net.*

$$ ✕ **Mi Casa Supper Club.** Mi Casa evolved out of a unique underground
MOROCCAN dining alternative that literally originated in the "casa" of the owners, Dennis and Bo Bendana. The menu reflects their international back-ground as do the Balinese influences of the decor. Dennis, a knowl-edgeable wine connoisseur, sets the tone with refreshing margaritas like mango-habanero or prickly pear. They also offer a wide selection of single-malt scotches and Mi Casa's private label Zinfandel from Guadalupe Valley. Moroccan-born Chef Bo Bendana incorporates the spices of her childhood with the bold flavors of Mexico to create unique "Moraxican" dishes. The menu changes regularly, but you might find Moroccan tortillas with smoked habanero lentil dip or grilled octopus over couscous with cochinita pibil sauce. The slow-cooked chicken tagine and the lamb with caramelized plums are the stars of the show. Pace yourself for the decadent desserts like flourless chocolate cake with salted caramel ice cream. Saturday night features a six-course Chef's Dinner and live entertainment, which can vary from belly dancing to tango ($60, reservations essential). To learn Bo's tricks of the kitchen, ask about her cooking classes held Wednesday and Thursday from 9:30 am to 1 pm. ⑤ *Average main: $16* ⊠ *Estero 54, San Antonio Del Mar* ☎ *664/609–3459* ⊕ *www.micasasupperclub.com* ⌀ *Reservations essential* ☉ *Closed Mon. and Tues.*

$$ ✕ **Susanna's.** In addition to the fresh Southern California cuisine, many
ECLECTIC come to this restaurant to connect with the charming owner Susanna who moved to Rosarito in 2004 to open a high-end furniture shop. Her love for fine food prevailed, thus turning her store into a restaurant that makes people feel right at home. From the moment you try the fresh baked bread with homemade butter and tapenade, you know you're in for a memorable meal (don't bother asking her the secret recipe!). Every-thing here is made from scratch including salsas and vinaigrettes that top her beautiful salads. The asparagus salad with strawberries, field greens, feta, and pine nuts is remarkably fresh. Entrées are beautifully prepared, like the pork chop seasoned with brown sugar and cumin and covered in a mound of apple chipotle salsa. Susanna's rich flan is made with Grand Marnier and three types of milk, a dessert perfect to share. Larger groups can request the private table in the wine cellar, ideal for private parties. ⑤ *Average main: $15* ⊠ *Blvd. Benito Juarez 4356, Publo*

9

Plaza, Playas de Rosarito ☎ *661/613–1187* ⊕ *www.susannasinrosarito. com* ⊗ *Closed Tues.*

WHERE TO STAY

$$$

B&B/INN

Fodor's Choice

★

🔲 **Casa Farolito.** Sheltered within the beachfront gated community of San Antonio del Mar, this B&B is the perfect introduction to Baja Norte with bright rooms, ocean views, delightful breakfasts, and welcome margaritas the moment you step foot in the door. **Pros:** gracious hosts; rates include breakfast and calls to the U.S.; beachfront location. **Cons:** two-night minimum stay; no children under 16. ⑤ *Rooms from: $260* ✉ *299 Bahia, San Antonio Del Mar* ☎ *619/786–8000* ⊕ *www. casafarolito.com* ↩ *4 rooms, 1 studio* ⦿ *Breakfast.*

$$

HOTEL

🔲 **Rosarito Beach Hotel and Spa.** Charm and location have the slight edge over comfort at this landmark hotel built in 1925. **Pros:** close to the beach; antique charm; good Sunday brunch. **Cons:** older furnishings; overpriced; slow elevator. ⑤ *Rooms from: $190* ✉ *Blvd. Benito Juárez 1207, south end of town* ☎ *661/612–0144, 800/343–8582* ⊕ *www. rosaritobeachhotel.com* ↩ *495 rooms* ⦿ *No meals.*

NIGHTLIFE

Papas and Beer. Papas and Beer, one of the most popular bars in Baja Norte, draws a young, energetic spring-break crowd for drinking and dancing on the beach and small stages. The $3 beers and mechanical bull make for an entertaining combination. ✉ *On beach off Blvd. Benito Juárez, near Rosarito Beach Hotel* ☎ *661/612–0444* ⊕ *www. rosarito.papasandbeer.com.*

SPORTS AND THE OUTDOORS

Rosarito Ocean Sports. The ocean sports center in the heart of Rosarito rents kayaks, mountain bikes, snorkeling gear, Jet Skis, and scuba-diving equipment. ✉ *Blvd. Benito Juarez, 890-7, Playas de Rosarito* ☎ *661/100–2196* ⊕ *www.rosaritooceansports.com* ⧠ *Guided kayak from $35; diving trips from $160.*

PUERTO NUEVO

19 km (12 miles) south of Rosarito.

Southern Californians regularly cross the border to indulge in the classic Puerto Nuevo meal: lobster fried in hot oil and served with refried beans, rice, homemade tortillas, salsa, and lime. At least 20 restaurants are packed into this village; nearly all offer the same menu, but the quality varies drastically; some establishments cook up live lobsters, while others swap in frozen critters. In most places prices are based on size; a medium lobster with all the fixings will cost you about $15.

Though the fried version is the Puerto Nuevo classic, some restaurants also offer steamed or grilled lobsters—why not try one of each and pass

BAJA HISTORY

It's believed the first humans arrived in Baja some 11,000 years ago, having followed the Pacific coast down from present-day Alaska. The Yumano (northern Baja), Cochimí (central Baja), and Guaycura (southern Baja) were hunter-gatherers who slept in caves and waged frequent wars among one another. In stark contrast to the well-organized Aztec and Mayan communities of mainland Mexico, Baja's Amerindians lived this way until the arrival of the Spanish.

Led by explorer Francisco de Ulloa, the Spanish came to the peninsula in 1539, believing they had landed on an island. Ulloa, who had been commissioned by Hernán Cortés to find proof of the infamous Northwest Passage, reconnoitered the entire eastern coast of the peninsula and drafted a number of early maps, laying the groundwork for further exploration in the following century.

By 1751, Jesuits had begun establishing the first Roman Catholic missions among the Amerindian tribes of Baja California, and over the next hundred years Spain used these religious outposts as a means of extending its stronghold on the territory.

But even after Mexico won its independence from Spain in 1821, Baja California remained an underdeveloped and largely uninhabitable desert. It was only with the completion of the Carretera Transpeninsular in 1973 that many towns began blossoming alongside the region's rattlesnakes and giant cardón cacti. Today, Baja California is not just a route of passage to Cabo San Lucas but a burgeoning vacation destination in its own right for fishermen, surfers, sunbathers, and culture fiends from all over the world.

'em around? Each October, to mark the start of the season (which ends in March), the town holds a wine-and-lobster festival.

The town itself is tired and dated, with waiters standing curbside begging tourists in passing cars to stop in for the day's catch. Still, it's the best spot along the coast to try fresh lobster at an unbeatable price. For lodging, you're better off renting a beach house in the neighboring community of Las Gaviotas or heading to a hotel north in Rosarito or south in Ensenada. Most accommodations in the town of Puerto Nuevo are in desperate need of a face-lift.

Artisans' markets and stands throughout the village sell serapes and T-shirts; the shops closest to the cliffs have the best selection.

GETTING HERE AND AROUND
Puerto Nuevo sits just beside Highway 1. When you pull off the highway and enter the town, find a parking spot (free unless otherwise marked) and hop out. There's no other transport to speak of (or needed) in this five-block hamlet.

WHERE TO EAT

$$$ ✕ **La Casa de la Langosta.** Seafood soup and grilled fish are options at the
SEAFOOD "House of Lobster," but clearly lobster is the star. It's served in omelets and burritos or steamed with a wine sauce. Most wooden tables in the

large, noisy dining room are covered with platters of fried or grilled lobster and all the standard accompaniments like rice, beans or tortillas. Start with the clam chowder or jumbo shrimp wrapped in bacon. The medium-size lobsters tend to be a bit more flavorful than the larger ones. There's an actual wine list here, and it has several Baja wines. ⑤ *Average main: $25* ⊠ *Avenida Renteria 3, Km 44* ☎ *661/614–1072* ⊕ *www.casadelalangosta.com.*

$$ ✕ **Rosamar.** This two-story establishment is well patronized by locals, SEAFOOD but not so much by tourists. Perhaps it's because of the bright, unromantic lighting, blaring TV, and well-stocked bar. But amble up to the open-air second floor, and you'll be treated to ocean views and fresh lobster and shrimp at some of the best prices in town. Plates come with all-you-can-eat beans, rice, and fresh chips and salsa. The handmade flour tortillas and drawn butter are just about as good as it gets. Wash down your meal with one of their margaritas. The live lobsters here are so fresh (they come in off the fishing boats each morning) that the restaurant sells its B-list lobsters to other places around town. ⑤ *Average main: $15* ⊠ *Calle Anzuelo and Barracuda, Km 44* ☎ *661/614–1210.*

WHERE TO STAY

$ 🏨 **Puerto Nuevo Baja Hotels and Villas.** If you're a lobster fanatic, consider RESORT spending a relaxing night just steps away from Puerto Nuevo after your enormous dinner and pitchers of margaritas. **Pros:** nice-size rooms; convenient location. **Cons:** rooms a little spartan; property needs renovation; photos on website not a fair representation; only decent hotel option in town. ⑤ *Rooms from: $125* ⊠ *Carretera Tijuana–Ensenada, Km 44.5, just past Puerto Nuevo in Ensenada direction* ☎ *661/614– 1488, 877/315–1002* ⊕ *www.grandbaja.com* ⌖ *60 villas, 40 suites* ⓘ❑ *No meals.*

VALLE DE GUADALUPE

80 km (50 miles) southeast of Rosarita.

The Valle de Guadalupe, northeast of Ensenada on Carretera 3, is filled with vineyards, wineries, and rambling hacienda-style estates. Although Mexican wines are still relatively unknown in the United States, the industry is exploding in Mexico, and the Valle de Guadalupe is responsible for some 90% of the country's production. In 2004, there were five wineries in production, and less than a decade later there are more than 100.

With a region that combines the right heat, soil, and a thin morning fog, some truly world-class boutique wineries have developed in the Valle de Guadalupe, most in the past decade. Many of these are open to the public; some require appointments. Several tour companies, including Bajarama (☎ *646/178–3252* ⊕ *www.bajarama.com*), leave from Ensenada on tours that include visits to wineries, a historical overview, transportation, and lunch. Better yet, visit the wineries yourself by car, as they all cluster in a relatively small area. Also worth a look is winemaker Hugo D'Acosta's school, which brings in some 30 young winemakers to use common facilities to make their own blends. The facilities are on the site of an old olive oil press (a few antique presses remain in the outlying buildings), and the grounds are augmented with artwork made from recycled wine bottles and other materials.

Several changes are in store, which may alter the isolation of the valley, and in five years the place may have a different, more upscale, feel. The newly constructed El Cielo winery has announced plans to build a 50-villa resort and spa on its property overlooking the vineyards. It seems that it's not only Mexican wine that's being discovered, but the potential of Guadalupe as a "wine destination," along with the mixed blessings that accompany such discovery. Still, many locals are fighting to keep it from becoming the next Napa Valley.

WHEN TO GO
The ideal time to visit Valle de Guadalupe's wine country is in August during the Harvest Festival (Las Fiestas de la Vendimia). This 21-day celebration brings in thousands of wine lovers who commemorate the harvest with wine tastings, cultural blessings, live music, and elaborate feasts. Be sure to make hotel reservations well in advance.

GETTING HERE AND AROUND
If you're not on a tour, a private car (or hired taxi) is essential for touring the wine country. West of the town of Francisco Zarco (also called Guadalupe), the road is paved past Monte Xanic and the small village of Porvenir; after that, it is mainly gravel. The turnoffs for the major wineries are well marked; if you're looking for a smaller destination, you may end up doing a few loops or asking a friendly bystander. The general area is not too spread out; still, you will need to drive from one winery to the other. Watch out for hidden stop signs at nearly every street crossing. You can arrange a half- or full-day tour with many of the taxi drivers in Ensenada, and some drivers in Tecate may also be willing to take you.

ESSENTIALS
Banks are few and far between in this area, so get cash before arriving if you think you'll need it. Nearly every business accepts credit cards. There are two gas stations in town, one at the entrance to the valley near Ensenada, and the second where Highway 3 meets Highway 1.

EXPLORING

TOP ATTRACTIONS
Adobe Guadalupe. One of the most up-and-coming small wineries in Baja, Adobe Guadalupe is making an array of fascinating high-end blends named after angels. Don't miss the Kerubiel, which is a blockbuster blend; the Serafiel, Gabriel, and Miguel are also excellent. The owner's passion for wine has made the production consistently superior from year to year. Gaining notoriety is the Rosé Uriel and of course the powerful Mezcal, appropriately named Lucifer. Owner Tru also runs a bed-and-breakfast, and her beautiful horses are available for riding tours. Tastings are available daily from 11 to 4 and include four reds and one Rosé for $12 (free to hotel guests). Be sure to visit the

Continued on page 209

VIVA VINO

About an hour south of San Diego, just inland from Ensenada, lies a region that's everything Ensenada is not. The 14-mile-long Valle de Guadalupe is charming, serene, and urbane, and—you might find this hard to believe if you're a wine buff—is a robust producer of quality vino.

There's no watered-down tequila here. Red grapes grown include Cabernet Sauvignon, Merlot, Tempranillo, and Syrah, while whites include Chardonnay, Sauvignon Blanc, and Viognier. Drive down and spend a day at the vineyards and wineries that line la Ruta del Vino, the road that stretches across the valley, or better yet (and to avoid talking to border guards if passengers are slightly intoxicated on your way back into the States), base yourself here. The inns and restaurants in the Valle de Guadalupe welcome guests with refined material comforts, which complement the region's natural desert-mountain beauty and lovely libations.

(top) Adobe Guadalupe, (bottom left) Grapes from the Guadalupe Valley, Ensenada, (bottom right) Adobe Guadalupe

WINERY-HOPPING

Some wineries along la Ruta del Vino are sizeable enterprises, while others are boutique affairs Here are a few choice picks.

THE FULL-BODIED EXPERIENCE

Serious oenophiles should visit the midsize **Monte Xanic,** which, with a new tasting, is a serious contender for Mexico's finest winery. In August, tastings are by appointment; don't miss the Gran Ricardo, a high-end Bordeaux-style blend. **L. A. Cetto** is bigger than Monte Xanic, but it offers a well-orchestrated experience with tastings. Free tours are offered daily every half-hour from 10–5. Look for celebrity winemaker Camillo Magoni's wonderful Nebbiolo. A spectacular terrazza overlooks Cetto's own bullring and a sweeping expanse of wine country.

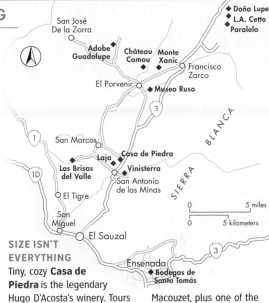

SIZE ISN'T EVERYTHING

Tiny, cozy **Casa de Piedra** is the legendary Hugo D'Acosta's winery. Tours and tastings of D'Acosta's high-end wines are by reservation only. Call ahead to visit the even smaller, but equally impressive, **Vinisterra**, where eccentric Swiss winemaker Christoph Gärtner turns out a small-production line of showstoppers called Macouzet, plus one of the only wines in the world made from mission grapes; these grapes come from vines descended from those planted by the Spanish in the 1500s for ceremonial services.

BACK TO THE BEGINNING

The imbibing of fermented fruit dates from the Stone Age (or Neolithic period; 8,500–4,000 BC), but the production of wine in the Americas is comparatively adolescent. Mexico actually has the New World's oldest wine industry, dating from 1574, when conquistadors and priests set off north from Zacatecas in search of gold; when none turned up, they decided to grow grapes instead. In 1597, they founded the Hacienda de San Lorenzo, the first winery in the Americas, in the modern-day state of Coahuila. By the late 1600s, Mexican wine production was so prolific, the Spaniards shut it down so it wouldn't compete with Spanish wine—sending Mexico's wine industry into a three-century hibernation from which it's just beginning to awaken. Now, most Mexican wine producers have moved to the Valle de Guadalupe (a cooler, more favorable climate for vineyards).

L.A. Cetto sparkling wines, Valle de Guadalupe

HOW TO EXPERIENCE WINE COUNTRY

LIVE THE VALLEY If you fancy tranquility and a perfectly starry sky, and don't mind an early bedtime, you're best off staying at one of the intimate, romantic haciendas in the middle of the valley itself, where you'll also benefit from your hosts' knowledge of the area. One of the most up-and-coming small wineries in Baja, **Adobe Guadalupe** is also a gracious bed-and-breakfast run by Tru Miller. A delightful and committed host—Tru might take you to neighboring wineries on horseback. **La Villa del Valle**, a newer American-run hotel-hacienda, is larger but just as nice, with spectacular countryside views and amenities like massage, a hot tub, and a restaurant with its own market garden. Be sure to visit its cellar at neighboring Vena Cava Winery, made entirely of recycled boats.

DO IT BY DAY If you can't live without city buzz and nightlife, Ensenada has tons of it, and staying there is another viable option. In downtown Ensenada you can also visit **Bodegas de Santo Tomás**, one of Baja's oldest wineries. The city is less than an hour's drive to most of the wineries. It's also possible to visit the valley on a long day trip from Tijuana or San Diego.

WINOS UNITE You can expect clear, sunny days in the valley for virtually the whole year, although evening temperatures dip into the 40s F (single digits Celsius) from December through March. A good time to visit is during the first two weeks of August, when the region comes alive for the **Fiestas de la Vendimia** (646/178–3136, www.fiestasdelavendimia.com), a harvest festival that's full of special wine tastings, dinners, and parties—both at the wineries and in Ensenada proper.

(pictured top and bottom) Adobe Guadalupe

wine store and tapas food truck on your way out. ✉ *Off Carretera Tecate–Ensenada, turn at sign and drive 6 km (4 miles), Guadalupe* ☎ *646/155–2094, 949/733–2744 in U.S.* ⊕ *www.adobeguadalupe.com.*

Fodor's Choice
★
Baron Balché. Having won more than 270 awards for its blends, this winery is considered the Rolls-Royce of Valle de Guadalupe's wineries. Logos on the premium line are based on Mayan numbers, with outstanding selections like the Balché UNO, a Grenache with hints of raspberry and caramel. The Balché CERO, 100% Nebbiolo is the king of their wines, having aged four years in the barrel. Even their younger wines are exceptional, but expect to pay a hefty price to try them. Tastings for top selections will cost you about $50, but considering you are sampling $250 bottles of wine, it just might be worth it. Be sure to end your wine tour here, otherwise the rest of your tastings might pale in comparison. ✉ *Ej. El Porvenir, Valle de Guadalupe* ☎ *646/155–2141* ⊕ *www.baronbalche.com.*

El Cielo. Considered the new giant among the region's vineyards, this winery currently produces 4,000 cases of wine but is slated to reach 20,000 by 2018. Making up the property is Latitude 32 restaurant and a soon to be resort with luxury villas. For now, most stop by to sample the fine blends named after constellations in honor of the owner's love for astronomy. Behind the barrel is winemaker Jesus Rivera, responsible for much of the success of neighboring wineries where he previously consulted. For an elegant Chardonnay, try Capricornius, or for an Italian grape blend of Nebbiolo and Sangiovese, the Perseus aged 24 months in French oak barrels is also wonderful. The Copernicus is one of their most popular reds. Tastings and tours are available daily for $6. ✉ *Parcela 118, Km 7.5, Valle de Guadalupe* ☎ *646/155–2220* ⊕ *www.vinoselcielo.com.*

Fodor's Choice
★
La Lomita. Owned by Fernando Pérez Castro, this new generation winery creates rich wines made with 100% local grapes. As one of the smaller wineries, their blends are sold to top restaurants and hotels in Mexico City, Rivera Maya, and Cabo. The preferred Sacro—a mix of Cabernet Sauvignon and Merlot—has hints of pomegranate, cherry, pepper, berries, and maple syrup, while the Tinto de la Hacienda has characteristics of compote and jam. The tasting room is one of the nicest in the region with wood crate ceilings with dangling vintage bulbs and a chalkboard wall sharing tales of the grapes. Tastings are Wednesday to Sunday from 11 to 4 and until 6 on the weekends. The cost is $10 and includes four wines, snacks, and a tour of the winery. ✉ *Plot 13, San Marcos Village, San Antonio de las Minas* ☎ *646/156–8459* ⊕ *www.haciendalalomita.com.mx.*

WORTH NOTING

Casa de Piedra. The brainchild of Hugo D'Acosta, Casa de Piedra is part of an impressive portfolio that includes Paralelo, Aborigen, and La Borde Vieille, known for its México and French blends. Try Casa de Piedra's flagship wine Contraste or their newer sparkling wines. The space is interesting and modern, designed by the winemaker's architect brother. This is the area's last winery to still offer free wine tastings. Visits are by reservation only. ✉ *Carretera Tecate–Ensenada, Km 93.5,*

9

San Antonio de las Minas ☎ 646/155–5267 ⊕ *www.vinoscasadepiedra. com* ⊘ *Closed Sun.*

L.A. Cetto. L.A. Cetto is another giant, but this is the closest thing to a California wine country experience south of the border. When tasting or buying, avoid the more affordable wines, and go straight for the premiums. They make a lovely Nebbiolo and Chardonnay, and their Don Luis Concordia is nicely balanced. Three levels of tastings (Traditional, Private Reserve, Premium) increase by $5 per level, making the Premium a good deal considering tastings are offered in a private VIP room away from the crowds. Popular with tour groups, this is one of the busiest wineries in the area. Tours take place daily 10–5 on the half hour. ⊠ *Carretera Tecate–Ensenada, Km 73.5* ☎ 646/155–2179 ⊕ *www.cettowines.com.*

Liceaga. Neighboring Casa de Piedra, this winery produces a variety of Merlot- and Cabernet-heavy blends, as well as a line of grappa. Try Liceaga's "L", a complex and elegant wine with hints of cherry, blackberry, cassis, plum and pepper. The tasting room is open most days from 11 to 5, and they have live music every Saturday. ⊠ *Carretera Tecate–Ensenada, Km 93, San Antonio de las Minas* ☎ 646/178–2922 ⊕ *www.vinosliceaga.com.*

Mogor Badan. One of the area's only vineyards to offer organic wines, this 1950's ranch has gained notoriety for whites such as their remarkably fragrant Chasselas de Mogar. Their newer Pirineo blends a contemporary Mexican Grenache with a French Syrah. Wine tastings are available daily from 11 to 5 in their underground cave. Owner Natalia Badan hosts the local Farmer's Market on Wednesday and Saturday from 11 to 1, making this *the* place to buy fresh eggs, honey, jams, breads, and salsas. If you're fortunate enough to visit between July and October, you can dine at their garden restaurant, operated by the talented Chef Drew Deckman. ⊠ *Rancho El Mogor, Federal Highway # 3 Tecate-Ensenada; Km 85.5, San Antonio de las Minas* ☎ 646/156–8156 🍷3 tastings, $7 ⊘ *Daily 11–5.*

Monte Xanic. Tastings at Monte Xanic take place at the edge of a lovely pond and include four reds and four whites for $10. Most impressive is their consistency, right down to the cheapest table wines. During the month of August, tastings and tours are available by appointment only. Be sure to check out the impressively styled cellar. ⊠ *Carretera 3, Km 70* ☎ 646/117–0027 ⊕ *www.montexanic.com.mx.*

Paralelo. Paralelo was built by the Hugo d'Acosta clan as "parallel" to Casa de Piedra. The winery makes two red blends—the excellent and balanced Arenal and the heavier, minerally Colina—as well as a Sauvignon Blanc Emblema. A reservation is necessary (ask for Gloria in the office), and construction is underway for a formal tasting room. For now, tastings remain a casual and friendly affair, conducted around a big table. ⊠ *Carretera Tecate–Ensenada, Km 73.5, Valle de Guadalupe* ☎ 646/156–5268 ⊕ *www.paralelo.com.mx.*

Vena Cava. Even if you're not into wine, a visit to this unique winery is well worth a visit. Winemaker Phil Gregory blended his passion for sustainable practices and wine making into the architecture of this funky wine cave made from old fishing boats. Bursting with character, these 1930s vessels once sailed the waters off the coast of Ensenada. Today they serve as the domes that cap the wine cellar, housing Vena Cava's seven labels; most popular are the Tempranillo and the Cabernet Sauvignon. Wines here have a tendency to be spicy, fruity, floral, and well balanced. Tours and tastings are offered from 11 to 5 on the hour for $16. Stay awhile and enjoy a meal at the food truck out front, serving an urban take on the cuisine from the neighboring Corazon de Tierra. ✉ *Rancho San Marcos, Valle de Guadalupe* ☎ *646/156–8007* ⊕ *www. venacavawine.com.*

Vinisterra. Within Vinisterra, expect to find Tempranillo and Cabernet-Merlot blends that are big and juicy. Tastings are available Saturday and Sunday from 11 to 5, and Tuesday through Friday by reservation only. Four tastings will run you about $8. Call well ahead. ✉ *Carretera Tecate–Ensenada, Km 94.5, San Antonio de las Minas* ☎ *646/178– 3350, 646/155–3233* ⊕ *www.vinisterra.com.*

Wine Museum (*Museo de la Vid y el Vino*). For a better understanding of the wine-making process, the Museo de la Vid y el Vino in the heart of Valle de Guadalupe has exhibits on wine history, viticulture, and wine-inspired art. The museum showcases a vast collection of agricultural tools, more than 100 wines from the region, and a wine-tasting room where local blends are introduced on Saturday. Don't miss the spectacular panoramic view of the valley and the outdoor amphitheater surrounded by vineyards. ✉ *Carretera Tecate–Ensenada, Km 81.37, Valle de Guadalupe* ☎ *646/156–8165, 646/156–8166* ⊕ *www. museodelvinobc.com* ✉ *$4* ⊗ *Closed Mon.*

WHERE TO EAT

$$ × **Almazara Gastrobar.** This former olive oil refinery is reminiscent of a
MEXICAN FUSION Manhattan loft with its high ceilings, concrete floors, white brick walls, and chalkboard bar surrounding the open kitchen. It's here where Chef Alejandro Alvarez prepares a Mexican-Spanish fusion utilizing organic ingredients from his on-site garden. Having trained under Basque Chef Martín Berasategui, Alejandro gives a Spanish flair to his menu with hints of Manchego cheese and papas bravas. Start your experience with the refreshing roasted beet salad with watermelon *salmorejo* (tomato puree), followed by the Bluefin tuna tartare with mango and quinoa. If there's one place to try lamb in Valle de Guadalupe, it's here. Far from gamey, the sheep are given a diet of olive branches, making this New York cut beyond flavorful and tender. Try pairing it with their homemade brew, a rich imperial brown. The outdoor terrace overlooking the vineyard makes an idyllic backdrop to the savory dessert—wine-cooked pears bathed in a Belgian chocolate green tea soup. ⑤ *Average main: $18* ✉ *Carretera 3, Km 84.5, at Rancho Olivares, San Antonio de las Minas* ☎ *646/156–8048* ⊕ *www.almazaragastrobar.com* ⊗ *Closed Mon.–Wed.*

$$$$ × **Corazon de Tierra.** A glass box restaurant surrounded by rows of veg-
ECLECTIC etables and sunflowers that are plucked and brought to the chef—and hours later to your table—is the true essence of "Heart of Earth."

Adding to the rustic charm are beamed ceilings and floors recycled from an old pier, refurbished hand-stitched chairs, and burlap curtains that blow in the wind. The menu changes daily based on the harvest, but it always features six courses that are local, organic, and fresh. You might find microgreens with a dollop of whipped beet or the daily catch topped with broccoli sprigs and pumpkin puree. Meat dishes usually come with a flavorful "mother sauce," the chef's unique take on a beef reduction. Unlike typical desserts, those served here leave you perfectly satisfied (rather than stuffed) like the fennel leaf sorbet or the parsley coconut cake with sweet New Zealand spinach and just a tablespoon of chocolate ice cream. Don't be surprised when your six-course meal turns into nine; the generous Chef Diego Hernandez has been known to lose track when sharing the "earth" with his guests. ⑤ *Average main: $68* ✉ *Toros Pintos s/n, Km 88.3, Rancho San Marcos, Valle de Guadalupe* ☎ *646/156–8030* ⊕ *www.corazondetierra.com* ⌑ *Reservations essential.*

$$$$ ✕ **Laja.** One sign that the Valle de Guadalupe has its sights on Napa
MEXICAN is this extraordinary restaurant set inside a cozy little house. Celebrity
Fodor's Choice chef Jair Téllez's ambitious prix-fixe menus (there are four-course and
★ seven-course versions) change frequently, but may include cucumber gazpacho, yellowtail tartare, and Swiss chard ravioli with ranch egg and beef juice, all served with excellent regional wines. After the main entrée, cleanse your palate with refreshing orange-carrot-mint sorbet and then sink your teeth into one of their savory desserts like mandarin ice cream with white chocolate and pineapple coulis. Don't be surprised if a bonus course suddenly appears at some point throughout your meal. If you aren't satisfied with the portions, simply ask for more at no extra charge. Polished woods and windows overlooking the valley make the dining room and outdoor plaza as sleek as the menu. A meal here is well worth the drive. ⑤ *Average main: $120* ✉ *Carretera 3, Km 83* ☎ *646/155–2556* ⊕ *www.lajamexico.com* ⌑ *Reservations essential* ⊘ *Closed Sun.–Tues. and late Nov.–early Jan. No dinner Wed. Last orders taken at 8:30 pm Thurs.–Sat.*

$$ ✕ **Latitud 32.** Named for its location on the map, this restaurant at El
STEAKHOUSE Cielo Vineyards specializes in Baja cuisine and grilled cuts like flavorful skirt steak with rosemary potatoes and a chipotle sauce. For an ideal introduction to the meal, try the scallop carpaccio with sea asparagus and avocado cream. South African Chef Ryan Steyn brings his grandmother's recipe to the table with the apricot bread pudding that has been soaked in milk, honey, sugar, and nutmeg. If you come by for Sunday brunch, you'll likely see a hot air balloon or helicopter landing on the lawn just in front of your table. This is one of the most prestigious forms of arrival for weekend wine tasters coming from San Diego. ⑤ *Average main: $20* ✉ *Parcela 118, Km 7.5, at El Cielo, Valle de Guadalupe* ☎ *646/155–2220* ⊕ *www.vinoselcielo.com.*

$$ ✕ **Malva.** With sprawling views of vineyards, this restaurant is sur-
ECLECTIC rounded by acres of farmland where Chef Roberto Alcocer gathers
Fodor's Choice ingredients for nearly 100% of what is served, making this the most sus-
★ tainable restaurant in the region and a true "table to farm" experience. Beer, wine, vegetables, fruit, cheese, bread, meat, eggs, honey—nearly

everything he serves is from the on-site farm. Setting the scene are wooden tables adorned with rosemary-filled mason jars and paper menus showcasing the daily harvest. Each plate is a work of art, including the tender lamb with a black bean crust and broth that is poured at your table. Fresh fish is adorned with edible flowers, like the catch of the day with tomato rosemary salsa on a bed of beets with a tangy lemon sauce. Tastings are available in four, seven, and 10 courses, and prices are very reasonable considering the quality of the food. The homemade horchata ice cream and the crème brûlée are not overly sweet, allowing you to taste the flavors rather than just the sugar. $ *Average main: $18* ✉ *Carretera Ensenada–Tecate, Km 96, at Mina Penelope Vinicola, San Antonio de las Minas* ☎ *646/155–3085* ⊕ *www.minapenelope.com* ⊗ *Closed Mon. and Tues.*

WHERE TO STAY

$$

B&B/INN

Fodor's Choice

★

🛏 **Adobe Guadalupe.** Brick archways, white-stucco walls, and fountains set a tone of endless pleasure and relaxation at Tru Miller's magnificent country inn surrounded by vineyards. **Pros:** lovely setting; engaging owner; rates include wine tasting and breakfast. **Cons:** weekends usually booked six months in advance; chilly pool; no children under 12. $ *Rooms from: $194* ✉ *Off Carretera 3 through Guadalupe village, 6 km (4 miles) along same road, right turn at town of Porvenir, Valle de Guadalupe* ☎ *646/155–2094, 949/733–2744 in U.S.* ⊕ *www.adobeguadalupe.com* ↝ *6 rooms* ❑*Breakfast.*

$$$$

HOTEL

🛏 **Encuentro Guadalupe** (*Endemico*). With freestanding steel box-cabins perched on a boulder-strewn hill, this property has architect Jorge Gracia to thank for its success. **Pros:** pet-friendly; unique design; rate includes Continental breakfast and welcome cocktail; 50% discounts available in November. **Cons:** no kids under 13; must sign liability waivers at check-in; room rates don't match quality of service. $ *Rooms from: $420* ✉ *Carretera Tecate–Ensenada, Km 75, San Antonio de las Minas* ☎ *646/155–2775* ⊕ *www.encuentroguadalupe.com* ↝ *20 rooms, 2 suites* ❑*Breakfast.*

$$

B&B/INN

🛏 **La Villa del Valle.** Perched on a hilltop overlooking the valley, this luxury inn is part of a country retreat comprised of Vena Cava winery and the restaurant, Corazon de Tierra. **Pros:** attention to detail; charming; excellent breakfasts. **Cons:** no kids under 13; guests are not given keys to lock rooms. $ *Rooms from: $245* ✉ *Off Carretera 3, Km 88, between San Antonio de las Minas and Francisco Zarco, exit at Rancho Sicomoro and follow signs, Valle de Guadalupe* ☎ *646/156–8007, 818/207–7130 in U.S.* ⊕ *www.lavilladelvalle.com* ↝ *6 rooms* ❑*Breakfast.*

SHOPS AND SPAS

La Casa de Doña Lupe. Near L.A. Cetto, Dona Lupe's boutique sells berry jams, chili marmalades, olive spreads, cheeses, wines, and other local delicacies. ✉ *Off Carretera 3, turn left and follow road past L.A. Cetto to small yellow building), San Antonio de las Minas* ☎ *646/155–2323* ⊕ *www.lacasadonalupe.com.*

9

Viniphera Spa. The creative makers of Quinta Monasterio winery combine wine and pampering with wine tastings following spa treatments incorporating grapes, lavender, citrus, and olive oil directly from their vineyard. Housed in an innovative two-story container, the small spa accommodates one to two guests and includes massages, facials, exfoliations, manicures, pedicures, and aromatherapy in the sauna created from old wine barrels. Some spa packages include lunch; appointments are by reservation only. ⊠ *Quinta Monasterio, Hwy. 3 to el Ejido Porvenir, turn right and follow signs, San Antonio de las Minas* ☎ *646/156–8055* ⊕ *www.viniphera.com.*

ENSENADA

65 km (40 miles) south of Puerto Nuevo.

In 1542 Juan Rodríguez Cabrillo first discovered the seaport that Sebastián Vizcaíno named Ensenada-Bahía de Todos Santos (All Saints' Bay) in 1602. Since then the town has drawn a steady stream of explorers and developers. After playing home to ranchers and gold miners, the harbor gradually grew into a major port for shipping agricultural goods, and today Baja's third-largest city (population 369,000) is one of Mexico's largest sea and fishing ports.

There are no beaches in Ensenada proper, but sandy stretches north and south of town are satisfactory for swimming, sunning, surfing, and camping. Estero Beach is long and clean, with mild waves; the Estero Beach Resort takes up much of the oceanfront, but the beach is public. Although not safe for swimming, the beaches at several of the restaurants along Highway 1 are a nice place to enjoy a cocktail with a view. Surfers populate the strands off Highway 1 north and south of Ensenada, particularly San Miguel, Tres Marías, and Salsipuedes, while scuba divers prefer Punta Banda, by La Bufadora. Lifeguards are rare, so be cautious. The tourist office in Ensenada has a map that shows safe diving and surfing beaches.

Both the waterfront and the main downtown street are pleasant places to stroll. If you're driving, be sure to take the Centro exit from the highway, since it bypasses the commercial port area.

GETTING HERE AND AROUND

If you're flying into Tijuana, from Aeropuerto Alberado Rodriguez (TIJ) you can find buses that also serve Rosarito and Ensenada. Or you can hop on a bus at Tijuana Camionera de la Línea station, just inside the border, with service to Rosarito and Ensenada along with city buses to downtown. To head south from Tijuana by car, follow the signs for Ensenada Cuota, the toll road (i.e., Carretera Transpeninsular or Highway 1) along the coast. Tollbooths accept U.S. and Mexican currency; there are three tolls of about $2.50 each between Tijuana and Ensenada. Restrooms are available near toll stations. Ensenada is an hour south of Tijuana on this road. The alternative free road—Carretera 1D or Ensenada Libre—is curvy and not as well maintained. (Entry to it is on a side street in a congested area of downtown Tijuana.)

Highway 1 continues south of Ensenada to Guerrero Negro, at the border between Baja California and Baja Sur, and on to Baja's southernmost resorts; there are no tolls past Ensenada. Highway 1 is fairly well maintained and signposted.

Although there are several rental car companies in Tijuana, Alamo is one of the few that includes insurance and tax in the quoted rate, rather than tacking on hidden fees at arrival. Rates start at $60 per day. In 2013, the Mexican government passed a law stating that drivers must carry mandatory Third Party Liability, an expense that is not covered by U.S. insurance policies or by credit card companies.

If driving your own vehicle across the San Ysidro border, ask your hotel if they offer a Fast Pass, which helps eliminate the long border wait on the return. Otherwise expect to wait two to three hours on an average weekend.

Taxis are a reliable means of getting around Ensenada, and you can flag them down on the street.

Taxi Alamo ✉ *Blvd Sanchez Taboada, Zona Río, Tijuana* ☎ *664/686–4040* ⊕ *www.alamomexico.com.mx.*

Visitor and Tour Info Ensenada Tourist Information Office ✉ *Blvd. Sertuche 152, Valle Dorado, Ensenada* ☎ *800/025–3991 toll-free in Mexico, 800/310–9687* ⊕ *www.enjoyensenada.com.*

EXPLORING

TOP ATTRACTIONS

Fodor's Choice
★
La Cava de Marcelo. For many a visit to Baja Norte must include an afternoon drive to the cheese caves of Marcelo, in Ojos Negros 45 minutes outside of Ensenada. With Swiss-Italian roots, Owner Marcelo Castro Chacon is now the fourth generation to carry on the *queso* tradition since it first began in 1911. A visit to the farm includes a tour of the milking facilities and a tasting of seven cheeses and their signature Ramonetti red wine. Milder selections seasoned with basil, black pepper, and rosemary are more popular with locals than their sharper cheeses, aged up to 2½ years, loved by foreigners. As Mexico's only cheese cave (and the first in Latin America), this beloved factory produces 450 pounds of cheese per day. Milking takes place at 5 pm daily and the small on-site shop sells the remarkable marmalade and wine that accompany your cheese tasting. Those with time and an appetite can dine under the shade of a peppertree for a lunch menu integrating Marcelo's cheeses and organic fruits and vegetables from his farm. The cactus salad and portobello mushrooms with melted cheese make the ideal starters to the regional trout served with roasted garlic. The fig mousse alone is worth a visit. ✉ *Rancho La Campana, 48 km (30 miles) east of Ensenada, off Hwy. 3, follow signs to La Cruz de Quarez, Ojos Negros* ☎ *646/175–7073* 🛒 *$10 tour and tasting* ☉ *Thurs.–Sun. 1–6 pm.*

Mercado de Mariscos. At the northernmost point of Boulevard Costero, the main street along the waterfront, is an indoor-outdoor fish market where row after row of counters display piles of shrimp, tuna, dorado, and other fish caught off Baja's coasts. Outside, stands sell grilled or smoked fish, seafood cocktails, and fish tacos. You can pick up a few souvenirs, eat well for very little money, and take some great photographs. Fish taco stands line the dirt path to the fish market; around lunchtime, cooks will stand outside to vie for your attention (and your pesos). If your stomach is delicate, try the fish tacos at the cleaner, quieter Plaza de Mariscos in the shadow of the giant beige Plaza de Marina that blocks the view of the traditional fish market from the street.

WORTH NOTING

Las Bodegas de Santo Tomás. One of Baja's oldest wine producers gives tours and tastings at its downtown winery and bottling plant. Santo Tomás's best wines are the Alisio Chardonnay, the Cabernet, and the Tempranillo; avoid the overpriced Unico. The winery also operates the enormous wine shop, a brick building across the avenue. The Santo Tomás Vineyards can be found on the eastern side of Highway 1 about 50 km (31 miles) south of Ensenada, fairly near the ruins of the Misión Santo Tomás de Aquino, which was founded by Dominican priests in 1791: only a few pieces of adobe remain of the old church. ⊠ *Av. Miramar 666, Centro* ☎ *646/178–3333* ⊕ *www.santo-tomas.com* 🗐 *$19* ☽ *Tours, tastings daily 9–5 on the hour.*

Paseo Calle Primera (*Avenida López Mateos*). The renamed Avenida López Mateos is the center of Ensenada's traditional tourist zone. Highrise hotels, souvenir shops, restaurants, and bars line the avenue for eight blocks, from its beginning at the foot of the Chapultepec Hills to the dry channel of the Arroyo de Ensenada. The avenue also has cafés, American-style coffee shops, and most of the town's souvenir stores. ⊠ *Av. López Mateos.*

Riviera del Pacífico. Officially called the Centro Social, Cívico y Cultural de Ensenada, the Riviera is a rambling, white, hacienda-style mansion built in the 1920s. An enormous gambling palace, hotel, restaurant, and bar, the glamorous Riviera was frequented by wealthy U.S. citizens and Mexicans, particularly during Prohibition. You can tour some of the elegant ballrooms and halls, which occasionally host art shows and civic events. Many of the rooms are locked; check at the main office to see if someone is available to show you around. ⊠ *Blvd. Costero at Av. Riviera, Centro* ☎ *646/176–4310* ⊕ *www.rivieradeensenada.com.mx* 🗐 *Building and gardens free; museum entry $1* ☽ *Daily 8–7.*

WHERE TO EAT

$$$ ✗ **Belio.** Polished floors, stone pillars, and a staircase leading down to
MEXICAN FUSION an oceanfront terrace make this one of the best places in Ensenada to enjoy a meal with a view. Watch the crashing waves during a starter of grilled octopus with a spicy Asian sauce or a phyllo cone stuffed with ceviche. Presentations are impressive such as the baby quail in a nest of fried carrot, topped with apple caviar, or the dessert that looks like ham and eggs but is actually crepes and coconut custard with a mango filling. The lavender ice cream is a must. The menu changes every six months. Year-round favorites include the seared tuna medallions with a sesame crust. Even on cold nights, you can grab a table near the toasty

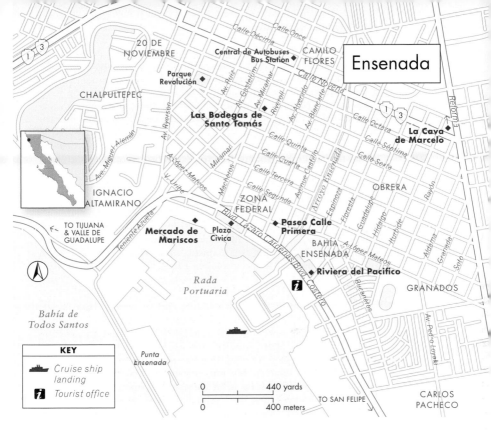

fire pits or head indoors to the more elegant dining room. There's a lavish buffet on Sunday starting at 8 am. $ *Average main: $25* ⊠ *Carretera Tijuana–Ensenada, Km 104, north of downtown Ensenada on Hwy. 1* ☎ *646/216–3912.*

$$ ✕ **El Rey Sol.** From its chateaubriand *bouquetière* (garnished with a bouquet of vegetables) to the savory chicken chipotle cooked with brandy, port wine, and cream, this French restaurant has been family-owned since 1947. It's considered one of the top restaurants in Mexico and has won the Five Diamond Award every year since 2004. Louis XIV–style furnishings and an attentive staff make it both comfortable and elegant. Impressive preparations of Caesar salad, crêpes Suzette, and café flambé create a show at your table. The sidewalk tables are a perfect place to dine and people-watch. The small café in the front sells pastries that are made on the premises. $ *Average main: $20* ⊠ *Av. López Mateos 1000, Centro* ☎ *646/178–1733* ⊕ *www.elreysol.com.*

FRENCH
Fodor's Choice
★

$ ✕ **El Charro.** Platters of chiles rellenos, enchiladas, tamales, and guacamole are served on El Charro's heavy wooden picnic tables below enormous piñatas dangling from the rafters. Plump chickens slowly turn over a wood fire by the front window, and the aroma of simmering beans fills the air here. A spiral staircase leads to a second floor of this hacienda-style restaurant, known as much for its margaritas as for its moles. Offering a hearty taste of traditional fare, the Mexican

MEXICAN

combo comes with enchiladas, tacos, tamales, rice and beans. If you still have room, try the soft caramel flan. $ *Average main: $10* ✉ *Av. López Mateos 454, Centro* ☎ *646/178–2144.*

$
SEAFOOD
Fodor'sChoice
★

× **La Guerrerense.** This food-cart stall off of Ensenada's bustling Calle Primera is *the* place where locals get a solid helping of the region's seafood. Established in 1960, La Guerrerense has been featured on international shows like Anthony Bourdain's *No Reservation.* Crowds line up at all hours and ogle a small army of cooks cracking open clams, shucking oysters, and piling the freshest fish onto tostadas and into oversize clam shells. After you choose from the day's catch—shrimp, uni, clams, lobster, octopus—stand back and wait while your dish is prepared. Once it's ready, make your way through the throng of hungry patrons, and dress your plate from the selection of bottled salsas and condiments on display, which are also for sale. Most-loved is the salsa made with toasted peanuts, oil, garlic, and fresh chilies. Owned by Sabina and Luis Eduardo Oviedo, the spot is a mainstay on the Ensenada food scene, and not to be missed. $ *Average main: $10* ✉ *Corner of Calle Primera and Alvarado* ☎ *646/206–0445* ⊕ *www.laguerrerense.com* ⊘ *Closed Tues. No dinner.*

$$
ECLECTIC

× **Manzanilla.** Two of the most exciting chef-owners in Baja Norte, Benito Molina and Solange Muris, have taken a truly modern approach to Mexican cuisine at Manzanilla, integrating the freshest catches from the local waters—oysters, mussels, and clams, for instance—and integrating ingredients like ginger, saffron, smoked tomato marmalade, and *huitlacoche* (corn fungus). The ahi with ginger strawberry vinaigrette melts in your mouth and the white clam with Gorgonzola is delicious. A local ranch sources their beef, grilled and served on a cutting board with warm tortillas. Next to the port, this hip joint is popular for its pleasant atmosphere and eclectic style of concrete floors, pink chandeliers, and an intricately carved wooden bar from the 1930s brought over from Los Angeles (notice the hand-carved lions blowing smoke). It's *the* place to be and a must-visit on any trip through Ensenada. The chefs have a smaller version of the restaurant next to Encuentro Hotel in Valle de Guadalupe, open weekends June through September. $ *Average main: $20* ✉ *Recinto Portuario, Teniente Azueta 139, Centro* ☎ *646/175–7073* ⊕ *www.rmanzanilla.com* ⊘ *Closed Mon. and Tues.*

$$
ECLECTIC

× **Ophelia.** For a bit of Asian flair along Carretera 1, check out Ophelia, opened by Rosendo Ramos. It's a favorite among the Ensenada foodie crowd. Shiitake mushrooms, pork, and ginger glazes make somewhat unexpected, but welcome, appearances for this seaside town. At the root of all that's good about Ophelia is a blending of European, American, and Asian cuisines and a handful of dependable flavors and ingredients: fresh fish, tomatoes, chilies, and cilantro. Top sellers include the seared bluefin tuna, the fried wontons, and the grilled pork chops with a balsamic glaze. Daily specials usually come with regional vegetables and rosemary potatoes. A good stop on the way home after a long day touring Valle del Guadalupe's wineries, this spot highlights many of the region's wines. $ *Average main: $16* ✉ *Carretera Tijuana–Ensenada, Km 103* ☎ *646/175–8365* ⊘ *Closed Mon.*

$$$ ✗ **Sano's.** This elegant restaurant, with its white linens and soft candle-
STEAKHOUSE light, is the best steak house in Baja California. Aged for 21 days, the
Fodor's Choice black Angus is juicy, flavorful, and tender, cooked beautifully rare (or
★ done) and can be served with spinach, lentils rigatoni, or potatoes au
gratin. Awaken your appetite with tuna ceviche bathed in olive oil or
mussels in white wine and butter sauce. For something from the earth,
try the spinach salad with green apple, fig, almonds, and local goat
cheese. They also serve pastas, grilled quail, and a lovely chicken in
a plum sauce. Service is impeccable and the wine list extensive. For
a less formal setting, grab a table on the outdoor patio. ⑤ *Average
main: $30* ✉ *Carretera Tijuana–Ensenada, Km 108, just after Playitas
Club del Mar, heading south to Ensenada* ☎ *646/174–4061* ⊕ *www.
sanosrestaurant.com.*

WHERE TO STAY

$$ ⛺ **Cabañas Cuatrocuatros.** Situated among vineyards is this peaceful set-
B&B/INN tlement of 14 luxury tents with creature comforts like air-conditioning,
a minibar, fireplace, king-size beds, and private sundecks. **Pros:** the
ultimate in Baja "glamping"; pet- and child-friendly; mountain bikes
for exploring; private beach. **Cons:** 15 minutes from town; restaurant
closes at 6 pm. ⑤ *Rooms from: $200* ✉ *Transpeninsular Hwy., Km 89*
☎ *646/174–6780* ⊕ *www.cabanascuatrocuatros.com.mx* ⟷ *14 Cabañas* ⑪ *No meals.*

$$ ⛺ **Estero Beach Resort.** Families love this long-standing resort on Ensena-
RESORT da's top beach, especially because of its private location and endless
FAMILY activities like horseback riding, tennis, volleyball, kayaking, and jet
skiing. **Pros:** wonderful breakfasts; right on the beach; good for fami-
lies. **Cons:** rooms by parking lot aren't great. ⑤ *Rooms from: $150*
✉ *Carretera Tijuana–Ensenada, intersection of Lazaro Cardenas and
Lupita Novelo, 10 km (6 miles) south of Ensenada, Estero Beach*
☎ *646/176–6235, 646/176–6225* ⊕ *www.hotelesterobeach.com* ⟷ *94
rooms, 2 suites* ⑪ *No meals.*

$$ ⛺ **Hotel Coral & Marina.** As the most upscale accommodations in
RESORT Ensenada, this all-suites resort has indoor-outdoor pools, a spa, ten-
nis courts, a water-sports center, and a marina with slips for 350
boats. **Pros:** midweek discounts; spacious rooms; outstanding Sunday
brunch; guests receive Fast Pass for border crossing. **Cons:** pool can get
noisy with kids; patchy Wi-Fi; slow elevator; often full on weekends.
⑤ *Rooms from: $150* ✉ *Carretera Tijuana–Ensenada, Km 103, Zona
Playitas* ☎ *646/175–0000, 800/862–9020 from U.S.* ⊕ *www.hotelcoral.
com* ⟷ *147 suites* ⑪ *No meals.*

$$ ⛺ **Las Rosas Hotel & Spa.** This intimate hotel north of Ensenada has
RESORT rooms facing the ocean and pool, and some even have fireplaces and
hot tubs. **Pros:** laid-back and relaxing; great ocean views. **Cons:** dated
rooms; rocky beach; some street noise; Wi-Fi in common areas only.
⑤ *Rooms from: $190* ✉ *Carretera Tijuana–Ensenada, Km 105.5, just
north of Ensenada, Zona Playitas* ☎ *646/174–4310, 646/174–4360*
⊕ *www.lasrosas.com* ⟷ *48 rooms* ⑪ *No meals.*

$$ ⛺ **Punta Morro Resort.** In one of Ensenada's most beautiful settings, this
RESORT 24-room hotel has charm and tranquillity to spare. **Pros:** great views;

9

excellent restaurant; Fast Pass for border. **Cons:** no bathtubs; uncomfortable couches in rooms; rocky beach not suitable for swimming. ⑤ *Rooms from: $198* ✉ *Carretera Tijuana–Ensenada, Km 106, Zona Playitas* ☎ *646/178–3507* ⊕ *www.hotelpuntamorro.com* ⇱ *24 rooms* ⦿ *No meals.*

NIGHTLIFE

Hussong's Cantina. Hussong's Cantina has been an Ensenada landmark since 1892, and has changed little since then. Ask anyone here and they'll tell you that this is where the margarita was invented by bartender Don Carlos Orozco in October 1941; however, this is just one of several local establishments that state that claim to fame. Regardless, come by Saturday when you can get two margaritas for the price of one, or 2-for-1 beers every Tuesday and Thursday. A security guard stands by the front door to handle the often-rowdy crowd—mostly local men. The floor is covered with sawdust, and the noise is usually deafening, pierced by mariachi and ranchera musicians and the whoops and hollers of the pie-eyed. There's live music Tuesday through Sunday. ✉ *Av. Ruíz 113, Centro* ☎ *646/178–3210* ⊕ *www.cantinahussongs.com* ⊗ *Closed Mon.*

Papas and Beer. The massive Papas and Beer attracts a rowdy college crowd. There are daily specials on shots and cocktails, as well as beach parties and regular drinking contests. Live music takes place on weekends. Consider yourself warned. ✉ *Av. Ruíz 102, Centro* ☎ *646/178– 8826* ⊕ *www.papasandbeer.com.*

Fodor'sChoice ★   Wendlandt Cerveceria. For a casual, yet more refined bar scene, this chic bar is a favorite of Ensenada's many vintners, chefs, and brewers. Showcasing the local craft beers in the region, as well as wines from nearby Valle del Guadalupe, the friendly owners also brew their own cervezas on-site. Beer tastings in their brewery are available by reservation only. If you're hungry, Wendlandt serves elevated bar food using local ingredients. The nondescript bar is simply marked by their logo and an antique door. ✉ *Blvd. Costero 248-1, Centro* ☎ *646/178–2938* ⊕ *www.wendlandt.com.mx* ⊗ *Tues.–Thurs. 6–12; Fri. and Sat. 2–12.*

SHOPPING

Most of the tourist shops hold court along Avenida López Mateos beside the hotels and restaurants. There are several two-story shopping arcades, some with empty spaces for rent. Dozens of curio shops line the street, all selling similar selections of pottery, serapes, and the tackier trinkets and T-shirts.

Bazaar Casa Ramirez. Bazar Casa Ramirez sells high-quality Talavera pottery and other ceramics, wrought-iron pieces, jewelry, wooden carvings, and papier-mâché figurines. Everything here is made in Mexico. Be sure to check out the displays upstairs. ✉ *Av. López Mateos 498, Centro* ☎ *646/178–8209.*

Centro Artesanal de Ensenada. The Centro Artesanal de Ensenada has a smattering of galleries and shops, and it's a good place to buy quality souvenirs. ✉ *Blvd. Costero 1094–39, Centro.*

Tourism helps to keep the local economy afloat in Ensenada.

Fausto Polanco. A former hotel from 1948, this furniture store features lovely handcrafted wood pieces and other home accessories. Meander the historical landmark where works of art are displayed throughout each room, reminiscent of an old Mexican hacienda. ⊠ *Av. López Mateos 1100, at the corner of Castillo, Centro* ☎ 646/174–0336 ⊕ *www.faustopolanco.com.mx.*

Los Castillo. Operated by the renowned Sanchez-Macfarland family for nearly four decades, this jewelry store has the highest quality and most unique silver pieces from famous designers from the Taxco region. ⊠ *Lopez Mateos 1084, Centro* ☎ 646/156–5274 ⊕ *www. loscastillosilver.com.*

Los Globos. Los Globos is a daily open-air swap meet. Vendors and shoppers are most abundant on weekends. ⊠ *Calle 9, 3 blocks east of Av. Reforma, Centro.*

SPORTS AND THE OUTDOORS

SPORTFISHING

The best angling takes place from April through October, with bottom fishing the best in winter. Charter vessels and party boats are available from several outfitters along Avenida López Mateos and Boulevard Costero and off the sportfishing pier. Mexican fishing licenses for the day or year are available at the tourist office or from charter companies.

Sergio's Sportfishing. One of the best sportfishing companies in Ensenada, Sergio's Sportfishing has year-round private charter or open party boats. Whale-watching tours are available from December 15 to April 15.

✉ *Sportfishing Pier, Blvd. Lázaro Cárdenas #6, Centro* ☎ *646/178–2185, 619/399–7224 in U.S.* ⊕ *www.sergiosfishing.com* ✉ *Fishing $70 per person on a group boat, including the cost of a license; whale watching $30 per person.*

WATER SPORTS

Estero Beach and Punta Banda (en route to La Bufadora, south of Ensenada) are both good kayaking areas, although facilities are limited. A small selection of water-sports equipment is available at the Estero Beach Resort.

WHALE-WATCHING

Boats leave the Ensenada sportfishing pier for whale-watching trips from December through March. The gray whales migrating from the north to bays and lagoons in southern Baja pass through Todos Santos Bay, often close to shore. Binoculars and cameras with telephoto capabilities come in handy. The trips last about three hours. Vessels are available from several outfitters at the sportfishing pier. Expect to pay about $30 for a three-hour tour.

DETOUR TO LA BUFADORA

La Bufadora. Legend has it that La Bufadora, an impressive tidal blowhole (*la bufadora* means the buffalo snort) in the coastal cliffs at Punta Banda, was created by a whale or sea serpent trapped in an undersea cave; both these stories, and the less romantic scientific facts, are posted on a roadside plaque.

The road to La Bufadora along Punta Banda—an isolated, mountainous point that juts into the sea—is lined with olive, craft, and tamale stands; the drive gives you a sampling of Baja's wilderness. If you're in need of some cooling off, turn off the highway at the sign for La Jolla Beach Camp. The camp charges a small admission fee for day use of the beach-side facilities, but it's a great place to do a few "laps" of lazy freestyle or breaststroke at La Jolla Beach. At La Bufadora, expect a small fee to park, and then a half-mile walk past T-shirt hawkers and souvenir stands to the water hole itself. A public bus runs from the downtown Ensenada station to Maneadero, from which you can catch a minibus labeled "Punta Banda" that goes to La Bufadora. ✉ *Carretera 23, 31 km [19 miles] south of Ensenada, Punta Banda.*

UNDERSTANDING
LOS CABOS

VOCABULARY

SPANISH VOCABULARY

ENGLISH	SPANISH	PRONUNCIATION

BASICS

ENGLISH	SPANISH	PRONUNCIATION
Yes/no	Sí/no	see/no
Please	Por favor	pore fah-**vore**
May I?	¿Me permite?	may pair-**mee**-tay
Thank you (very much)	(Muchas) gracias	(**moo**-chas) **grah**-see-as
You're welcome	De nada	day **nah**-dah
Excuse me	Con permiso	con pair-**mee**-so
Pardon me	¿Perdón?	pair-**dohn**
Could you tell me?	¿Podría decirme?	po-dree-ah deh-**seer**-meh
I'm sorry	Lo siento	lo see-**en**-toh
Good morning!	¡Buenos días!	**bway**-nohs **dee**-ahs
Good afternoon!	¡Buenas tardes!	**bway**-nahs **tar**-dess
Good evening!	¡Buenas noches!	**bway**-nahs **no**-chess
Good-bye!	¡Adiós!/¡Hasta luego!	ah-dee-**ohss/ah** -stah **lwe**-go
Mr./Mrs.	Señor/Señora	sen-**yor**/sen-**yohr**-ah
Miss	Señorita	sen-yo-**ree**-tah
Pleased to meet you	Mucho gusto	**moo**-cho **goose**-toh
How are you?	¿Cómo está usted?	**ko**-mo es-**tah** oo-**sted**
Very well, thank you.	Muy bien, gracias.	**moo**-ee bee-**en**, **grah**-see-as
And you?	¿Y usted?	ee oos-**ted**
Hello (on the telephone)	Diga	**dee**-gah

NUMBERS

ENGLISH	SPANISH	PRONUNCIATION
1	un, uno	oon, **oo**-no
2	dos	dos
3	tres	tress
4	cuatro	**kwah**-tro
5	cinco	**sink**-oh

ENGLISH	SPANISH	PRONUNCIATION
6	seis	saice
7	siete	see-**et**-eh
8	ocho	**o**-cho
9	nueve	new-**eh**-vey
10	diez	dee-**es**
11	once	**ohn**-seh
12	doce	**doh**-seh
13	trece	**treh**-seh
14	catorce	ka-**tohr**-seh
15	quince	**keen**-seh
16	dieciséis	dee-**es**-ee-**saice**
17	diecisiete	dee-**es**-ee-see-**et**-eh
18	dieciocho	dee-**es**-ee-**o**-cho
19	diecinueve	d**ee**-**es** ee ncw-**ev**-eh
20	veinte	**vain**-teh
21	veinte y uno/veintiuno	**vain**-te-**oo**-noh
30	treinta	**train**-tah
32	treinta y dos	train-tay-**dohs**
40	cuarenta	kwah-**ren**-tah
43	cuarenta y tres	kwah-**ren**-tay-**tress**
50	cincuenta	seen-**kwen**-tah
54	cincuenta y cuatro	seen-**kwen**-tay **kwah**-tro
60	sesenta	sess-**en**-tah
65	sesenta y cinco	sess-**en**-tay **seen**-ko
70	setenta	set-**en**-tah
76	setenta y seis	set-**en**-tay **saice**
80	ochenta	oh-**chen**-tah
87	ochenta y siete	oh-**chen**-tay see-**yet**-eh
90	noventa	no-**ven**-tah
98	noventa y ocho	no-**ven**-tah-**o**-choh

ENGLISH	SPANISH	PRONUNCIATION
100	cien	see-**en**
101	ciento uno	see-**en**-toh **oo**-noh
200	doscientos	doh-see-**en**-tohss
500	quinientos	keen-**yen**-tohss
700	setecientos	set-eh-see-**en**-tohss
900	novecientos	no-veh-see-**en**-tohss
1,000	mil	meel
2,000	dos mil	dohs meel
1,000,000	un millón	oon meel-**yohn**

COLORS

black	negro	**neh**-groh
blue	azul	ah-**sool**
brown	café	kah-**feh**
green	verde	**ver**-deh
pink	rosa	**ro**-sah
purple	morado	mo-**rah**-doh
orange	naranja	na-**rahn**-hah
red	rojo	**roh**-hoh
white	blanco	**blahn**-koh
yellow	amarillo	ah-mah-**ree**-yoh

DAYS OF THE WEEK

Sunday	domingo	doe-**meen**-goh
Monday	lunes	**loo**-ness
Tuesday	martes	**mahr**-tess
Wednesday	miércoles	me-**air**-koh-less
Thursday	jueves	hoo-**ev**-ess
Friday	viernes	vee-**air**-ness
Saturday	sabado	sah-bah-doh

	ENGLISH	SPANISH	PRONUNCIATION

MONTHS

	ENGLISH	SPANISH	PRONUNCIATION
	January	enero	eh-**neh**-roh
	February	febrero	feh-**breh**-roh
	March	marzo	**mahr**-soh
	April	abril	ah-**breel**
	May	mayo	**my**-oh
	June	junio	**hoo**-nee-oh
	July	julio	**hoo**-lee-yoh
	August	agosto	ah-**ghost**-toh
	September	septiembre	sep-tee-**em**-breh
	October	octubre	oak-**too**-breh
	November	noviembre	no-vee-**em**-breh
	December	diciembre	dee-see-**em**-breh

USEFUL PHRASES

	English	Spanish	Pronunciation
	Do you speak English?	¿Habla usted inglés?	**ah**-blah oos-**ted** in-**glehs**
	I don't speak Spanish	No hablo español	no **ah**-bloh es-pahn-**yol**
	I don't understand (you)	No entiendo	no en-tee-**en**-doh
	I understand (you)	Entiendo	en-tee-**en**-doh
	I don't know	No sé	no seh
	I am American/British	Soy americano (americana)/inglés(a)	soy ah-meh-ree-**kah**-no (ah-meh-ree- **kah**-nah)/ in-**glehs(ah)**
	What's your name?	¿Cómo se llama usted?	koh-mo seh **yah**-mah oos-**ted**
	My name is . . .	Me llamo . . .	may **yah**-moh
	What time is it?	¿Qué hora es?	keh **o**-rah es
	It is one, two, three o'clock	Es la una./Son las dos, tres	es la **oo**-nah/sohnahs dohs, trehs
	Yes, please/No, thank you	Sí, por favor/No, gracias	**see** pohr fah-**vor**/no **grah**-see-us
	How?	¿Cómo?	**koh**-mo

ENGLISH	SPANISH	PRONUNCIATION
When?	¿Cuándo?	**kwahn**-doh
This/Next week	Esta semana/ La semana que entra	**es**-teh seh-**mah**- nah/ lah seh-**mah**-nah keh **en**-trah
This/Next month	Este mes/El próximo mes	**es**-teh mehs/el **proke**-see-mo mehs
This/Next year	Este año/El año que viene	**es**-teh **ahn**-yo/el **ahn**-yo keh vee-**yen**-ay
Yesterday/today/ tomorrow	Ayer/hoy/mañana	ah-**yehr**/oy/ mahn-**yah**-nah
This morning/ afternoon	Esta mañana/ tarde	**es**-tah mahn-**yah**- nah/ **tar**-deh
Tonight	Esta noche	**es**-tah **no**-cheh
What?	¿Qué?	keh
What is it?	¿Qué es esto?	keh es **es**-toh
Why?	¿Por qué?	pore **keh**
Who?	¿Quién?	kee-**yen**
Where is . . . ?	¿Dónde está . . . ?	**dohn**-deh es-**tah**
the train station?	la estación del tren?	la es-tah-see-on del trehn
the subway station?	la estación del tren subterráneo?	la es-ta-see-**on** del trehn la es-ta-see-**on** soob-teh-**rrahn**-eh-oh
the bus stop?	la parada del autobus?	la pah-**rah**-dah del ow-toh-**boos**
the post office?	la oficina de correos?	la oh-fee-**see**- nah deh koh-**rreh**-os
the bank?	el banco?	el **bahn**-koh
the hotel?	el hotel?	el oh-**tel**
the store?	la tienda?	la tee-**en**-dah
the cashier?	la caja?	la **kah**-hah
the museum?	el museo?	el moo-**seh**-oh
the hospital?	el hospital?	el oliss-pee-iul
the elevator?	el ascensor?	el ah-**sen**-sohr
the bathroom?	el baño?	el **bahn**-yoh

ENGLISH	SPANISH	PRONUNCIATION
Here/there	Aquí/allá	ah-**key**/ah-**yah**
Open/closed	Abierto/cerrado	ah-bee-**er**-toh/ ser-**ah**-doh
Left/right	Izquierda/derecha	iss-key-**er**-dah/ dare-**eh**-chah
Straight ahead	Derecho	dare-**eh**-choh
Is it near/far?	¿Está cerca/lejos?	es-**tah sehr**-kah/ **leh**-hoss
I'd like . . .	Quisiera . . .	kee-see-ehr-ah
a room	un cuarto/ una habitación	oon **kwahr**-toh/ **oo**-nah ah-bee- tah-see-**on**
the key	la llave	lah **yah**-veh
a newspaper	un periódico	oon pehr-ee-**oh**- dee-koh
a stamp	un sello de correo	oon **seh**-yo deh korr-ee-oh
I'd like to buy . . .	Quisiera comprar . . .	kee-see-**ehr**-ah kohm-**prahr**
cigarettes	cigarrillos	ce-ga-**ree**-yohs
matches	cerillos	ser-**ee**-ohs
a dictionary	un diccionario	oon deek-see-oh- **nah**-ree-oh
soap	jabón	hah-**bohn**
sunglasses	gafas de sol	**ga**-fahs deh sohl
suntan lotion	Loción bronceadora	loh-see-**ohn** brohn- seh-ah-**do**-rah
a map	un mapa	oon **mah**-pah
a magazine	una revista	**oon**-ah reh-**veess**-tah
paper	papel	pah-**pel**
envelopes	sobres	**so**-brehs
a postcard	una tarjeta postal	**oon**-ah tar-**het**-ah post-**ahl**
How much is it?	¿Cuánto cuesta?	**kwahn**-toh **kwes**-tah
It's expensive/ cheap	Está caro/barato	es-**tah kah**-roh/ bah-**rah**-toh

ENGLISH	SPANISH	PRONUNCIATION
A little/a lot	Un poquito/ mucho	oon poh-**kee**-toh/ **moo**-choh
More/less	Más/menos	mahss/**men**-ohss
Enough/too much/too little	Suficiente/ demasiado/ muy poco	soo-fee-see-**en**-teh/ deh-mah-see-**ah**- doh/ **moo**-ee poh-koh
Telephone	Teléfono	tel-**ef**-oh-no
Telegram	Telegrama	teh-leh-**grah**-mah
I am ill	Estoy enfermo(a)	es-**toy** en-**fehr**- moh(mah)
Please call a doctor	Por favor llame a un medico	pohr fah-**vor ya**-meh ah oon **med**-ee-koh

ON THE ROAD

Avenue	Avenida	ah-ven-**ee**-dah
Broad, tree-lined boulevard	Bulevar	boo-leh-**var**
Fertile plain	Vega	**veh**-gah
Highway	Carretera	car-reh-**ter**-ah
Mountain pass	Puerto	poo-**ehr**-toh
Street	Calle	**cah**-yeh
Waterfront promenade	Rambla	**rahm**-blah
Wharf	Embarcadero	em-bar-cah-**deh**-ro

IN TOWN

Cathedral	Catedral	cah-teh-**dral**
Church	Templo/Iglesia	**tem**-plo/ ee-**glehs**- see-ah
City hall	Casa de gobierno	kah-sah deh go-bee-**ehr**-no
Door, gate	Puerta portón	poo-**ehr**-tah por-**ton**
Entrance/exit	Entrada/salida	en-**trah**-dah/ sah-**lee**- dah
Inn, rustic bar, or restaurant	Taverna	tah-**vehr**-nah
Main square	Plaza principal	plah-thah prin- see-**pahl**

ENGLISH	SPANISH	PRONUNCIATION

DINING OUT

Can you recommend a good restaurant?	¿Puede recomendarme un buen restaurante?	**pweh**-deh rreh-koh-mehn-**dahr**-me oon bwehn rrehs-tow-**rahn**-teh?
Where is it located?	¿Dónde está situado?	**dohn**-deh ehs-**tah** see-**twah**-doh?
Do I need reservations?	¿Se necesita una reservación?	seh neh-seh-**see**-tah **oo**-nah rreh-sehr-bah-**syohn**?
I'd like to reserve a table . . .	Quisiera reservar una mesa . . .	kee-**syeh**-rah rreh-sehr-**bahr oo**-nah **meh**-sah . . .
for two people.	para dos personas.	**pah**-rah dohs pehr- **soh**-nahs
for this evening.	para esta noche.	**pah**-rah **ehs**-tah **noh**-cheh
for 8 pm	para las ocho de la noche.	**pah**-rah lahs **oh**-choh deh lah **noh**-cheh
A bottle of . . .	Una botella de . . .	**oo**-nah bo-**teh**-yah deh
A cup of . . .	Una taza de . . .	**oo**-nah **tah**-thah deh
A glass of . . .	Un vaso de . . .	oon **vah**-so deh
Ashtray	Un cenicero	oon sen-ee-**seh**-roh
Bill/check	La cuenta	lah **kwen**-tah
Bread	El pan	el pahn
Breakfast	El desayuno	el deh-sah-**yoon**-oh
Butter	La mantequilla	lah man-teh-**key**-yah
Cheers!	¡Salud!	sah-**lood**
Cocktail	Un aperitivo	oon ah-pehr-ee-**tee**-voh
Dinner	La cena	lah **seh**-nah
Dish	Un plato	oon **plah**-toh
Menu of the day	Menú del día	meh-**noo** del **dee**-ah
Enjoy!	¡Buen provecho!	bwehn pro-**veh**-cho
Fixed-price menu	Menú fijo o turistico	meh-**noo fee**-hoh oh too-**ree**-stee-coh

ENGLISH	SPANISH	PRONUNCIATION
Fork	El tenedor	el ten-eh-**dor**
Is the tip included?	¿Está incluida la propina?	es-**tah** in-cloo-**ee**-dah lah pro-**pee**-nah
Knife	El cuchillo	el koo-**chee**-yo
Large portion of savory snacks	Raciónes	rah-see-**oh**-nehs
Lunch	La comida	lah koh-**mee**-dah
Menu	La carta, El menú	lah **cart**-ah, el meh-**noo**
Napkin	La servilleta	lah sehr-vee-**yet**-ah
Pepper	La pimienta	lah pee-me-**en**-tah
Please give me	Por favor déme	pore fah-**vor deh**-meh
Salt	La sal	lah sahl
Savory snacks	Tapas	**tah**-pahs
Spoon	Una cuchara	**oo**-nah koo-**chah**-rah
Sugar	El azúcar	el ah-**thu**-kar
Waiter!/Waitress!	¡Por favor Señor/ Señorita!	pohr fah-**vor** sen- **yor**/ sen-yor-**ee**-tah

TRAVEL SMART
LOS CABOS

GETTING HERE AND AROUND

■ AIR TRAVEL

You can now fly nonstop to Los Cabos from Southern California, Atlanta, Charlotte, Chicago, Dallas/Fort Worth, Denver, Houston, Las Vegas, Los Angeles, Mexico City, New York, Phoenix, Portland, Sacramento, Salt Lake City, San Diego, San Francisco, and Seattle. From most other destinations, you will have to make a connecting flight, either in the United States or in Mexico City. Via nonstop service, Los Cabos is about 2 hours from San Diego, about 2¼ hours from Houston, 3 hours from Dallas/Fort Worth, 2½ hours from Los Angeles, and 2½ hours from Phoenix. Flying time from New York to Mexico City, where you must switch planes to continue to Los Cabos, is 5 hours. Los Cabos is about a 2½-hour flight from Mexico City.

Airlines and Airports Airline and Airport Links.com ⊕ www.airlineandairportlinks.com.

Airline Security Issues Transportation Security Administration ⊕ www.tsa.gov.

AIRPORTS

Aeropuerto Internacional de San José del Cabo (SJD) is 1 km (½ mile) west of the Transpeninsular Highway (Highway 1), 13 km (8 miles) north of San José del Cabo, and 48 km (30 miles) northeast of Cabo San Lucas. The airport has restaurants, duty-free shops, and car-rental agencies. Los Cabos flights increase in winter with seasonal flights from U.S. airlines, and, despite growing numbers of visitors to the area, the airport manages to keep up nicely with the crowds.

Aeropuerto General Manuel Márquez de León serves La Paz. It's 11 km (7 miles) northwest of the Baja California Sur capital, which itself is 188 km (117 miles) northwest of Los Cabos.

Airport Information Aeropuerto Internacional Los Cabos ⊠ Hwy. 1, Km. 43.5, San José del Cabo, Baja California Sur

☎ 624/146–5111 ⊕ www.aeropuertosgap.com. mx. **Aeropuerto General Manuel Márquez de León** ⊠ Hwy. 1, Km. 13, La Paz, Baja California Sur ☎ 612/124–6307.

FLIGHTS

AeroCalafia flies charter flights from Los Cabos for whale-watching. Aeroméxico has service to Los Cabos from San Diego; and to La Paz from Los Angeles, Tucson, Tijuana, and Mexico City.

Alaska Airlines flies nonstop to Los Cabos from Los Angeles, San Diego, Seattle, Portland, and San Francisco; and three times a week to La Paz from Los Angeles. Frontier flies nonstop from Denver. US Airways has nonstop service from Phoenix, San Diego, and Las Vegas. American flies nonstop from Dallas/Fort Worth, Chicago, Los Angeles, and New York JFK. British Airways and other European airlines fly to Mexico City, where connections are made for the 2½-hour flight to Los Cabos.

United has nonstop service from Houston. Delta flies to Los Cabos from Atlanta and Ontario, California, and has daily flights from Los Angeles to La Paz.

Airline Contacts AeroCalafia ☎ 624/143–4302 in Los Cabos ⊕ www.aereocalafia.com. mx. **Aeroméxico** ☎ 800/237–6639 in U.S., 624/146–5097 in Los Cabos, 612/124–6366 in La Paz ⊕ www.aeromexico.com. **Alaska Airlines** ☎ 800/252–7522, 624/146–5103 in Los Cabos ⊕ www.alaskaair.com. **American Airlines** ☎ 800/433–7300, 624/146–5302 in Los Cabos ⊕ www.aa.com. **British Airways** ☎ 800/AIRWAYS in U.S. ⊕ www.britishairways. com. **Delta Airlines** ☎ 800/221–1212, 624/146–5005 in Los Cabos ⊕ www.delta.com. **Frontier Airlines** ☎ 800/432–1359 ⊕ www. flyfrontier.com. **US Airways** ☎ 800/428–4322, 624/146–5380 in Los Cabos ⊕ www.usairways. com. **United Airlines** ☎ 800/241–6522, 800/900–5000 in Mexico ⊕ www.united.com.

GROUND TRANSPORTATION

If you have purchased a vacation package from an airline or travel agency, transfers are usually included. Otherwise, only the most exclusive hotels in Los Cabos offer transfers. Fares from the airport to hotels in Los Cabos are expensive. The least expensive transport is by shuttle buses that stop at various hotels along the route; fares run $16 to $25 per person. Private taxi fares run from $80 to $100. Some hotels can arrange a pickup, which is much faster and might cost about the same as a shuttle. Ask about hotel transfers, especially if you're staying in the East Cape, La Paz, or Todos Santos and not renting a car—cab fares to these areas are astronomical.

If you're renting a car and driving say, to the East Cape, make sure you get detailed directions on how to locate where you'll be staying.

Unless you want to tour a time-share or real estate property, ignore the offers for free transfers when you first come out of customs. The scene can be bewildering for first timers. Sales representatives from various time-share properties compete vociferously for clients; often you won't realize you've been suckered into a time-share presentation until you get in the van. To avoid this situation, go to the official taxi booths inside the baggage claim or just outside the final customs clearance area and pay for a ticket for a regular shuttle bus. Private taxis, often U.S. vans, are expensive and not metered, so always ask the fare before getting in. Rates change frequently, but it costs about $55 to get to San José del Cabo, $70 to a hotel along the Corridor, and $80 to Cabo San Lucas. After the fourth passenger, it's about an additional $3 per person. Usually only vans accept more than four passengers. At the end of your trip, don't wait until the last minute to book return transport. Make arrangements a few days in advance for shuttle service, and then reconfirm the morning of your departure. Or, again, at least a day in advance, sign up at your hotel's front desk to share a cab with other travelers, reconfirming the morning of your departure.

■ BUS TRAVEL

In Los Cabos, the main Terminal de Autobus (Los Cabos Bus Terminal) is about a 10-minute drive west of Cabo San Lucas. Express buses, including Aguila and ABC, have air-conditioning and restrooms and travel frequently from the terminal to Todos Santos (one hour) and La Paz (three hours). One-way fare is $10 (payable in pesos or dollars) to Todos Santos, $23 to La Paz. From the Corridor, expect to pay about $25 for a taxi to the bus station.

SuburBaja can provide transport for $3 between San José del Cabo and Cabo San Lucas. The bus is located to the left, outside the airport, about a five-minute walk along the main road. Pay 32 pesos (or $3) when you get on the bus, and press the stop button near the back door when you need to get off. The ride from the airport to Cabo San Lucas takes about 90 minutes due to frequent stops. If you're going to Cabo San Lucas, the main stop is Puerto Paraíso Shopping Mall, and for San José del Cabo, the bus stops at the Mega grocery store.

In La Paz the main Terminal de Autobus is 10 blocks from the *malecón*, the seaside promenade.

Bus Information ABC ☎ *800/025-0222* ⊕ *www.abc.com.mx.* **Aguila** ✉ *Direccion-Alvaro Obregon # 125, entre 5 de Mayo e Independencia, La Paz, Baja California Sur* ☎ *800/824-8452.* **Los Cabos Terminal de Autobus** ✉ *Hwy. 19, Heroes at Morales, Cabos San Lucas, Baja California Sur* ☎ *624/143-7880.* **SuburBaja** ☎ *624/143-7880* ⊕ *www. suburcabos.com.*

■ CAR TRAVEL

Rental cars come in handy when exploring Baja. Countless paved and dirt roads branch off Highway 1 like octopus tentacles beckoning adventurers toward the mountains, ocean, and sea. Baja Sur's highways and city streets are under constant improvement, and Highway 1 is usually in good condition except during heavy rains. Four-wheel drive comes in handy for hard-core backcountry explorations, but isn't necessary most of the time. Just be aware that some car-rental companies void their insurance policies if you run into trouble off paved roads. If you are even slightly inclined to impromptu adventures, it's best to find out what your company's policy is before you leave the pavement.

GASOLINE

Pemex (the government petroleum monopoly) franchises all gas stations in Mexico. Stations are to be found in both towns as well as on the outskirts of San José del Cabo and Cabo San Lucas and in the Corridor, and there are also several along Highway 1. Gas is measured in liters. Prices run higher than in the United States. Premium unleaded gas (*magna premio*) and regular unleaded gas (*magna sin*) are available nationwide, but it's still a good idea to fill up whenever you can. Fuel quality is generally lower than that in the United States and Europe. Vehicles with fuel-injected engines are likely to have problems after driving extended distances.

Gas-station attendants pump the gas for you and may also wash your windshield and check your oil and tire air pressure. A tip of 5 or 10 pesos (about 50¢ or $1) is customary depending on the number of services rendered, beyond pumping gas.

ROAD CONDITIONS

Mexico Highway 1, also known as the Carretera Transpeninsular, runs the entire 1,700 km (1,054 miles) from Tijuana to Cabo San Lucas. Do not drive the highway at high speeds or at night—it is not lighted and is very narrow much of the way.

Highway 19 runs between Cabo San Lucas and Todos Santos and was widened in 2014 to two lanes in each direction, joining Highway 1 below La Paz. The four-lane road between San José del Cabo and Cabo San Lucas is usually in good condition. Roadwork along the highway is common and commonly frustrates locals and visitors alike. Take your time and don't act rashly if you encounter delays or if you need to drive several miles out of your way to turn around and re-approach a missed turnoff.

In rural areas, roads tend to be iffy and in unpredictable condition. Use caution, especially during the rainy season, when rock slides and potholes are a problem, and be alert for animals—cattle, goats, horses, coyotes, and dogs in particular—even on the highways. If you have a long distance to cover, start early, fill up on gas, and remember to keep your tank full as gas stations are simply not as abundant here as they are in the United States or Europe. Allow extra time for unforeseen obstacles.

Signage is not always adequate in Mexico, and the best advice is to travel with a companion and a good map. Take your time. Always lock your car, and never leave valuable items in the body of the car (the trunk will suffice for daytime outings, but be smart about stashing expensive items in there in full view of curious onlookers).

The Mexican Tourism Ministry distributes free road maps from its tourism offices outside the country. Guía Roji and Pemex publish current city, regional, and national road maps, which are available in bookstores and big supermarket chains for under $10; but stock up on every map your rental-car company has, as gas stations generally do not carry maps. Most car-rental agencies have GPS units available for $12 to $15 per day with regional maps preprogrammed.

ROADSIDE EMERGENCIES

The Mexican Tourism Ministry operates a fleet of more than 350 pickup trucks, known as the Angeles Verdes, or Green Angels. Bilingual drivers provide mechanical help, first aid, radio-telephone communication, basic supplies and small parts, towing, tourist information, and protection. Services are free; spare parts, fuel, and lubricants are provided at cost. Tips are always appreciated ($10–$15 for big jobs, $3–$5 for minor repairs). The Green Angels patrol sections of the major highways daily 8–8 (later on holiday weekends). If you break down, call Green Angels, or if you don't have a cell phone, **pull off the road as far as possible,** lift the hood of your car, hail a passing vehicle, and ask the driver to **notify the patrol.** Most bus and truck drivers will be quite helpful. If you witness an accident, do not stop to help—it could be a ploy to rob you or could get you interminably involved with the police. Instead, notify the nearest official.

Contacts Federal Highway Patrol 📞 624/122–5735, 624/125–3584. **Green Angels, La Paz** 📞 800/987–8224 in Mexico, 078 from any Baja Phone.

SAFETY ON THE ROAD

The mythical *banditos* are not a big concern in Baja. Still, **do your very best to avoid driving at night,** especially in rural areas. Cows and burros grazing alongside the road can pose as real a danger as the ones actually *in* the road—you never know when they'll decide to wander into traffic. Other good reasons for not driving at night include potholes, cars with no working lights, road-hogging trucks, and difficulty with getting assistance. Despite the temptation of margaritas and cold cervezas, do not drink and drive; choose a designated driver. Plan driving times, and if night is falling, find a nearby hotel or at least slow down your speed considerably.

Though it isn't common in Los Cabos, police may pull you over for supposedly breaking the law, or for being a good prospect for a scam. If it happens to you, remember to **be polite**—displays of anger will only make matters worse—tell the officer that you would like to talk to the police captain when you get to the

station. The officer will usually let you go. If you're stopped for speeding, the officer is supposed to hold your license until you pay the fine at the local police station. But he will always prefer taking a *mordida* (small bribe) to wasting his time at the police station. Corruption is a fact of life in Mexico, and the $10 or $20 it costs to get your license back is supplementary income for the officer who pulled you over with no intention of taking you to police headquarters.

RENTAL CARS

When you reserve a car, ask about cancellation penalties, taxes, drop-off charges (if you're planning to pick up the car in one city and leave it in another), and surcharges (for being under or over a certain age, for additional drivers, or for driving across state or country borders or beyond a specific distance from your point of rental). All these things can add substantially to your costs. Request car seats and extras such as GPS when you book.

Rates are sometimes—but not always—better if you book in advance or reserve through a rental agency's website. There are other reasons to book ahead, though: for popular destinations, during busy times of the year, or to ensure that you get certain types of cars (vans, SUVs, exotic sports cars). We've also found that car-rental prices are much better when reservations are made ahead of travel, from the United States. Prices can be as much as 50% more when renting a car upon arrival in Los Cabos. Shockingly low rates through third-party sites usually result in hidden fees when you actually pay for the car on-site. Alamo and Cactus Car include insurance, taxes, and unlimited mileage in the quoted rate and have a solid fleet of compact cars, SUVs, and vans. The Los Cabos-based Cactus Car has some of the best prices in the area and includes 20% discounts on local attractions when booking through their website.

■**TIP→** Make sure that a confirmed reservation guarantees you a car. Agencies sometimes overbook, particularly for busy weekends and holiday periods.

Taxi fares are especially steep in Los Cabos, and a rental car can come in handy if you'd like to dine at the Corridor hotels, travel frequently between the two towns, stay at a hotel along the Cabo Corridor, spend more than a few days in Los Cabos, or plan to see some of the sights outside Los Cabos proper, such as La Paz, Todos Santos, or even farther afield. If you don't want to rent a car, your hotel concierge or tour operator can arrange for a car with a driver or limousine service.

Convertibles and jeeps are popular rentals, but beware of sunburn and windburn and remember there's nowhere to stash your belongings out of sight. Specify whether you want air-conditioning and manual or automatic transmission. If you rent from a major U.S.-based company, you can find a compact car for about $60 per day ($420 per week), including automatic transmission, unlimited mileage, and 10% tax; however, having the protection of complete coverage insurance will add another $19 to $25 per day, depending on the company, so you should figure the cost of insurance into your budget. You will pay considerably more (probably double) for a larger or higher-end car. Most vendors negotiate considerably if tourism is slow; ask about special rates if you're renting by the week.

To increase the likelihood of getting the car you want and to get considerably better car-rental prices, make arrangements before you leave for your trip. You can sometimes, but not always, find cheaper rates on the Internet. No matter how you book, rates are generally much lower when you reserve a car in advance outside Mexico.

In Mexico your own driver's license is acceptable. In most cases, the minimum rental age is 25, although some companies will lower it to 22 for an extra daily charge. A valid driver's license, major credit card, and Mexican car insurance are required.

Contacts Alamo ⊠ *Hwy. 1, Km. 43.5, at Los Cabos Intl Airport, San José del Cabo, Baja California Sur* ☎ *624/146–1900* ⊕ *www. alamo.com.* **Cactus Car** ⊠ *Hwy. 1, Km 45, at Aeropuerto Intl de Los Cabos, San José del Cabo, Baja California Sur* ☎ *624/146–1839, 866/225–9220 from U.S.* ⊕ *www.cactuscar.com.*

CAR-RENTAL INSURANCE

Everyone who rents a car wonders whether the insurance that the rental companies offer is worth the expense. In 2013, the Mexican government passed a law stating that drivers must carry mandatory Third Party Liability, an expense that is not covered by U.S. insurance policies or by credit card companies. Just to be on the safe side, agree to at least the minimum rental insurance. It's best to be completely covered when driving in Mexico.

If you own a car, your personal auto insurance may cover a rental to some (very limited) degree, though not all policies protect you abroad; always read your policy's fine print.

Even if you have auto insurance back home, you should buy the collision- or loss-damage waiver (CDW or LDW) from the car-rental company, which eliminates your liability for damage to the car. Some credit cards offer CDW coverage, but it's only supplemental to your own insurance and rarely covers SUVs, minivans, luxury models, and the like. If your coverage is secondary, you may still be liable for loss-of-use costs from the car-rental company. But no credit-card insurance is valid unless you use that card for *all* transactions, from reserving to paying the final bill. In general, U.S. and Canadian auto insurance policies are not recognized in Mexico, and the few that are only cover specific coverage like damage and theft. Rather than fear what *might* happen, it is best to purchase a Mexican liability insurance package from your rental car company so that you know you're covered.

■TIP→ American Express offers primary CDW coverage on all rentals reserved and paid for with the card. This means that the American Express company—not your own car insurance—pays in case of an accident. This does not cover Third Party Liability, nor does it mean your car-insurance company won't raise your rates once it discovers you had an accident—but it provides a welcome amount of security for travelers.

▌TAXI TRAVEL

Taxis are plentiful throughout Baja Sur, even in the smallest towns. Government-certified taxis have a license with a photo of the driver and a taxi number prominently displayed. Fares are exorbitant in Los Cabos, and the taxi union is very powerful. Some visitors have taken to boycotting taxis completely, using rental cars and buses instead, the latter of which can be most time-consuming. The fare between Cabo San Lucas and San José del Cabo runs about $50–$60—more at night. Cabs from Corridor hotels to either town run at least $30 each way. Expect to pay at least $55 from the airport to hotels in San José, and closer to $85 to Cabo.

In La Paz, taxis are readily available and inexpensive. A ride within town costs under $5; a trip to Pichilingue costs between $7 and $10. Illegal taxis aren't a problem in this region.

ESSENTIALS

■ COMMUNICATIONS

PHONES

Los Cabos is on U.S. Mountain Time. The region has good telephone service and wide cell-phone reception. Phone numbers in Mexico change frequently; a recording may offer the new number, so it's useful to learn the Spanish words for numbers 1 through 9. Beware of pay phones and hotel-room phones with signs saying "Call Home" and other entice-ments. Some of these phone companies charge astronomical rates. Some all-inclu-sive resorts include free calls to the U.S. and Canada, which will be clearly stated in your amenities upon check-in.

The country code for Mexico is 52. When calling a Mexico number from abroad, dial the country code and then the area code and local number. At this writing, the area code for all of Los Cabos is 624. All local numbers have seven digits.

CALLING WITHIN MEXICO

For local or long-distance calls, one option is to contact your cell phone pro-vider and add the Mexico plan to your account for the days you are traveling. From your computer or a smartphone you can download Skype onto your device and purchase $10 to $20 of talk time, which will actually go quite far. Alternatively, if the person you are call-ing has Skype, it will be free for both parties. If you are tech-savvy, purchase a local SIM card for an "unlocked" cell phone and use a prepaid phone card to deduct minutes from your talk time. Tel-Cel is a reliable Mexican company that offers this service. When all else fails, you can always use the phone in your hotel room.

Contact TelCel ☎ 552/581–3300, 888/350–4035 ⊕ www.telcel.com.

CALLING OUTSIDE MEXICO

To make a call to the United States or Canada, dial 001 before the area code and number. For operator assistance in mak-ing an international call dial 090.

AT&T, MCI, and Sprint access codes make calling long-distance relatively con-venient, but you may find the local access number blocked in many hotel rooms. First ask the hotel operator to connect you. If the hotel operator balks, ask for an international operator, or dial the inter-national operator yourself. One way to improve your odds of getting connected to your long-distance carrier is to travel with more than one company's calling card (a hotel may block Sprint, for example, but not MCI). If all else fails, call from a pay phone.

Access Codes AT&T Direct ☎ 800/331–0500 ⊕ www.att.com. **MCI WorldPhone** ☎ 800/674–7000 ⊕ www.mci.com. **Sprint International Access** ☎ 866/866–7509 ⊕ www.sprint.com.

DIRECTORY AND OPERATOR ASSISTANCE

Directory assistance in Mexico is 040 nationwide. For international assistance, dial 020 first for an international operator and most likely you'll get one who speaks English; indicate in which city, state, and country you require directory assistance and you will be connected with directory assistance there.

MOBILE PHONES

If you have a multiband phone (some countries use different frequencies from what's used in the United States) and your service provider uses the world-standard GSM network (as do T-Mobile, AT&T and Verizon), you can probably use your phone abroad. Roaming fees can be steep, however: 99¢ a minute is considered rea-sonable. And overseas you normally pay the toll charges for incoming calls. It's almost always cheaper to send a text message than to make a call, since text messages have a very low set fee (often less than 5¢). Verizon offers very reasonable Mexican calling plans that can be added to your existing plan.

If you just want to make local calls, consider buying a new SIM card (note that your provider may have to unlock your phone for you to use a different SIM card) and a prepaid service plan in the destination. You'll then have a local number and can make local calls at local rates. If your trip is extensive, you could also simply buy a new cell phone in your destination, as the initial cost will be offset over time.

■**TIP➜** If you travel internationally frequently, save one of your old mobile phones or buy a cheap one on the Internet; ask your cell phone company to unlock it for you, and take it with you as a travel phone, buying a new SIM card with pay-as-you-go service in each destination.

There are now companies that rent cell phones (with or without SIM cards) for the duration of your trip. You get the phone, charger, and carrying case in the mail and return them in the mailer. **Contacts Cellular Abroad** ☎ 800/287–5072 ⊕ www.cellularabroad.com. **Mobal** ☎ 888/888–9162 ⊕ www.mobalrental.com. **Planet Fone** ☎ 888/988–4777 ⊕ www.planetfone.com.

PUBLIC PHONES

Although uncommon, you may see pay phones with an unmarked slot for prepaid phone cards called Telmex cards. The cards are sold in 30-, 50-, or 100-peso denominations at newsstands or pharmacies. Credit is deleted from the Telmex card as you use it, and your balance is displayed on a small screen on the phone. Some phones have two unmarked slots, one for a Telmex card and the other for a credit card. These are primarily for Mexican bank cards, but some accept Visa or MasterCard.

TOLL-FREE NUMBERS

Toll-free numbers in Mexico start with an 800 prefix. To reach them, you need to dial 01 before the number. *In this guide, Mexico-only toll-free numbers appear as follows: 01–800/123–4567 (numbers have seven digits).* Most of the 800 numbers *in this book* work in the United States only and are listed simply: 800/123–4567; you cannot access a U.S. 800 number from Mexico. Some U.S. toll-free numbers ring directly at Mexican properties. Don't be deterred if someone answers the phone in Spanish. Simply ask for someone who speaks English. Toll-free numbers that work in other countries are labeled accordingly.

■ CUSTOMS AND DUTIES

Upon entering Mexico, you'll be given a baggage declaration form and asked to itemize what you're bringing into the country. You are allowed to bring in 3 liters of spirits or wine for personal use; 400 cigarettes, 25 cigars, or 200 grams of tobacco; a reasonable amount of perfume for personal use; one video camera and one regular camera and 12 rolls of film for each; and gift items not to exceed a total of $300. If driving across the U.S. border, gift items shouldn't exceed $50, although foreigners aren't usually hassled about this. ⚠ Although the much-publicized border violence doesn't usually affect travelers, it is real. To be safe don't linger long at the border.

You aren't allowed to bring firearms, ammunition, meat, vegetables, plants, fruit, or flowers into the country. You can bring in one of each of the following items without paying taxes: a cell phone, a beeper, a radio or tape recorder, a musical instrument, a laptop computer, and portable copier or printer. Compact discs are limited to 20 total and DVDs to 10.

Mexico also allows you to bring one cat or dog, if you have two things: (1) a pet health certificate signed by a registered veterinarian in the United States and issued not more than 72 hours before the animal enters Mexico; and (2) a pet vaccination certificate showing that the animal has been treated (as applicable) for rabies, hepatitis, distemper, and leptospirosis.

For more information or information on bringing other animals or more than one type of animal, contact the Mexican consulate, which has branches in many major American cities as well as border towns. To find the consulate nearest you, check the Ministry of Foreign Affairs website (go to the "Servicios Consulares" option).

Information in Mexico Mexican Embassy ☎ 202/728–1600 ⊕ www.embassyofmexico. org. **Ministry of Foreign Affairs** ☎ 55/3686–5100 ⊕ www.sre.gob.mx.

U.S. Information U.S. Customs and Border Protection ☎ 877/CBP–5511 in U.S., 202/325–8000 outside the U.S. ⊕ www.cbp. gov.

■ ELECTRICITY

For U.S. and Canadian travelers, electrical converters are not necessary because Mexico operates on the 60-cycle, 120-volt system; however, many Mexican outlets have not been updated to accommodate three-prong and polarized plugs (those with one larger prong), so to be safe bring an adapter. If your appliances are dual-voltage you'll need only an adapter. Don't use 110-volt outlets, marked "for shavers only," for high-wattage appliances such as blow dryers. Most laptops operate equally well on 110 and 220 volts and so require only an adapter. It is well worth bringing a small surge protector if you're going to be plugging in your laptop, unless you have a newer computer with a battery and power adapter that handles both 120V/220V.

■ EMERGENCIES

The state of Baja California Sur has instituted an emergency number for police and fire: 060. A second number, 065, is available to summon medical assistance. Both numbers can be used throughout the state, and there are English-speaking operators. Another option is air medical services—find a provider through the Association of Air Medical Services (AAMS); several of the U.S.-headquartered operations have bases around Mexico, so they can reach you more quickly.

Emergency Services AAMS ☎ 703/836–8732 ⊕ www.aams.org. **Highway Patrol** ☎ 624/143–0135 in Los Cabos, 612/122–0429 in La Paz. **Police** ☎ 624/142–0361 in San José del Cabo, 624/143–3977 in Cabo San Lucas, 612/122–0477 in La Paz.

Foreign Consulates Consular Agent in Cabo San Lucas ✉ Hwy. 1 Km 27.5, Shoppes at Palmilla, Corridor, Baja California Sur ☎ 624/143–3566.

Hospitals and Clinics AmeriMed ✉ Av. Cárdenas at Paseo Marina, in front of Seven Crown Resort, Cabo San Lucas, Baja California Sur ☎ 624/105–8500 ⊕ www.amerimed.com. mx ✉ Plaza Patio Cabo Ley, near Burger King, San José del Cabo, Baja California Sur ☎ 624/105–8550 ⊕ www.amerimedloscabos. com. **Centro de Especialidades Médicas** ✉ Calle Delfines 110, La Paz, Baja California Sur ☎ 612/124–0400.

■ HEALTH

FOOD AND DRINK

In Mexico the biggest health risk is *turista* (traveler's diarrhea) caused by consuming contaminated fruit, vegetables, or water. To minimize risks, avoid questionable-looking street stands and bad-smelling food even in the toniest establishments; and if you're not sure of a restaurant's standards, pass up ceviche (raw fish cured in lemon juice) and raw vegetables that haven't been, or can't be, peeled (e.g., lettuce and tomatoes).

In general, Los Cabos does not pose as great a health risk as other parts of Mexico. Nevertheless, watch what you eat, and drink only bottled water or water that has been boiled for a few minutes. Water in most major hotels is safe for brushing your teeth, but to avoid any risk, use bottled water. Hotels with water-purification systems will post signs to that effect in the rooms.

When ordering cold drinks at establishments that don't seem to get many tourists, skip the ice: *sin hielo.* (You can usually identify ice made commercially from purified water by its uniform shape.)

Stay away from uncooked food and unpasteurized milk and milk products. Mexicans excel at grilling meats and seafood, but be smart about where you eat—ask locals to recommend their favorite restaurants or taco stands, and if you have the slightest hesitation about cleanliness or freshness, then skip it. This caution must extend to ceviche, which is a favorite appetizer, especially at seaside resorts. The Mexican Department of Health warns that marinating in lemon juice does not constitute the "cooking" that would make the shellfish safe to eat. Fruit and *licuados* (smoothies) stands are wonderful for refreshing treats, but again, ask around, be fanatical about freshness, and watch to see how the vendor handles the food. Mexico is a food-lover's adventureland, and many travelers wouldn't dream of passing up the chance to try something new and delicious.

Mild cases of turista may respond to Imodium (known generically as loperamide), Lomotil, or Pepto-Bismol (not as strong), all of which you can buy over the counter. Keep in mind though, that these drugs can complicate more serious illnesses. You'll need to replace fluids, so drink plenty of purified water.

Chamomile tea (*té de manzanilla*) and peppermint tea (*té de menta/hierbabuena*) can be good for calming upset stomachs, and they're readily available in restaurants throughout Mexico.

It's smart to bring down a few packets of drink mix, such as EmergenC, when you travel to Mexico. You can also make a salt-sugar solution (½ teaspoon salt and 4 tablespoons sugar per quart of water) to rehydrate. Drinking baking soda dissolved in water can neutralize the effects of an acidic meal and help with heavy indigestion or an upset stomach. It might also help prevent a painful hangover if taken after excessive drinking.

If your fever and diarrhea last longer than a day or two, see a doctor—you may have picked up a parasite or disease that requires prescription medication.

DIVERS' ALERT
⚠ Do not fly within 24 hours of scuba diving.

SHOTS AND MEDICATIONS
According to the U.S. National Centers for Disease Control and Prevention (CDC), there's a limited risk of dengue fever and other insect-carried or parasite-caused illnesses in some rural parts of Mexico, though Baja California Sur is not one of the major areas of concern.

Health Information National Centers for Disease Control & Prevention (*CDC*) ☎ *800/232–4636 international travelers' health line* ⊕ *www.cdc.gov/travel.* **World Health Organization** (*WHO*) ☎ *41–22/791–2111* ⊕ *www.who.int.*

MEDICAL INSURANCE AND ASSISTANCE
Consider buying trip insurance with medical-only coverage. Neither Medicare nor some private insurers cover medical expenses anywhere outside the United States. Medical-only policies typically reimburse you for medical care (excluding that related to pre-existing conditions) and hospitalization abroad, and provide for evacuation. You still have to pay the bills and await reimbursement from the insurer, though.

Another option is to sign up with a medical-evacuation assistance company. Membership gets you doctor referrals, emergency evacuation or repatriation, 24-hour hotlines for medical consultation, and other assistance. International SOS Assistance Emergency and AirMed

International provide evacuation services and medical referrals. MedjetAssist offers medical evacuation.

Medical Assistance Companies AirMed International ☎ 800/356-2161 in U.S., 205/443-4840 from Mexico ⊕ www. airmed.com. **International SOS Assistance Emergency** ☎ 800/523-8662 ⊕ www.internationalsos.com. **MedjetAssist** ☎ 800/527-7478 ⊕ www.medjetassist.com.

Medical-Only Insurers International Medical Group ☎ 800/628-4664 ⊕ www. imglobal.com. **Wallach & Company** ☎ 800/237-6615, 540/687-3166 ⊕ www. wallach.com.

▌ HOLIDAYS

Mexico is the land of festivals; if you reserve lodging well in advance, they present a golden opportunity to have a thoroughly Mexican experience. Banks and government offices close during Holy Week (the week leading to Easter Sunday) and on Cinco de Mayo, Día de la Raza, and Independence Day. Government offices usually have reduced hours and staff from Christmas through New Year's Day. Some banks and offices close for religious holidays.

Official holidays include New Year's Day (January 1); Constitution Day (February 5); Flag Day (February 24); Benito Juárez's Birthday (March 21); Good Friday (Friday before Easter Sunday); Easter Sunday (the first Sunday after the first full moon following spring equinox); Labor Day (May 1); Cinco de Mayo (May 5); St. John the Baptist Day (June 24); Independence Day (September 16); Día de la Raza (Day of the Race; October 12); Dia de los Muertos (Day of the Dead; November 2); Anniversary of the Mexican Revolution (November 20); Christmas (December 25).

Festivals include Carnaval (February and March, before Lent); Semana Santa (Holy Week; week before Easter Sunday); Día de Nuestra Señora de Guadalupe (Day of Our Lady of Guadalupe; December 12); and Las Posadas (pre-Christmas religious celebrations; December 16–25).

▌ HOURS OF OPERATION

Banks are usually open weekdays 8:30–3 (although sometimes banks in Cabo and San José stay open until 5). Government offices are usually open to the public weekdays 8–3; they're closed—along with banks and most private offices—on national holidays. Stores are generally open weekdays and Saturday from 9 or 10 to 7 or 8. In tourist areas, some shops don't close until 10 and are open Sunday. Most galleries are closed on Sunday. Some shops close for a two-hour lunch break, usually from 2 to 4. Shops extend their hours when cruise ships are in town.

▌ MAIL

Airmail letters from Baja Sur can take up to two weeks and often much longer to reach their destination. The *oficina de correos* (post office) in San José del Cabo is open 8–7 weekdays (with a possible closure for lunch) and 9–1 Saturday. Offices in Cabo San Lucas and La Paz are open 9–1 and 3–6 weekdays; La Paz and San Lucas offices are also open 9–noon on Saturday.

Post Offices Cabo San Lucas Oficina de Correo ⊠ Av. Cárdenas s/n ☎ 624/143-0048. **San José del Cabo Oficina de Correo** ⊠ Mijares and Margarita Maya de Juárez.

SHIPPING PACKAGES

FedEx does not serve Los Cabos area. DHL has express service for letters and packages from Los Cabos to the United States and Canada; most deliveries take three to four days (overnight service is not available). To the United States, letters take three days and boxes and packages take four days. Cabo San Lucas, San José del Cabo, and La Paz have a DHL drop-off location. Mail Boxes Etc. can help with DHL and postal services.

Major Services DHL Worldwide Express
✉ *Blvd. Mauricio Castro 1738, San José del Cabo, Baja California Sur* ☎ *624/130–7887* ⊕ *www.dhl.com* ✉ *Plaza Los Arcos, Leona Vicario, Cabo San Lucas, Baja California Sur* ☎ *624/146–4184* ⊕ *www.dhl.com*. **Mailbox Store** ✉ *Plaza las Palmas, Hwy. 1, Km 31, San José del Cabo, Baja California Sur* ☎ *624/142–4355* ⊕ *www.mbstorecabo.com* ✉ *Blvd. Lazaro Cárdenas, Esq. 20 de Nov. Col. Benito Juarez, Cabo San Lucas, Baja California Sur* ☎ *624/143–3032* ⊕ *www.mbstorecabo.com*.

▌ MONEY

Mexico has a reputation for being inexpensive, but Los Cabos is one of the most expensive places to visit in the country. Prices rise from 10% to 18% annually and are comparable to those in Southern California.

Prices in this book are quoted most often in U.S. dollars, which are readily accepted in Los Cabos (although you should always have pesos on you if you venture anywhere beyond the walls of a resort). ⇨ *For information on taxes, see Taxes.*

Prices here are given for adults. Substantially reduced fees are almost always available for children, students, and senior citizens.

ATMS AND BANKS

ATMs (*cajas automáticas*) are commonplace in Los Cabos and La Paz. If you're going to a less-developed area, though, go equipped with cash. Cirrus and Plus cards are the most commonly accepted. The ATMs at Banamex, one of the oldest nationwide banks, tend to be the most reliable. Bancomer is another bank with many ATM locations.

Many Mexican ATMs cannot accept PINs with more than four digits. If yours is longer, change your PIN to four digits before you leave home. If your PIN is fine yet your transaction still can't be completed, chances are that the computer lines are busy or that the machine has run out of money or is being serviced. Don't give up.

Expect to pay a $5 withdrawal fee with each ATM transaction.

CREDIT CARDS

When shopping, you can often get better prices if you pay with cash, particularly in small shops. But you'll receive wholesale exchange rates when you make purchases with credit cards. These exchange rates are usually better than those that banks give you for changing money. The decision to pay cash or to use a credit card might depend on whether the establishment in which you are making a purchase finds bargaining for prices acceptable, and whether you want the safety net of your card's purchase protection. To avoid fraud or errors, it's wise to make sure that "pesos" is clearly marked on all credit-card receipts.

Before you leave for Mexico, contact your credit-card company to let them know you'll be using your card abroad, and get lost-card phone numbers that work in Mexico; the standard toll-free numbers often don't work abroad. Carry these numbers separately from your wallet so you'll have them if you need to call to report lost or stolen cards. American Express, MasterCard, and Visa note the international number for card-replacement calls on the back of their cards.

CURRENCY AND EXCHANGE

The currency in Los Cabos is the Mexican peso (MXP), though prices are often given in U.S. dollars. Mexican currency comes in denominations of 20-, 50-, 100-, 200-, and 500-peso bills. Coins come in denominations of 1, 2, 5, 10, and 20 pesos and 20 and 50 centavos (20-centavo coins are only rarely seen). Many of the coins are very similar, so check carefully; bills, however, are different colors and easily distinguished.

At this writing, US$1 was equivalent to approximately MXP 12.98.

■ PASSPORTS AND VISAS

A passport, or other WHTI (Western Hemisphere Travel Initiative) compliant document, is required of all visitors to Mexico, including U.S. citizens who may remember the days when only driver's licenses were needed to cross the border. Upon entering Mexico all visitors must get a tourist card (FMT card). If you're arriving by plane from the United States or Canada, the standard tourist card will be given to you on the plane. They're also available through travel agents and Mexican consulates and at the border if you're entering by land.

■TIP➜ You're given a portion of the tourist card form upon entering Mexico. Keep track of this documentation throughout your trip: you will need it when you depart. You'll be asked to hand it, your ticket, and your passport to airline representatives at the gate when boarding for departure.

If you lose your tourist card, plan to spend some time (and about $60) sorting it out with Mexican officials at the airport on departure.

A tourist card costs about $23. The fee is generally tacked onto the price of your airline ticket. If you enter by land or boat you'll have to pay the fee separately. You're exempt from the fee if you enter by sea and stay less than 72 hours, or by land and do not stray past the 26- to 30-km (16- to 18-mile) checkpoint into the country's interior.

Tourist cards and visas are valid from 15 to 180 days, at the discretion of the immigration officer at your point of entry (90 days for Australians). Americans, Canadians, New Zealanders, and the British may request up to 180 days for a tourist card or visa extension. The extension fee is about $20, and the process can be time-consuming. There's no guarantee that you'll get the extension you're requesting. If you're planning an extended stay, plead with the immigration official for the maximum allowed days at the time of entry. It will save you time and money later.

■TIP➜ Mexico has some of the strictest policies about children entering the country. Minors traveling with one parent need notarized permission from the absent parent.

If you're a single parent traveling with children up to age 18, you must have a notarized letter from the other parent stating that the child has his or her permission to leave his or her home country. The child must be carrying the original letter—not a facsimile or scanned copy—as well as proof of the parent-child relationship (usually a birth certificate or court document), and an original custody decree, if applicable. If the other parent is deceased or the child has only one legal parent, a notarized statement saying so must be obtained as proof. In addition, you must fill out a Tourist Card for each child over the age of 10 traveling with you.

Info Mexican Embassy ☎ *202/728–1600* ⊕ *www.embassyofmexico.org.*

U.S. Passport Information U.S. Department of State ☎ *877/487–2778, 888/407–4747* ⊕ *www.state.gov.*

■ RESTROOMS

Expect to find clean flushing toilets, toilet tissue, soap, and running water in Los Cabos. An exception may be small roadside stands or restaurants in rural areas. If there's a bucket and a large container of water sitting outside the facilities, fill the bucket and use it for the flush. Some public places, such as bus stations, charge 1 or 2 pesos for use of the facility, but toilet paper is included in the fee. Still, it's always a good idea to carry some tissue. Throw your toilet paper and any other materials into the provided waste bins rather than the toilet. Mexican plumbing simply isn't equipped to deal with the volume of paper Americans are accustomed to putting in toilets.

▌ SAFETY

Although Los Cabos area is one of the safest in Mexico, it's still important to be aware of your surroundings and to follow normal safety precautions. Everyone has heard some horror story about highway assaults, pickpocketing, bribes, or foreigners languishing in Mexican jails. Reports of these crimes apply in large part to Mexico City and other large cities; in Los Cabos, pickpocketing is usually the biggest concern.

General Information and Warnings Transportation Security Administration (TSA) ☎ 866/289-9673 ⊕ www.tsa.gov. **U.S. Department of State** ☎ 202/501-4444 from Mexico, 888/407-4747 from the U.S. ⊕ www.travel.state.gov.

▌ TAXES

Mexico charges a departure and airport tax of about US$13 and US$8.50, or the peso equivalent, respectively, when you leave the country. This tax is almost universally included in the price of your ticket, but check to be certain. Traveler's checks and credit cards are not accepted at the airport as payment for this fee.

A 2% tax on accommodations is charged in Los Cabos, with proceeds used for tourism promotion.

Baja California Sur has a Value-Added Tax of 10%, called I.V.A. (*impuesto de valor agregado*), which is occasionally (and illegally) waived for cash purchases. Other taxes and charges apply for phone calls made from your hotel room.

▌ TIME

Baja California Sur is on Mountain Standard Time, Baja California is on Pacific Standard Time. And the unofficial standard for behavior is "Mexican time"—meaning stop rushing, enjoy yourself, and practice being *tranquilo*.

▌ TIPPING

When tipping in Baja, remember that the minimum wage is equivalent to a mere $4.50 a day, and that the vast majority of workers in the tourist industry of Mexico live barely above the poverty line. However, there are Mexicans who think in dollars and know, for example, that in the United States porters are tipped about $2 a bag; many of them expect the peso equivalent from foreigners but are sometimes happy to accept 5 pesos (about 50¢) a bag from Mexicans. They will complain either verbally or with a facial expression if they feel they deserve more—you and your conscience must decide. Following are some guidelines. Naturally, larger tips are always welcome.

For porters and bellboys at airports and at moderate and inexpensive hotels, $1 (about 13 pesos) per bag should be sufficient. At expensive hotels, porters expect at least $2 (about 26 pesos) per bag. Leave at least $1 (13 pesos) per night for maids at all hotels. The norm for waiters is 15% to 20% of the bill, depending on service (make sure a 15% service charge hasn't already been added to the bill, although this practice is more common in resorts). Tipping taxi drivers is necessary only if the driver helps with your bags; 50¢ to $1 (6 to 13 pesos) should be enough, depending on the extent of the help. Tip tour guides and drivers at least $3 (39 pesos) per half day or 10% of the tour fee, minimum. Gas-station attendants receive 50¢ to $1 (6 to 13 pesos), more if they check the oil, tires, etc. Parking attendants—including those at restaurants with valet parking—should be tipped $1 to $3 (13 to 39 pesos).

▌ TRIP INSURANCE

Comprehensive trip insurance is valuable if you're booking a very expensive or complicated trip (particularly to an isolated region) or if you're booking far in advance. Comprehensive policies typically cover trip-cancellation and interruption, letting you cancel or cut your trip short because of a personal emergency, illness, or, in some cases, acts of terrorism in your destination. Such policies also cover evacuation and medical care. (For trips abroad you should at least have medical-only coverage). Some also cover you for trip delays because of bad weather or mechanical problems as well as for lost or delayed baggage. If you plan on engaging in extreme activities like surfing, bungee jumping, scuba diving, or zip-lining, consider buying an extended plan that covers such sports.

Another type of coverage to look for is financial default—that is, when your trip is disrupted because a tour operator, airline, or cruise line goes out of business. Generally you must buy this when you book your trip or shortly thereafter, and it's only available to you if your operator isn't on a list of excluded companies.

Always read the fine print of your policy to make sure that you are covered for the risks that are of most concern to you. Compare several policies to make sure you're getting the best price and range of coverage available.

Insurance Comparison Sites Insure My Trip. com ☎ 800/487–4722 ⊕ www.insuremytrip. com. **Square Mouth** ☎ 800/240–0369 ⊕ www. squaremouth.com.

Comprehensive Travel Insurers Allianz ☎ 800/284–8300 ⊕ www. allianztravelinsurance.com. **Travel Guard** ☎ 800/826–4919 ⊕ www.travelguard.com. **CSA Travel Protection** ☎ 877/243–4135 ⊕ www.csatravelprotection.com. **Travelex Insurance** ☎ 800/228–9792 ⊕ www.travelex-insurance.com. **Travel Insured International** ☎ 800/243–3174 ⊕ www.travelinsured.com.

❚ VISITOR INFORMATION

Avoid tour stands on the streets; they are usually associated with time-share operations. The *Gringo Gazette* newspaper and the *Baja Traveler Guide* are good resources for the Cabo scene, as

are *Los Cabos Magazine* and *What's Up Los Cabos*. These publications are free and easy to find in hotels and restaurants throughout the region. Discover Baja, a membership club for Baja travelers, has links and info at its website. Planeta.com has information about ecotourism and environmental issues.

The Baja California Sur State Tourist Office is in La Paz about a 10-minute drive north of the malecón, the seaside promenade. It serves as both the state and city tourism office. There's also an information stand on the malecón (no phone) across from Los Arcos hotel. The booth is a more convenient spot, and it can give you info on La Paz, Scammon's Lagoon, Santa Rosalia, and other smaller towns. Both offices and the booth are open weekdays 9–5.

Contacts Baja California Sur State Tourist Office ⊠ Mariano Abasolo s/n, La Paz, Baja California Sur ☎ 612/124–0100 ⊕ www.explorebajasur.com. **Discover Baja** ☎ 800/727–2252 ⊕ www.discoverbaja.com. **Gringo Gazette** ⊕ www.gringogazette.com. **Los Cabos Tourism Board** ⊠ Plaza Providencia, Hwy. 1, Km 4.3, next to Costco, Cabos San Lucas, Baja California Sur ☎ 624/143–5531 in Mexico, 01-800/746–2226 toll-free ⊕ www. visitloscabos.travel. **Mexican Government Tourist Board** ☎ 800/446–3942 from U.S. and Canada ⊕ www.visitmexico.com. **Planeta.com** ⊕ www.planeta.com. **TodosSantos-Baja.com** ⊕ www.todossantos-baja.com.

INDEX

PHOTO CREDITS

Front Cover: Buddy Mays/Alamy [Description: A tour boat carries passengers to El Arco, on the Sea of Cortez, Cabo San Lucas]. 1, carlos sanchez pereyra/Shutterstock. 2-3, Chad Ehlers/Alamy. 5, Jim Russi/age fotostock. Chapter 1: Experience Los Cabos: 8-9, Victor Elías/age fotostock. 10, Carolina K. Smith, M.D./ Shutterstock. 11, Bruce Herman/Mexico Tourism Board. 12 (top), Michael S. Nolan/ age fotostock. 12 (bottom) and 13, Bruce Herman/Mexico Tourism Board. 14, (left), Victor Elías/age fotostock. 14, (top right), ZUMA Press, Inc. / Alamy.14, (bottom right), alysta/Shutterstock. 15 (top left), Visual&Written SL/Alamy. 15 (right), csp/Shutterstock. 15 (bottom left), Kim Karpeles / Alamy. 16, Bruce Herman/Mexico Tourism Board. 17 (left), Esperanza Resort. 17 (right), Adobe Guadalupe. 20, TFoxFoto/Shutterstock. 21, john hoadley/Shutterstock. 22, SuperStock/age fotostock. 23, Bruce Herman/Mexico Tourism Board. 27 (left), Pete Saloutos/Shutterstock. 27 (right), SuperStock/age fotostock. 28, Luis Garcia Photography. Chapter 2: Beaches: 29, Heeb Christian/age fotostock. 30, Brian Florky/Shutterstock. 35 and 36 (top), Jim Russi/age fotostock. 36 (center), Kato Inowe/Shutterstock. 36 (bottom), RCPPHOTO/ Shutterstock. 37, Henry William Fu/Shutterstock. 38 and 40 (top), Kato Inowe/Shutterstock. 40 (bottom), Bruce Herman/Mexico Tourism Board. 44. Victor Elías/age fotostock. 46-47, Heeb Christian/ age fotostock. Chapter 3: Sports and Outdoor Activities: 51 and 52, Bruce Herman/Mexico Tourism Board. 58-59, Ralph Hopkins/age fotostock. 62, tonobalaguerf/Shutterstock. 63, Larry Dunmire. 64 (top), Sam Woolford/iStockphoto. 64 (bottom), Larry Dunmire. 66 (top), Bruce Herman/Mexico Tourism Board. 66 (bottom), csp/Shutterstock. 68, Robert Chiasson/age fotostock. 71, Michele Westmorland/age fotostock. 75, Adalberto Ríos Szalay/age fotostock. 76 (illustration), Pieter Folkens. 76 (bottom), Michael S. Nolan/age fotostock. 77, Ryan Harvey/Flickr. 78, Reinhard Dirscherl/age fotostock. Chapter 4: Where to Eat: 81, SIME/Grandadam Laurent/eStock Photo. 82, Matthieu Fiol. Chapter 5: Where to Stay: 105, Larry Dunmire. 106, Victor Elias. 117, Marbella en la Playa. 118, One&Only Palmilla. Chapter 6: Shops and Spas: 125, Terrance Klassen/age fotostock. 126, Tony Hertz/Alamy. 133, Jan Butchofsky-Houser/age fotostock. 140, Richard Cummins/age fotostock. 142, John Mitchell/Alamy. 143, María Lourdes Alonso/age fotostock. 144 (top), Danita Delimont/Alamy. 144 (bottom), María Lourdes Alonso/age fotostock. 145 (top), Ken Ross. 145 (bottom left), Ken Ross. 145 (bottom 2nd from left), Ken Ross. 145 (bottom 3rd from left), Ken Ross. 145 (right), Jane Onstott. 146 (top left), patti haskins/Flickr. 146 (bottom left), fontplaydotcom/Flickr. 146 (top right), Wonderlane/Flickr. 146 (center right), Jose Zelaya Gallery/ArtedelPueblo.com. 146 (bottom right), Jane Onstott. Chapter 7: Nightlife and the Arts: 151, Jay Reilly/Aurora Photos. 152, Elena Koulik/ Shutterstock. 163, Blaine Harrington III/Alamy. Chapter 8: Los Cabos Side Trips: 167, Photoshot/age fotostock. 168 (top), iStockphoto. 168 (bottom), William Katz/iStockphoto. 170, Sherwin McGehee/ iStockphoto. 179, San Rostro/ age fotostock. 180, Danita Delimont/Alamy. 192, Michael S. Nolan/age fotostock. Chapter 9: Baja California Beach Towns: 195, Photo Network / Alamy. 196, Jordan Hetrick / Alamy. 197, Witold Skrypczak / Alamy. 198, Peter Coombs / Alamy. 206 (top and bottom right), Adobe Guadalupe. 206 (bottom left), Tomas Castelazo/Wikipedia.org. 207, María Lourdes Alonso. 208 (top and bottom), Adobe Guadalupe. 221, Richard Cummins/age fotostock. Back cover (from left to right): nicksan; csp/Shutterstock; Solmar Hotels & Resorts. Spine: Khewey | Dreamstime.com

About Our Writers: Marlise Kast, courtesy of Benjamin Myers; Chris Sands, courtesy of Camilla Fuchs.

NOTES